IN MY SHOES

A MEMOIR

TAMARA MELLON

PORTFOLIO
PENGUIN

PORTFOLIO PENGUIN

UK | USA | Canada | Ireland | Australia
India | New Zealand | South Africa

Portfolio Penguin is part of the Penguin Random House group of companies
whose addresses can be found at global.penguinrandomhouse.com.

First published in the United States of America by Portfolio Penguin 2013
First published in Great Britain by Portfolio Penguin 2013
Published in this edition 2014
002

Printed in Great Britain by Clays Ltd, St Ives plc

ISBN: 978-0-670-92365-6

www.greenpenguin.co.uk

To the memory of my father, Thomas Yeardye, who inspired me through my darkest days, and to my daughter, Minty Mellon, who makes it all worthwhile

···· 1 ····

I had just dragged myself to my desk at *Vogue*, yet again two hours late, when Anna Harvey, the deputy editor, appeared ominously at my shoulder.

"I need to speak to you," she whispered.

Anna had been at Condé Nast forever and was very old school. Short dark hair. Wool suit and pearls. Cream Chanel blouse.

Eleven a.m. had become all too customary for my arrival, so I wasn't entirely surprised to find a senior person wanting to have a chat. A day of reckoning had long been in the cards, and now I was just so very, very tired.

I got to my feet and walked with just the slightest hint of effort down the long corridor that led to her office. To my right, the open room where we editors sat. To my left, the glass boxes all in a row for the higher-ups. The decor was gleaming white, and everything around me had such a clean, bright look that it could have been a hospital. Or maybe it just seemed that way because I felt so ill. Nauseous and a little gauzy, as if I were jet-lagged. In fact, I'd been up all night at Tramp consuming prodigious quantities of cocaine and vodka. Then again, it could have been L'Equipée Anglaise. After enough drugs and drink the clubs do tend to blur.

1

I'd been at *Vogue* for five years at this point, and despite my after-hours indiscretions, I'd always worked very hard. I'd started off as the assistant to Sarajane Hoare, the fashion director, but when she decamped for *Harper's Bazaar* in New York, I went to work for Jane Pickering. Eventually, I became accessories editor, a job that included putting together a page on belts and bags and shoes called "Last Look."

The feature was called "Last Look" because it came last in the book, but lots of people told me it was the page that they looked for first. It wasn't a fashion shoot with a model, but rather a collection with a theme. One month, it was Christmas gifts. Another, it would be "everything's going metallic silver." But now it appeared very likely that "Last Look" was going to be my last stand.

I followed Anna into her office and sat down across from her, confronting a woman with the exasperated mien of a schoolmistress pushed to the limit. I think what must have frustrated her most is that she could see that I had talent, but that talent alone was not going to save me.

"We think you've outgrown your job," she began.

At *Vogue* they never said, "You're fired." They came up with encouraging euphemisms framed in the language of personal development.

I nodded and let out a great sigh of relief. It was all very polite. We exchanged a moment of warm and well-meaning eye contact, and then, leaving my things to pack up another day, I went home and slept all afternoon.

Introspection and self-awareness were not my strong suits in those days, and as I trundled home I did not fully appreciate the huge favor Anna was doing me. She was setting me up to mend my ways. She was also setting forces in motion that, in time, would lead to success far beyond anything I could ever have imagined. But if my subsequent history came as a surprise to me, it must have been absolutely mystifying to those who knew me at this and at earlier stages of my development. Trust me. No one ever would have voted Tamara Yeardye "Most Likely to Succeed."

. . . .

VOGUE HOUSE IS IN HANOVER Square, near Oxford Circus, which is just across Hyde Park from Chester Square where, in 1995, I lived in the basement of my parents' house. London real estate, especially in Belgravia, is ridiculously expensive, and the large houses usually have staff apartments that the older generation makes available to their less affluent adult children. My rather dodgy quarters had a separate entrance with a door that connected to the main house, which I always tried to keep locked.

This modest attempt at privacy drove my mother nuts. Then again, my mother was unwell, which is a polite way of saying that she had severe emotional problems exacerbated by alcoholism, and though she was sober at this point, she was still not getting the help she needed. Certainly she has always been the most painful warp in the loom of my life. My very first memory is, in fact, of her pushing me across the bed and my hitting my head on a radiator. Had I spilled something? Made too much noise? All I remember is being so stunned that the pain took a moment to register, and then her loving words: "You're not hurt. You didn't even start crying until I came over."

My mother's alcoholic rants and cruelties were the bane of my childhood. But during the period of the Belgravia basement, her greatest perversity was in watching me follow the same path of chemical dependency and never saying a word.

For several years I'd been what you could call a functioning addict. When I wasn't going out to clubs, I was falling asleep at eight p.m., but it wasn't like ordinary sleep. What I did each night at home was a variation on passing out. Then the next morning I'd get up and drag myself in to work. If my child were living like that, I think I might have had something to say.

And it wasn't as if my mother was completely indifferent to my existence. Whenever I was out she would go down to my room and search through my things, then make inappropriate comments to others about whatever she had found. I was with my boyfriend's family once at their house in France and his father said to me, "Is it true that your mother has to go down and tidy up your underwear drawer?"

Cedric Middleton, the boyfriend, worked in finance, but that aside, he wasn't the typically pale and priggish English public school boy. Cedric had gone to school in Switzerland, which is where the people who can afford it go when they can't quite navigate a place like Eton or Harrow. He had an edge to him.

Cedric came from a lower aristocratic family and lived just around the corner—also in the basement of his parents' home. It really was quite the fashion. A few years younger than I, he was handsome and tall with floppy brown hair, and he was really a lot of fun. We hung around with a crowd that was similarly favored by genealogy: Lucas White, Lord White's son; Emily Oppenheimer, whose family once owned most of the diamonds in South Africa; Tara Palmer-Tomkinson, goddaughter to Prince Charles; and all-purpose "It girl" Tamara Beckwith, now a fixture in the British tabloids.

Our nocturnal habitat ranged from L'Equipée Anglaise in Marylebone to Tramp on Jermyn Street, a private club that had been around since "Swinging London" in the sixties. Johnny Gold, the owner, had played host to everyone from Sinatra and the Beatles to Lindsay Lohan and Dodi Fayed. He'd even known my father back in the day when Dad owned a similar venue and was still quite the man about town.

But by the time I'd reached the end of my career as a fashion editor, being "fabulous" on the dance floor but never quite sure of my exact whereabouts had become more trouble than it was worth. I had given my all to dissipation, and now, in a predictable twist to the unsavory plot, I was unemployed. The only reason I'd been living unhappily under my parents' roof was because, on a *Vogue* salary, I couldn't afford to move out. Now I had no salary at all.

Lounging in my subterranean lair in the days just after my chat with Anna Harvey, I realized more and more that I had slipped into the realm of personal crisis. With *Vogue* out of the picture, what exactly was I going to do with my life? I had made good progress up from the depths of a less than stellar school career, and now I had pissed all that away.

More to the point, how was I going to get by? Was I going to live off my parents forever, piled on the sofa, wrapped in a duvet, eating guacamole and chips in a Belgravian version of *Wayne's World*?

I needed a plan. So what did the self-help books advise us to do? Ask yourself, they say, "What do you love? What are you good at?"

Well, fashion, certainly. With perhaps a particular fixation on shoes that long predated "Last Look." On *Vogue* shoots in Nepal I used to obsess over which pair of mukluks to wear. As a child of four, I'd finagled my way onto a school trip to Paris with the older girls, where I broke down in tears over a pair of red cowgirl boots, so much so that the nuns were forced to buy them for me.

For the past year or so I'd been germinating an entrepreneurial idea, and, necessity being the mother of many good things, now might just be the time to get on with it. There was a cobbler in the East End of London who had made a name for himself creating bespoke shoes for women of a certain pedigree. If Lady Windermere-Smythe or her daughter needed a shoe to match the exact hue of her dress, and assuming that she was content to wear either a pump or a slingback (those were the only two options), he was the go-to guy.

This cobbler, whose name was Jimmy Choo, worked out of a small shop in a Dickensian building on Kingsland Road that had once housed London's Metropolitan Hospital. There was a tiny showroom with an old dirty carpet, a few wooden shelves with sample shoes on display, a sewing machine, and a worktable. It was hideous, but the Bentleys would pull up, the ladies would sit down and draw an outline of their feet on a piece of cardboard, and their shoes would be ready in time for the coming-out party, the wedding, or the viscount's ball.

Jimmy had emerged as cobbler to the well-heeled in the 1980s, when the major fashion houses did not yet have the shoe lines they do today. Sergio Rossi was making high fashion footwear on the Continent, but the only fabulous, sexy shoes available in London were from

Manolo Blahnik. Thus Jimmy became a service provider not only for society ladies in need of one-off shoes, but for editors as well.

Whenever we were planning a shoot at *Vogue*, one of us junior people would go down to his hideous little workshop in Hackney, past all the barbed wire and the metal grates, and we'd describe what we were doing. "It's a gladiator story. . . . We need some flat gladiator sandals, only with silver metallic studs." Just before the shoot—always at the last minute—his niece, Sandra, would show up to deliver the goods. We'd give him a fashion credit on the page, and then even more well-heeled ladies who read the fine print would find their way to his shop.

Jimmy was from Malaysia, where he had apprenticed to his cobbler father at the age of nine, cooking rice and running errands as well as learning to make shoes. As a teenager he'd come to London to attend the leather trade school, Cordwainers College, part of the London College of Fashion. The name "cordwainers" is derived from Cordoba, as in Spain, as in Cordoba leather. Ever since the London shoemaker's guild was organized in 1271, they called themselves the Worshipful Company of Cordwainers. What I never realized until much later, and much to my regret, was that students at Cordwainers learned everything about how to make shoes, but not necessarily anything about how to design them. But that gets us ahead of our story.

Elizabeth Stuart-Smith was another Cordwainers graduate who back in the mid-eighties worked next door to Jimmy. She was doing much better than he was commercially, and she asked him to make shoes for her. It was she who then spread the word among fashion editors that Jimmy was available to make one-offs on short notice. For a while the two of them produced shoes for Elizabeth's line, but then in 1988, when her brand really took off, she moved production to Italy, leaving Jimmy somewhat adrift. Certainly I think it left him feeling ill-used.

Jimmy's next venture was a partnership with three Turkish brothers whose father had opened a shoe factory in the fifties, on Abbot Street, very near the Hospital. The father's name was Mehmet Kurdash, and supposedly he'd introduced the stiletto to the UK. He named his brand Gina, after the actress Gina Lollobrigida.

Mehmet's sons began manufacturing a ready-to-wear line for Jimmy at the Gina factory, and in 1991 they opened a store on Sloane Street carrying Emma Hope, Gina, and Jimmy Choo. I remember going in and seeing the shoes they made for Jimmy, and I thought they were hideous—nothing distinctive or edgy or fun at all. These were "mother of the bride" shoes so, needless to say, the venture did not succeed. And once again the bad experience seemed to reinforce Jimmy's innate conservatism, validating in his mind what must have been the Chinese equivalent of "Cobbler, stick to thy last."

But advancement continued to come Jimmy's way, next in the person of Anouska Hempel, who noticed that he was making shoes for many of her clients, and so she brought Jimmy in to make the shoes for her own couture label. This led to the ultimate cachet booster when Kensington Palace called and asked Jimmy to make shoes for Princess Diana. He would go to her with his pieces of cardboard for the fittings. She didn't have to come to him.

Jimmy was thus committed to and doing nicely in the world of "one-of-a-kind" when, shortly after my departure from *Vogue*, I got

Cedric to drive me down to Hackney so that I could have my first serious conversation with him about starting a business.

Although Jimmy's building had been given over to odd craftsmen from all over the world (and to the occasional fashion star like Alexander McQueen), it was still known as the Hospital. There were no brass plaques directing you to the various businesses inside. You went past the chain-link fence, the barbed wire, and the metal grates, past a brick shed surrounded by weeds and rubble, and asked around. It was like something out of *Blade Runner* or *Mad Max*.

On the day that Cedric and I came to call, we sat in the small fitting room with the threadbare carpet, and Jimmy served us tea. Sandra sat at a table nearby, her head bent over her work but clearly listening, while I explained what I had in mind. Jimmy would design a line of exquisite shoes, and I would find a factory to make them and manage the sales and marketing. We would open stores and start a wholesale line to be carried in high-end stores all over the world, and we both would become incredibly rich.

Cedric thought it was a fine plan, but Jimmy didn't say much. He had been around this block once or twice before, and exposure to the royal family notwithstanding, he was still very much an immigrant living on not so much money in a council flat with his wife and baby. His English was terrible, and I think he was still largely dismayed by London and Londoners, and by Western ways in general.

He smiled a lot in that polite, Asian way, but despite his repeated, "Yes, yes, yes," I had no idea how much of what I was saying was actually sinking in. Sandra never looked up until we were leaving, and then she nodded and gave a faint smile.

Desperate as I was to find a new direction for my life, I was not going to be easily deterred. Still, I knew that building a business with this reclusive, even resistant, Chinese cobbler was not going to happen overnight. Even getting him to participate was not going to happen overnight.

. . . .

IN THE MEANTIME, I WAS still working out a number of personal issues and adhering to my own well-established, though self-destructive, regime of treatment.

A few days after my first, post-*Vogue* meeting with Jimmy, Damian Aspinall, son of the casino owner John Aspinall, flew a bunch of us to Paris for a weekend at the Crillon. Damian was a few years older than the rest of us, but of far greater distinction, he had entirely given up drugs and drink. He could still enjoy himself at a party, but he did so while remaining sober.

The rest of the guys on that trip were also abstaining, at least from drugs, but not me. On the second night we were at Les Bains Douches in the Marais, the house music blaring, and I was fighting my way through the boney elbows of fashion models to do lines in the ladies' room. I'd just come back to our table near the dance floor when Damian turned to me and said, "You've got a problem. You need to go to rehab."

I was gobsmacked. This comment came at me completely out of the blue. Yet I was also touched that he'd noticed. We didn't have any kind of special relationship, so why was Damian suddenly taking an interest?

All my life people had described me as being remote, as if living behind glass. In case of emergency, break glass. Damian had just thrown a brick, and the sudden honesty and clarity cut through years of passivity and denial.

"You're absolutely right," I said.

It was simply the perfect moment for me to hear a statement of the obvious, and my mind was utterly receptive. I was at a point of surrender, not in a spiritual or romantic way, but in the B movie way of "You've got me surrounded. I give up."

"Brilliant," I went on. "I'll do that. I'll check into rehab and get well. Where should I go?"

Damian mentioned the name of a place down in Surrey, and I breathed another great sigh of relief. There was a solution to my problem after all—I'd simply never thought of it. So that was that. I'd get myself into rehab as soon as I was back in London. But then the sudden clarity itself was cause for further celebration, and whatever my plans for sobriety, there was still plenty of coke in my bag and limitless vodka at the bar.

On Sunday, our very hungover group had a late lunch and then flew back to England, and on Monday I contacted the treatment facility Damian had recommended. After that, Cedric and I went to Spain for a couple of weeks, staying with friends in Marbella. I did cartloads of drugs, partly because I knew this was going to be my last hurrah, and not just coke but Ecstasy, all with my preferred chaser from the Russian steppes. It's a wonder I made it out alive.

We returned to London, and Cedric took me to dinner at San Lorenzo in Knightsbridge. I had a last glass of red wine—a fond farewell, that one—and the next morning we were in his little Golf GTI, motoring out the A24 to Surrey.

Farm Place is in the village of Ockley, and though it's only a short distance south of the city, it is profoundly "English countryside" in the manner of picture postcards. Roses twine along old rambling houses and boys amble in cricket whites on the village green.

The rehab center itself is in a shabby Tudor house with cigarette burns in the sofas in the drawing room, neglected green lawns, and a filthy swimming pool that no one ever used.

In the driveway I said good-bye to Cedric with slight trepidation. This was a little like being left at school, but I was ready to clean up on day one without any kicking and screaming. In fact, the therapists were quickly amazed by my enthusiasm and resolve—they said they'd never seen anyone so determined to get well.

I didn't know why I'd been acting out, but I did know that it wasn't just for the "fun" of it, because at this stage of the game it was anything but fun. I couldn't articulate what they were, maybe I couldn't even see them, but certainly I had more than my share of demons. One of them was, of course, my mother and the enigma of why she so often seemed to despise me. But the other force at play was a demonic drive for the financial security I hoped would keep me out of her clutches.

I had spent my childhood in preferred postal codes—Beverly Hills, Belgravia—but somehow along the way I had inherited the fear of destitution that sometimes comes from growing up in an entrepreneurial household. My father had made a lot of money, but it never flowed in a steady stream, and it never seemed to be quite enough. In the late eighties he'd been heavily invested in London real estate, but in the crash of the early nineties, he had to unload his properties at half value. But no matter my parents' circumstance, feast or famine, I didn't want to remain dependent on them. My worst fear was remaining under my mother's thumb. My second worst fear was giving her the satisfaction of seeing me wind up in a council flat, which some of the well-born girls I did drugs with actually managed to do.

Other than Damian and Cedric, nobody knew about my sudden conversion to the cause of sobriety. When I mentioned rehab to my father, he told me not to do it. At that time, residential treatment was still virtually unknown in the UK. "You'll be branded a junkie," he said, "and no one will ever talk to you." He also refused to pay, but, happily, Damian agreed to cover my costs, and I agreed to repay him later.

For the first two weeks at Farm Place we weren't allowed to contact anyone, but as soon as that quarantine was lifted I rang my parents. My mother answered, and when I told her where I was she said, "This is not our cup of tea." Then she hung up.

Nevertheless, I remained genuinely excited by the prospect of moving beyond the slough of despond into which I had fallen. Rehab, of course, was not only an escape from drugs but from certain relationships. I welcomed six weeks without the temptation to self-medicate, and six weeks without any of the stimuli that had encouraged my destructive patterns in the first place. The "time-out" in this rural confinement gave me the cozy, protective feeling that I assume most people associate with home. I also knew that it was the only chance for me to get my life together. Certainly it was the only chance for me if I wanted to start a business with Jimmy Choo, or with anyone else for that matter.

Farm Place dealt with only a couple dozen patients at a time, with roughly an equal mix of men and women. The treatment began with a five-day detox, which I didn't really need, because I'd never drunk enough to create a physical addiction. I was a party girl, not the kind of alcoholic who would sit at home, *Lost Weekend* style, scheming to get my hands on a bottle of booze. I never had a drink alone my whole life, but when it came time to binge, I could keep up with the best of them.

The housing was four to a room, and my particular ménage seemed like a setup for Bridget Jones. There were three beds in a row: an anorexic on one side, a compulsive overeater on the other, and me in the middle. The codependent was over by herself, near the window.

The only one of us still in denial was the anorexic, who had been forced in by family and friends. She was horribly thin, but she thought she looked fantastic. She'd nibble a few morsels of food, then speed walk around the grounds. We all had to share one bathroom, so happily she was not bulimic. And just as happily she and the overeater got along famously.

Each of us began the day by making her own bed. We also did the dishes, mopped the floors, cleaned the bathrooms, and did our own laundry. This was new for me, this concept of chores—known in the vernacular of recovery as "therapeutic duties"—but I sort of enjoyed it. It all seemed in keeping with my newfound motivation to change, and the need to dig my way out with my fingernails if need be.

After this spot of housekeeping we'd have morning readings, with affirmations, daily meditation, and then breakfast. Then we'd break into groups for discussion and lots of assignments, working hard on the twelve steps, with emphasis on step #1: Admit you're powerless over your addiction and that your life has become unmanageable. The irony, of course, was that there were so many other ways in which I remained voiceless and powerless—even as I began to acquire the trappings of success, which, as you'll see, made my path to redemption a somewhat bumpy road.

The residents of Farm Place came from all classes, ranging from wealthy brats like me to those whose fees were paid for by the local health authorities. In group meetings for peer evaluation, one person would tell his or her life story and the rest would give feedback, and I was fascinated by listening to their problems, knowing that while there might be cheap seats and luxury boxes, out on the playing field we were all the same. The focus was on the feeling, never the material stuff, and the strangest combinations of people got on.

Other than go to meetings, just about all we did was eat and sleep. We consumed mountains of pork chops and mashed potatoes, fresh from the farm, but I don't think anyone gained weight because there was still a net reduction in calories due to the subtraction of alcohol. (Cases of mineral water were stacked in the kitchen.) Exercise was not encouraged, mostly because those with food issues might use it to try to control their weight.

Every Saturday was visiting day, and though my parents never came, Cedric drove out each and every weekend to bring me cigarettes, to walk around the grounds with me, and to make increasingly awkward conversation. He was very sweet and very supportive, but he really didn't understand what I was doing or why I was doing it.

And I must say I found my whole predicament rather bewildering myself. "How did I end up here?" I kept asking myself. But then I'd rearrange the grammar. I hadn't "ended up" here. I was determined to make sure this was the beginning.

The most productive thoughts available to me to punctuate my long periods of self-doubt and self-loathing were about my business plan. The idea of starting a luxury shoe line was my one ray of hope, a beacon toward which I could steer. I can do this, I told myself. This is something meaningful I can apply myself to and accomplish.

The therapists tried to be helpful in keeping my mind on a positive track, but their horizons were always remarkably limited. When I'd say, "I'm going to start a luxury shoe brand," they'd say, "Perhaps you might take a job in a shoe store." In other words—don't be grandiose. Think small. One day at a time.

My response to that was, "No fucking way. I've put in nearly ten years in the fashion industry. I'm not getting clean and sober just to go backwards!"

Their analysis of my condition was also far too reductive for my taste. They wanted to focus on my chemical addiction. "You are helpless in the face of this compulsion," they said, and fair enough. But then they went on to insist, "You can't blame your parents. We don't want to hear about your crazy, alcoholic mother who tormented you. You're just an addict—that's it."

That one-size-fits-all, no-need-to-look-beyond-the-brain-chemistry assessment didn't sit well with me because to me it simply didn't ring true. I wanted my own particular experience to be validated. And validating my experience would mean someone saying to me, "It's not all just chemicals. Your mother's always been a nightmare where you're concerned. That demon is not in your head, and it's going to take more than therapy to get rid of it."

Most people go to halfway houses after rehab. Instead, when I got out, I threw myself into trying to win over Jimmy Choo. This was still part of my therapeutic effort to shut down the old habits and rebuild the new, and it was still propelled in large part by fear. I was determined not to get stuck in my mother's world. I was determined not to end up as a junkie in a council flat. And yet it still took every bit of my strength. At times my energy seemed so depleted that it was all I could do to get out of bed, but I had nothing to lose and everything to gain.

. . . .

WHILE I'D BEEN AT FARM PLACE my parents had sold their big house in Chester Square and bought two smaller ones nearby, one on Chester Row and one on Gerald Road, which were sort of back-to-back. We'd probably lived in about seven different houses in Belgravia at one time or another because my father would buy a place, do it up, live in it for a while, and then sell it for a profit.

When I came out of rehab, I moved into the main house on Chester Row, my parents lived in the place on Gerald Road, and now my brother Daniel took up residence in their basement. The free rent was good for keeping my overhead low, but not so good for my state of mind. My mother still came around every day, and still let herself in, unannounced, presumably to explore my underwear drawer and God knows what else.

At night I went to Narcotics Anonymous meetings, and then each morning I'd take the tube from Sloane Square to Hackney to spend the day with Jimmy. He still seemed incredibly nervous and guarded, and to this day I don't think he ever fully understood what I was proposing, and where it might lead. So my first task, really, was to convince him that I was serious and that I meant him no harm. Quite the opposite, my most heartfelt intent was to make him a lot of money. But I couldn't win him over by taking him to a smart restaurant for lunch. He needed to get a better sense of me as a person and to see a demonstration of my commitment in action. He wanted me to "smell the leather," or perhaps the glue, so the only way to demonstrate what I was about was to hang around down there with him and to really get my hands dirty.

Every day, then, for three months, I went down to get my trade school education, but also, in a way, to continue my therapy. My past defenses had been stripped away at Farm Place—I was now experienced at making beds and cleaning toilets—which had indeed left me ready to rebuild on a more solid foundation.

Meanwhile, to continue my actual therapy, I immersed myself in the world of Narcotics Anonymous. I made new friends, but I also ran into a lot of people I'd known previously, never realizing until now that they, too, struggled with addiction. I still wanted to keep in touch with my old crowd, too, but I remember one night, going out to a club with Tara and Emily, then feeling so uncomfortable once I got there that I burst into tears and ran out.

Given my obsessive nature, being embedded in Jimmy's world meant spending a fair amount of time just trying to organize and tidy up. The place was always a mess, and as I pushed my broom, I observed Jimmy as he molded lasts in the back with a couple of Malaysian workers or stretched the uppers on the shoes. Meanwhile, his niece,

Sandra—young, skinny, with long dark hair and bangs—sat at the worktable cutting patterns and stitching.

As I was to learn, Sandra was a key player in Jimmy's operation, and in his psyche. She had been born on the Isle of Wight where her father and mother owned a Chinese restaurant. She'd wanted to go to fashion school but her parents refused, so she went to live with her mother's sister Rebecca, who was Jimmy's wife. Sandra spent a year at Central Saint Martins College of Arts and Design, then went to work for her uncle in 1989.

Throughout my trade school time in Hackney, I was turning to my father for a sort of kitchen MBA. I even brought Jimmy over to Chester Row for a business lesson or two. My dad told him, "You should never accept a deal where your share isn't on par with the investors. Fifty-fifty." It was solid advice, but in just a few years it would come back to haunt us.

At the outset my dad made it clear that he wasn't interested in being the investor who owned the other 50 percent. He wanted me to go out and raise the capital myself. So I pitched the idea to my friend Dodi, the son of Mohamed al-Fayed, owner of Harrods, and then to several of my dad's wealthier friends. I made up a press book with all the clippings from *Vogue* that included credits for Jimmy, but everyone said no. Neither Jimmy nor I had the kind of track record that investors look for.

At the same time I felt a bond growing between my father and me that had never been allowed to flourish during my childhood. He had been very successful as an entrepreneur, and it remained to be seen whether or not I had inherited any of those skills. But I brought other skills and other talents, as well as knowledge of this particular world, and of the particular generation I wanted to sell to.

After three months down in Hackney, I think I'd demonstrated all the determination that Jimmy—or my father—needed to see, but I still hadn't raised any outside money. Dad lined up his friends David and Frederick Barclay, owners of the Ritz and the Telegraph newspapers and other prestige properties. They agreed to invest £100,000 and my dad would invest £50,000. Then I think my father reflected for a moment and said, "You know what? For that amount of money, I'm going to do it myself." So he declined the Barclays' offer and lined up lawyers to start negotiating a contract. We were going to launch a line of ready-to-wear shoes, as well as a chain of boutiques, organized under the company name Jimmy Choo Limited.

Jimmy's role was to design the collection, and he would retain his couture business, which stood apart from this agreement. Our role was to provide the start-up money, management, and business expertise. Each party—my father and I being one, Jimmy the other—would own a 50 percent stake. (Jimmy nominally agreed to our suggestion that he give Sandra some shares from his half, but he never did.) Dad would be chairman. I would be managing director in charge of manufacturing, promotion, and marketing.

In May 1996, we all sat in the living room of the Chester Row house and signed the agreement. It was a big, fat booklet with enormously complicated legalese, which only added to Jimmy's intense anxiety. He looked terrified, as if he could still bolt at any minute. Luckily, he had a lawyer from Schillings in London who kept turning to him to say, "Jimmy, this is a good deal. You should sign this. This is a really good deal."

My father set up a corporate entity called Thistledown International Limited in the Virgin Islands as the vehicle for his investment. He then engaged a company called CI Law Trustees on the island of Jersey to hold the shares.

I simply assumed that these elaborate financial structures were a good idea—who was I to question my father's judgment about money? And we both "assumed" that Jimmy Choo, cobbler to the upper crust, would flourish as Jimmy Choo the fashion-forward shoe designer. But as the saying goes, we live and learn.

Unwarranted assumptions in both cases led to unbelievably painful consequences, and yet we not only kept on going—we thrived. Truth be told, if we'd done everything right, if there had never been any sharp reversals and internecine battles, this story would not be nearly so interesting.

. . . .

MANY YEARS LATER, AFTER I'D launched Jimmy Choo to become a global brand, gone through three private-equity deals, and survived a hostile takeover; made headlines by getting my playboy ex-husband off the hook in a wiretapping case by testifying to his lovable incompetence; then become embroiled in another courtroom drama to keep my own mother from cheating me out of millions, Giles Hattersley wrote in the *Sunday Times* that I seemed "less an actual person than the heroine of some dicey Danielle Steel bonkathon."

Looking back now, I suppose there's some small bit of justice in the characterization.

The basic Danielle Steel conceit is to take a plucky heroine, set her

HARROW COLLEG
Learning Centre

on a quest, then subject her to every villain and viper and pitfall imaginable, which is not an entirely bad summary of my life so far.

The formula came of age in silent movie serials like *The Perils of Pauline*, in which the always imperiled young woman did battle with pirates and rampaging Apaches, with each twelve-minute reel leading to a cliff-hanger. Danielle Steel's version provides more sophisticated villains who often lurk in boardrooms and wear bespoke suits, and the perils lead more often to financial ruin than to the wheels of an oncoming train. Danielle's damsel in distress must also have a certain look, her goals must involve the latest trends in business or media, and her environment must be saturated with bold-faced names, fabulous fashions, and other luxury goods. But what's most essential is that this plucky young woman ultimately makes it through, and so much the better if her beginnings were inauspicious.

To the extent that any of that attaches to me, I have made it through, yet, oddly enough, the vulnerabilities that led to my mistakes, and to my being susceptible to the bullying of certain "villains" along the way, were born of the very same early experiences that fueled the life-and-death determination that allowed me to survive.

I simply never imagined when I started this journey just how many backstabbings, cliff-hangers, and oncoming trains lay ahead.

.... 2 ....

haven't kept many photographs from my early life, but I did manage to hang on to a watercolor painting I did in primary school when I must have been about seven years old. It's of a house and two stick figures, and on the back I wrote, "My parents hate me."

Uncertainty about parental love is, unfortunately, a fact of life for many children. But my mother's raging lunacy flared up so routinely that it left me in a constant state of bewilderment. I could never understand what I'd done to deserve her wrath.

Her animosity rarely escalated into violence. It was more of a steady drip, drip, drip of psychological assaults and my impression that she took pleasure in hurting me. I was stupid. I was lazy. I was ugly. I was a hypochondriac. These were her endearments.

One Christmas—I was probably four or five—I woke up and walked into my parents' bedroom, only to have my mother look at me and say, "What are you so excited for? You haven't got anything." I went back to my room and cried my eyes out. Later I went downstairs and there were presents after all. So what was the point of the cruelty?

The randomness of the little digs, as well as the raging invectives, left me like a lab mouse pressing the bar, hoping to get the food pellet, but more often getting the electric shock, until I simply gave up in despair. At a very early age I simply learned to shut down and never show any emotion, either happy or sad.

The older I got, the more fully I internalized the lesson that the way to survive was to be invisible. Any time I showed up on her radar, whether because I was feeling good or feeling bad, I became a target. But the trigger for the most dramatic outbursts was any time my father showed me the least bit of attention. Whenever that happened, my mother would throw an absolute fit.

When I was small we lived in Berkshire, in a Tudor cottage with a swimming pool and tennis court. There were pretty gardens, a well-kept lawn, and six bedrooms, though two of them were the size of cupboards. My father, a big man, had to bend down to get through the door frame built in the era of Henry VIII.

Then we moved to California, and from the time I was about eight, television became the center of my existence. *Three's Company. The Brady Bunch. Mork and Mindy.* I never identified with any of the images I stared at so aimlessly, hours on end, but it did serve to introduce me to American culture.

We lived on Whittier Drive in Beverly Hills, next door to Nancy Sinatra, as it turned out. My father had come to the States to introduce Vidal Sassoon salons and hair care products as a national brand. This involved a dramatic surge in living standard for us, which was very exciting, especially with the blue skies and bougainvillea and the reflected glow of Hollywood. But despite the insistent sunshine, the move to California is when I remember things getting really bad for me, like a curtain coming down.

Just the other day I was tidying up my own daughter's room, rummaging through the board games, arts and crafts materials, pens and pencils, helping her organize it all, and I thought back to my childhood bedroom where there wasn't a desk, there weren't books, there were no games, certainly nothing for arts and crafts. There was a bed, and a TV, and a set of barren shelves. It was like a cell.

Psychologists say that women who have very narcissistic mothers often take one of two very different paths in life: They either go down the rabbit hole of drug addiction, or they become overachievers. In a way I followed both paths, one after the other. They've also discovered that the women who become overachievers usually have a strong connection with their dads. This was always the case, at least in terms of my emotional makeup. But it wasn't until we began to work together on Jimmy Choo that I began to feel that sense of connection being reciprocated.

. . . .

I GREW UP WITH TWO brothers—Gregory, three years younger than me, and Daniel, three years younger than he—and the three of us went to El Rodeo School, which was just at the foot of the hill below our house. My father drove us, and my mother would pick us up. It wasn't long, though, before I was transferred to Marymount, a Catholic girls' school a few miles away in Brentwood, and my mother began to drive me both ways. Our most memorable trip was the morning she was trying to mask the smell of liquor on her breath with a drop or two of Binaca. She was careening along through this exclusive neighborhood in her red Mercedes convertible, head back, bottle upended, when the cap came off and about three ounces of breath freshener gushed down her throat. She had to pull over to the side of the road and vomit.

As my mother's drinking escalated, my father had us go around putting Post-it notes on all the liquor bottles saying, "Please, Mummy, stop drinking." At other times he'd empty out the vodka and refill the containers with water. All the while we got the clear message that we were not supposed to talk about the drinking or about how crazy she was. The unspoken directive for the three of us children was to Keep the Family Secret and to, above all, Look Good and Act Normal.

The allure of being a "normal" family was so strong that my father once got it into his head that we should rent a recreational vehicle and go camping in Yosemite. So the five of us, plus another English couple, went off into the woods for this very "Ozzie and Harriet" adventure. Of course, my mother got stinking drunk, tripped over a log, and fell on her face, then began to rain long, obscene curses down on me. I think if a meteorite had struck the campsite, she would have similarly blamed me. When we got back to L.A., we had to make up some lie about what had happened to her face.

The joke, of course, was that this woman who devoted so much attention to how she looked went around the house wearing an unkempt dressing gown, no makeup, and her hair as frizzy as a fright wig. In her drunkenness she obsessed about the tiniest of imperfections, like the little fuzz balls that would appear on the carpet. Perhaps the finest moment of my childhood was the day she staggered down from the second floor, raging at me for God knows what, stooped to pick up a ball of lint, then slid headfirst and spread-eagled, all the rest of the way down. Shortly thereafter she was in a car crash, and she must have really erupted at the other driver, so much so that the man called my father at his office to ask, "Is your wife on drugs?"

Through it all I think my dad was simply overwhelmed, trying to keep the peace and make the best of it with three kids and a crazy wife. I didn't have to go too far into some Freudian fantasy to believe that getting away from my mom and being alone with my dad would make things better. I always wished they would get divorced and that I could live with him.

Divorce was not a great option from his perspective, though, because in those days, despite my mother's obvious shortcomings as a caretaker, custody almost certainly would have gone to her. As far as he was concerned, then, the only way it worked was for it to work, however superficially. And in his mind, I think he could rationalize the cruelties he saw visited on me as being merely verbal and emotional. As in, I wasn't being branded with cigarettes or beaten with coat hangers. In other words, I would survive.

My father did the best he could as a typical "man's man" of his time, someone for whom hugging and expressive conversation were simply not part of the repertoire. And that's before we factor in the whole matter of English culture, the stiff upper lip and all that. He had his hands full, and he simply wasn't equipped to cope with the fact that he had a severely depressed daughter.

Only once, and long after I'd grown up, do I remember him coming clean, as least to the extent of saying, "Your mother is the most selfish and self-obsessed woman I've ever come across."

Of course, she was also one of the most beautiful. She'd been a model when they met—the peak of her career was a print ad for

Chanel—and for her, life was still all about how she looked. Her mornings were a lengthy ritual of dressing and applying makeup. Then it would be lunch with a girlfriend, then picking us up from school. She had no particular passion for gardening, or tennis, or charity fundraisers, or any of the other things that wealthy women sometimes do. For her it was shopping, lunching, drinking. We had a pool, but she couldn't swim. As far as enjoying the Southern California lifestyle was concerned, we might as well have lived in Glasgow.

. . . .

MY BROTHERS WERE VERY CLOSE, and they shared a room and had the same friends. They were a team, and they used to go out in the street and play with other kids on the block. As the only girl, I inhabited a different planet, almost as if I were an only child, and definitely home alone.

On those rare occasions when I tried to bring over friends, it was a disaster. My mother would fly off the handle and kick them out of the house for making too much noise, or for some minor infraction like leaving a candy wrapper in the sink. After a while I stopped inviting anyone over, and I retreated to my bedroom, closed the door, and watched TV. There was no one saying, "Got any homework today? Let's sit down and maybe start into it. Are you hungry? Do you want a snack?"

My mother's primary form of engagement with me was an ongoing effort to humiliate. To her friends she would make cutting comments or play the victim, making the case that I was a terrible child. Then she would get these friends to come talk to me. I remember being at home on Whittier Drive when a woman I'd never seen before came up to me and said, "Can't you be nice to your mother?" Being older and more aware never helped me in understanding these strange psychological games. The more I thought about it, the more bewildered I became.

When I was about thirteen, a girlfriend invited me to go with her to the movies in Westwood. She was a little older, old enough to drive, with a nice family, a nice house in Beverly Hills, and a white VW Rabbit. She drove by and picked me up, we went to the movies, and then she dropped me off back at my house. At which point my mother came out on the lawn tearing her hair in a rage, screaming about how this girl was trying to seduce me into a lesbian relationship.

I never saw my friend again.

During my brief stint at El Rodeo I met two sisters and they were my most consistent social connection. I would go to their house, rather than the other way around, but what I saw there differed very little from what I experienced at home. It confirmed my belief that all the mothers in Beverly Hills were simply out of their minds.

My parents' own social circle extended into the English contingent in Hollywood. Michael Caine would have us over to his house for Sunday lunch, and I remember meeting Sean Connery once at the Beverly Hills Hotel, shortly before my parents took a trip with him to Morocco.

Because of my father's extensive business connections, there were long stretches when they would go out to dinner every night, leaving my brothers and me to eat at home with the Mexican housekeeper. In the movies there's always the nanny or the maid, usually a black woman but sometimes Hispanic, who gives the lonely child all the love she's not getting from her distant parents. Unfortunately, our domestic helpers came and went in an endless succession, and I never developed a relationship with any of them. For reasons that may appear obvious by now, none of them chose to stick around our household very long.

One evening I brought along a friend to a restaurant called Jimmy's, where my parents were having dinner with a group that included Phyllis Diller. My mother kept leaning over to stage-whisper in my ear, "Get that whore out of here." For an instant I thought she was talking about the comedienne, but then I realized she was talking about my friend. I didn't know what to do or even where to look. A little later I walked into the bathroom and there was my mother passed out on the floor. I went back to get my dad and he had to carry her out to the car. I remember he seemed very humiliated, even as he drove away in his white Rolls-Royce.

In these days before cell phones, she was missing for hours and my father was in a panic because he didn't know where she was. He was calling the airport frantically, and I remember standing there thinking why on earth would he want to look for this woman, much less find her? I know that a bit more compassion and forgiveness would reflect better on me. I will go so far as to say that I'm still working on it. But certainly those admirable qualities were not available to me as a teenager. At the time, I was barely able to process. And, of course, whenever one of these little dramas occurred, nobody ever said anything, much less offered an explanation. So all that was available to me was my own sense of shame and humiliation, while my mind struggled to make sense of it. Essentially, I was reduced to the primitive options of fight, flight, or freeze, and I chose the latter, which was to become my default response throughout life to any unexpected act of aggression or any "shocking" situation that defied easy explanation.

. . . .

WHEN I WAS FOURTEEN MY parents decided that I should go back to England for boarding school. Perhaps my father saw that putting a broad continent and an equally wide blue ocean between me and my mother was the only way I'd survive. Or maybe he thought getting me out of the house would make his wife easier to live with. I wanted to go to Beverly Hills High because one of my friends was going to go there, but as soon as a return to the UK was presented as an option, I saw that as a fine idea. I would have happily shipped off to join the Red Guard if that's what it took to get away from my mother.

Back when we'd lived in Berkshire, our local doctor also served as resident physician at Heathfield, in Ascot, the sister school to Eton. It's very English, of course, with lots of girls with titles and double-barreled names, but that wasn't my background at all. We were nouveau riche with a capital N. So my father called up his friend the doctor and asked if he could help get me in. The doctor rang up the school and said there's a girl who needs to come from California, and an interview was arranged.

My parents were planning to stay on in Beverly Hills, but we all flew over for the admissions interview with the headmistress, Mrs. Parry, and on the drive out from London, my mother hid a bottle under her seat, but not very well. I had no doubt that the clear liquid peeking out from inside the plastic bag was vodka.

We stopped first to see their friend the doctor, all three of us, and as my parents chatted in his drawing room, I went back outside, snatched the bottle from under the car seat, and hid it.

Later, all through our rather formal encounter with the rather formidable Mrs. Parry (her husband was a housemaster at Eton), I had the pleasure of watching my mother squirm and fidget, deprived of her tranquilizer. She went absolutely mad with twitching, after which she threw a raging fit, but she really couldn't go into why she was having the fit because she couldn't admit to having brought along the booze.

Heathfield was very adept at producing Sloane Rangers, the perfectly coifed, usually blond young women you see coming and going from the luxury shops near London's Sloane Square. It was incredibly snobby, but I was this sort of funny, alien thing from Beverly Hills, so I got a pass. If it hadn't been for my exotic American accent, I'm sure I would have been given the frostiest of cold shoulders.

I was also exotic because I arrived with hair curling combs and Calvin Klein underwear, which was an endless source of fascination to these daughters of the aristocracy still forced to wear granny pants under their pleated, navy skirts, white shirts, green ties, and navy V-neck sweaters.

The culture shock went both ways, of course, especially when they played sports like "netball," which I'd never even heard of. I missed my friends, and the L.A. lifestyle, but at least I'd escaped the insanity at home. Then again, I hadn't escaped at all. The damage had already been done.

···· 3 ····

ven though I was out of the house, and out from under my parents' direct control, I was by this time thoroughly embedded behind a wall of glass, the detached observer, emotionally flat. I felt that the girls liked me, but I also remember them teasing me with, "Hi, Tamara. Anybody there?" The only way I overcame the numbness and came to life was with the help of a chemical stimulant.

On my very first day the girls took me with them to the bushes, pulled out their cigarettes, and lit up. So I began smoking, too. As everyone who's ever done it knows all too well, the first cigarette is revolting, but you carry on because you want to be part of the group.

At night we broke out the wine, which was far more agreeable. There was a shop up the road where they'd sell us anything we wanted, and we'd go out into the woods and jam the cork down into the bottle with a stick. Why we never thought to buy a corkscrew, I don't know, because I'm sure they would have sold that to us quite happily as well.

With the exception of these brief moments devoted to sin, the days at Heathfield were nothing if not well organized. We'd get up in the morning, have breakfast (at least we were supposed to—I never made it), sit through chapel, do classes, then sports, then dinner, and more studies, until nine p.m., when it was time for bed. Each of us had her own room with a single bed, a desk, and a cupboard. What little time I had for introspection was spent in there daydreaming, staring into the mirror at a face that my mother had convinced me was quite ugly.

I survived, though, because outside of class I could have fun and act the clown and be silly. But at the same time, I was just so very dark inside. I dragged through all my courses, half asleep, which earned me the nickname "Vacant." There was absolutely nothing that spoke to me, no moment of great awakening in a literature class or a chemistry lab where I said, "Ah ha, this is what I want my life to be about." I had been dropped into this somewhat alien educational system with no real preparation, and having been told by my mother all my life that I was stupid, lazy, and unattractive, my self-confidence and sense of self-worth were not exactly rock solid.

Unfortunately, my record at Heathfield did nothing to counter my mother's assessment. I failed at everything, and still no one seemed to notice. No one ever called me aside or contacted my parents—not that my mother or father would have risen to the occasion. In England, in the seventies and early eighties, there still was the assumption that the primary purpose of educating girls was to prepare them for marriage, so why make a fuss?

I also think that all concerned readily assumed that I was indeed simply dumb, so maybe this was all that could be expected of me. What never seemed to occur to anyone—my teachers, my parents, or me— was that I was profoundly, clinically depressed.

IN THE ENGLISH SCHOOL SYSTEM the first separation of the sheep from the goats occurs when you're about sixteen and you take your "O"-level exams. The testing goes on for days and covers every subject. If you pass, you stick around for another two years to prepare for university in what's called Sixth Form, which is all about studying for your "A" levels in the hope of getting into Oxford or Cambridge. If you flunk those first tests at sixteen, of course, that's it. It's off to trade school with you, or the army, or a job as a waitress. That is, of course, unless you come from a family with money.

I failed all my "O" levels with flying colors, and thus I left school with no qualifications. But several of the girls in my set were also not going on to university. There was Arabella Johnson, as well as Lady Isabella Stanhope, daughter of the Eleventh Earl of Harrington, who later married Colin Campbell, the Seventh Earl of Cawdor, to become Countess of Cawdor, along with a few others whose names I can't remember. For reasons of their own, they were all going off to a Swiss finishing school, which is how the idea came up that I would do the same.

"Fine, dear," my parents said. I think I could have said I was going to join the trapeze act and it would have been, "Fine, dear." They really had no plan for me, certainly no expectations.

The school in question was the Institut Alpin Videmanette, in Rougemont, Switzerland. Going to one of these places was a little like being sent away to a convent, except that here the standard objective was not to avoid men, but to prepare yourself to meet and marry one who was proper and available. The assumption was that you were a dunce and that the only hope for you was to attach yourself to what was known as a "good provider." I didn't know or care, but Princess Diana had "finished" at Rougemont just a few years before, and she'd married Prince Charles. This dubious detail may have added a certain cachet as far as my parents were concerned.

L'Institut was a lingering anachronism even in my time, and by the mid-nineties it had closed for good. The curriculum, such as it was, included French, but was mostly centered on sewing, cooking, and otherwise learning how to be the lady of the house. We mastered the demands of etiquette, including how to curtsy in front of the Queen, should the need ever arise.

At the Institut the girls were treated much more as adults than we'd been at Heathfield. We had a smoking room, for instance, and we didn't have to go out into the bushes to drink, especially when there were such far more agreeable venues just a few miles down the winding Swiss roads.

The main attraction of Rougemont had always been its proximity to the ski resort of Gstaad, and in the winter we took lessons every afternoon. The ski instructor was dragooned into serving as our cooking instructor as well, which meant that our time in the kitchen was a bit of a joke. We would bake a cake and then eat it. That was the extent of the instruction.

The versatile young man who guided us in the kitchen as well as on the slopes had a habit of seducing his young charges, but he studiously avoided me. Maybe I just wasn't his type, but years later I learned that he'd also received a word to the wise from a most unlikely source—the actor Roger Moore, who was that era's James Bond and who lived nearby. Moore's son and this young man were mates, and supposedly Roger said to him one day, "You better give Tamara Yeardye a wide berth. I know her father and he'll break your legs."

Also nearby was the winter campus of Le Rosey, perhaps the most exclusive secondary school in the world. Several generations of Hohenzollerns, Rothschilds, Metternichs, and Borgheses have doodled in their textbooks there. Aga Khan IV is an alum, as is Prince Ranier III of Monaco, and various other monarchs. This is where Elizabeth Taylor, John Lennon, and Diana Ross sent their kids.

The boys from Le Rosey were entirely too *foreign* to be considered good husband material, but we girls weren't thinking in those terms anyway. These pampered boys had their uses, though, which included picking us up in their Ferraris after we'd jumped off the balcony into piles of snow. We'd drive down to our favorite Gstaad nightclub called the Gringo, located at the Palace Hotel, and then the Rosey boys would drop us off in the morning. On Saturday afternoons we'd simply hitchhike in to have hot chocolate at a tearoom called Charly's.

There were only sixty girls in the school, and when Madame Yersin, the headmistress, figured out that I was the ringleader for these escapades, she moved me to the chalet where she lived. I quickly found a new escape route through the basement boiler room and out a window. But for whatever reason, and despite my refusal to follow her rules, Madame and I seemed to get on. At a wedding years later, I ran into one of my partners in crime who told me she'd been back to see our former headmistress. Apparently Madame had said, "You two girls were some of the naughtiest I've ever had, but you were so endearing, I couldn't kick you out."

In 1984, with Madame's forbearance, I completed finishing school and was done with my formal education. I was seventeen, and I had no earthly idea what to do with myself.

. . . .

BY THIS TIME MY PARENTS had left California and established residence in Monaco. They also bought a country house in Wentworth and a mews house in Belgravia. My father's company, Vidal Sassoon, had just been sold for a tidy sum, and a fair portion of the proceeds went to my dad. He invested in London real estate, buying and selling properties, and working out of an office at his home, which is where I began to live camped out in the basement, anxious and insecure, and for a while indeed wrapped in the duvet, eating chips and guacamole, watching TV.

In Switzerland I'd begun to get high-tension headaches on a daily basis, and I was old enough now to know that I wasn't imagining things and that this wasn't normal. So when I came back to London I started seeing doctors to try to account for my symptoms. They checked me for anemia, and they did brain scans, but no one seemed at all curious about a link to depression and stress. My mother insisted that it was "all in my head," and men, even learned physicians, had a habit of accepting my mother's assessments without too much analysis.

All I knew was that I didn't feel well at all and that if I couldn't cure the problem, I needed to find a way to mask it.

The approach I took was to start hanging out with the kids at Crazy Larry's, just off Kings Road, which had a well-earned reputation for catering to dysfunctional Chelsea girls and South London black guys.

This was a much more music-oriented crowd than the Sloane Square types I'd known at school, and infinitely more creative. It felt "underground" to be with them, and very cool. There were people like Kay Montano, who was later to become the fashion industry's über makeup artist, the singer Neneh Cherry, Gavin Rossdale of the rock band Bush, and Nellee Hooper of Soul II Soul, who were breaking through at the time. I loved what these club kids were wearing, which was a very rough, street-chic, gangster look, which stylist Ray Petri began to market as Buffalo. He was the guiding force, style-wise, along with the model Nick Kamen. The idea was to create a smart and functional look that was nonfashion with a hard attitude. It paid tribute to rude boys, mods, blacks, punk whites, East Indians, ragamuffin Jamaicans, New Romantics à la Boy George, and bruised boxers. This was fashion up from the streets and from outside the fashion industry, which then infiltrated pretty much everything, from ad campaigns to magazines like *The Face*, *i-D*, and *Arena*. Buffalo made Petri a "fashion stylist" long before it became a coveted job description.

I loved the music that was emerging at the time, which included rap. Acid house music also became popular after it was essentially launched in a dungeon-like basement in the East End called Shoom. There were fog machines and strobe lights and the fashion was to wear Pumas and aviators. The music pulsed and people danced and blew whistles as if they were leading a procession at the Carnival in Rio. The smiley face was the symbol for this whole scene.

One night I met a guy called Barnzley who was from a council estate in Manchester or Leeds—somewhere up north. His real name was Simon Armitage, and he was friends with Nellee Hooper, and with all of his working-class grit he was definitely a go-getter, very trendy and cool, and we started dating. One day Barnzley said, "Let's set up a stall in the market on Portobello Road," and I agreed, so we began to make T-shirts with the yellow smiley face. I also began to sell my old clothes, along with things I'd pick up in thrift shops. It was fun, and I made a few pounds, but I was also just desperate for something to do, desperate for some way to break away from my parents.

An unintended consequence of the stall was that it stirred up a latent interest in fashion, and soon thereafter I started taking classes at the American University in London, which included courses in pattern cutting and other aspects of design.

My father thought that selling by hand was the way to learn retail, and he noted with approval that the entrepreneurial gene may have been passed on to me. He and I began to bat the ball back and forth, talking about business whenever we were together, and soon enough he encouraged me to move on.

"If you get a real job," he said, "I'll match what you earn."

A few days later we were walking down South Molton Street together and we bumped into Sidney Burstein, a friend of my father's from his days at Vidal Sassoon.

Sidney looked at the wastrel daughter and said, "What are you doing now?"

My father said, "She's studying fashion. Taking courses at American University."

Sidney said, "That's nonsense. You should come and work for me."

Sidney and his wife, Joan, owned Brown's, the legendary boutique that had been introducing the great designers to London since 1970.

Within the week I was selling Azzedine Alaia at their shop at 24 South Molton Street. I was much younger than the other girls, still a bit of a club kid, and occasionally I would show up wearing bike shorts, but of course made by Alaia. I also established the pattern of working all day, then staying up pretty much all night clubbing with Davina McCall and Samantha Robinson. Unfortunately, I also established a pattern of heavy dependence on the era's drugs of choice: cocaine and Ecstasy.

I was at Brown's through most of 1987, and it was a great education in retail. I worked the stockroom as well as the floor, I set up displays, and I manned the cash register. Of course, I also loved the clothes, and by the time I left the job I think I'd rung up a significant trade imbalance in Sidney and Joan's favor.

It was clear that I'd found my métier, and soon enough I was desperate to get off the selling floor and expand my horizons. Occasionally I'd have the chance to help a bit on the public relations side for Brown's, which led to my obtaining an interview with Phyllis Walters, who did PR for them as well as for many designers like Versace. In 1988, Phyllis hired me as her office runner, which meant that I would drop things off at fashion magazines—clothes or samples, whatever they wanted—then pick them up later. The fun part of the job was learning that a magazine was doing something with the theme of "spring roses," say, or "hothouse flowers," then rummaging through our clients' collections to find items that might be included. You could really use your own initiative to find just the right thing, then send it in for the shoot. Eventually, I graduated to working on a few accounts myself, including Marks and Spencer, Georges Rech, and Molton Brown, co-owned by Sidney and Joan's daughter.

My life as a courier in and out of editorial offices allowed me to see how the magazine business worked firsthand, and after about a year I felt ready to take another leap. Through Phyllis I learned that Rupert Murdoch was about to launch a UK version of *Mirabella*, the very smart, upscale women's magazine named after Grace Mirabella, the former editor of *Vogue*. I thought this would be just the place for me, and I approached getting a job there with a studiousness I had never applied back in school. I read everything about their vision, their ethos, and who they saw as their prospective reader.

Fashion magazines encompass two very different worlds: fashion and features. In London, the girls who work in features—the long, sometimes very substantive articles—have liberal arts degrees. The fashion department, which oversees the lavish and creative presentation of the clothing itself, hired girls like me who were less studious, perhaps, but more visually oriented. At *Mirabella*, the fashion director was Caroline Baker, already a legend in the industry for the radical shoots she'd done for *Nova*, and *The Face*, and *i-D* starting out in the sixties. *Mirabella* was more mainstream, but Caroline was still considered quite edgy. I was thrilled when she accepted me as her assistant.

Certainly I was now on a proper flight path, having left the duvet in the basement and the guacamole and the TV seemingly forever. But then came the financial crash of 1989–1990, Murdoch pulled the plug, and all hands at *Mirabella* were made redundant.

. . . .

DURING MY BRIEF TENURE IN the magazine world I'd become friends with a junior fashion editor named Charlotte Pilcher, who began to freelance as a stylist, with me freelancing as her assistant. Having gotten my foot in the door, I was not going to allow myself to be pushed back out so easily. Charlotte lived in Shepherd's Bush, and I was living in my Belgravia basement, and I would show up at her house most mornings with coffee and say, "Come on. Get dressed. Let's go." I was still not feeling well—I had sleep problems, and problems with lethargy and depression—but fear was a great motivator. To have any chance of staying in the game, we had to stay in the loop, which meant being out and about.

Press officers in London would have "open days" when they'd show their clients' new collections and invite the editors from the fashion magazines to come in to browse. The press officers hoped the editors would want to do a shoot featuring some part of their collection, and the editors like Charlotte hoped to be selected to style the shoot.

Charlotte happened to be friends with Jane Pickering, who knew Sarajane Hoare, another legend in the industry who was then fashion director at *Vogue*. Sarajane was looking for an assistant and in 1990, with a good word from Jane Pickering, I got the job. Sarajane had a well-deserved reputation for amazing photo shoots and always worked with the best photographers. Herb Ritts, Patrick Demarchelier, Peter Limbergh—these were her main collaborators. To give the fashions the right look, we would go to incredible lengths, setting up on a mountaintop in Nepal one season and on the beaches of Malibu the next.

On the downside, working this new job had many aspects of *The Devil Wears Prada*—with Sarajane in the Meryl Streep role.

I remember once, trekking up the side of a mountain in the Himalayas with Sarajane, Sherpas bringing up the rear with trunk after trunk of clothing and cameras and lighting equipment, and my boss going on about her boyfriend problems the entire time, all the way up and all the way down, for a solid seven hours. I was ready to shove her off a cliff. But we actually became friends, and she was instrumental in inculcating my attention to detail.

Once we were on a shoot in Central Park, and I'd run out of pins to gather in the dresses. Sarajane threw a red-faced screaming hissy fit every bit as good as anything my mother could have managed. I said I'd run back to the truck for more, but that wasn't good enough. She continued to berate me, and then with Christy Turlington, Naomi Campbell, and Linda Evangelista standing by like statues, she screamed, "You better run, Tamara! RUN!" I got to the point where I had every-thing provided in triplicate, sitting out, well ordered, and ready to go before she could even think about screaming. Years later after I'd started Jimmy Choo we ran into each other in New York. We got on very well, and she apologized for her behavior back when I worked for her.

Working at *Vogue* was a long way from hanging out with the club kids at Crazy Larry's, but biochemically it was very much the same. During the day I was focused on building a career, trying to get some-where in a glamorous and highly competitive field. At night it was all about self-medication for anxiety and depression, with verbal abuse as the constant drumbeat. To make matters worse, I was still living at home and under my mother's thumb and hating myself for doing it.

In prison they talk about EDR—the earliest date of release. For me there was no certain release date. I was going to have to earn my free-dom from my family, and from the uncertainties of working for someone else. Having grown up subject to relentless, emotional manipulation, I didn't want anyone ever to have control over me, so marrying well was never an appealing option. A husband's wealth might provide you luxury, but at best that would be a gilded cage. I knew it was going to be up to me to attain the life I wanted to have.

And after all those years of being told that I was useless, a dunce, and a thoroughly worthless human being, I had a desperate need to express myself. That's when the penny dropped: Jimmy Choo. I'd done my time in retail, in public relations, and in the fashion press. I had a father to advise me who'd succeeded in a similar business. I was also the customer I wanted to reach. I lived the life our prospective client lived. I had an emotional connection to her tastes and dreams because I shared her tastes and dreams.

In September 1996, less than a year after I went into rehab, *Tatler* ran the first story on me as an entrepreneur. Written by Vassi Chamberlain, it was all about the launch of Jimmy Choo and our plans for building a global brand. It even featured a picture of Jimmy and me. The hellion of Tramp and L'Equipée Anglaise had cleaned up her act and was finally trying to do something with her life.

...· 4 ····

Even after all my time at Brown's, at Phyllis Walters's, and at *Vogue*, working on the shop floor, in PR, and for a magazine, I had no idea just how much I knew about the business until I dug in and started applying what I had learned. I also had strong instincts, a certain entrepreneurial skill, and an incredible work ethic, some of which I inherited from my father.

No doubt my father also played a role in creating the drive—both by his unavailability and by the warmth and love that I always felt from him nonetheless, even when he could have been more demonstrative, or perhaps done more to "rescue" me from my mother. At least I always felt that he genuinely cared about me and loved me, so it was natural that I wanted to follow in his footsteps, even if only to prove my worth to him. There was the residual neediness that made me willing to do anything to prove myself worthy of love in his eyes. And there was the desperate drive to prove my mother wrong.

According to the cliché, all little girls have a sort of love affair with Dad, in which the daughter is Dad's little princess and Dad is, at least in her eyes, the big, strong hero, as handsome and rugged as a movie star. In my case, Dad really was heroically big and strong, and handsome enough to have a brief stint in the movies. Especially when you factor in where he came from, he was also sufficiently successful to be considered heroic by almost anyone's standards.

Owing nothing to Danielle Steel's sense of melodrama, my father, Tom Yeardye, was born in the Salvation Army home in Mill Hill, in the north of London. His mother was seventeen, unmarried, pregnant, and driven out of Ireland by the shame of it. She came to the capital to find better prospects, and she became a house cleaner. My father was put in a foster home, but after a few years my grandmother wanted him back, so she married George Yeardye, nineteen at the time, to round out the required nuclear family. Per the usual sad tale, this stepfather was an alcoholic who beat my father mercilessly, a pattern that stopped only when, at fourteen, my father grew big enough to fight back. My dad remained a fighter ever after.

Young Tom couldn't afford to go to university, and instead he did a two-year stint in the navy. Then in the early fifties, when he was in his early twenties, a film producer spotted him in a London club. Standing six foot four, and with a forty-seven-inch chest, he was pegged to be the stand-in for Rock Hudson in a film being shot in Ireland. It was a costume drama called *Captain Lightfoot*, about Irish rebels, set in Clogherhead during the Napoleonic era. The producers' problem was that their star didn't know how to ride a horse. The solution was to hire my father, who did.

Dad went on to appear in *Richard III*, *The Adventures of Robin Hood*, and then in 1957 he was the stand-in for Victor Mature during the torture scenes in *The Long Haul*. This is how he met Diana Dors, then being touted as the English Marilyn Monroe.

Diana and my father developed a thing, but inconveniently, she was already married to her manager, Dennis Hamilton Gittins. In an incident that was a tabloid editor's dream, the glamour girl and my dad went out for a drive, and when they got back, the irate husband was at the house. While Dad waited in the car, Diana went in alone to talk to Gittins. Dad waited, and waited, and then he heard screams. He rushed past the husband's two goons at the door, found Diana on the floor bleeding, with Gittins standing over her, holding a gun. As the story goes, my dad wrestled the gun out of Gittins's hand, pummeled him a bit, and left him whimpering on the floor. He rushed Diana to a doctor, and then brought her home to my grandmother's little house in Mill Hill. For the next several months my father was a fixture in the tabloids, known to every waitress and taxi driver in London as "Mr. Muscles."

He and Diana retired to an estate in Sussex that she'd purchased, and for a while she and my father raised horses. They formed a company, called Juliet Holdings, that allowed them to dabble in both agricultural and entertainment ventures. One of these was a touring cabaret show, written by the comedian Richard Dawson, who later found fame on *Hogan's Heroes*, and who more immediately found his way into Diana's heart, thereby displacing my father.

This was 1959, more or less. Swinging London was just around the corner, and my dad returned to the city to open a restaurant called the Paint Box. No one ever said much about the food, but no matter. The pièce de résistance was models who posed for the customers to sketch while they dined. "I'm bringing art to the common man," my father told reporters.

The Paint Box was a success, and a few months later my dad took what had once been a stuffy private club in the West End and turned it into a cabaret called Le Condor. He still carried the glamour of having been Diana Dors's boyfriend, not to mention her rescuer in a notorious scandal. But glamour attracted unwanted attention, and soon he had dodgy characters asking him to pay "insurance" on the club, as well as protection against "personal injury." A pretty tough guy himself, Dad refused. Soon after, a waiter was accosted by a man wielding a gun. My father was almost run down on the street, albeit by a Jaguar. Then the manager was attacked by a thug with a crowbar. My father decided to redirect his energies toward businesses less likely to attract that kind of attention.

He didn't retreat from glamour entirely, though, because he bought and subsequently lived in an apartment building in Kensington where most of the tenants where fashion models. He dated the B movie actress Sabrina Sykes—the English Jayne Mansfield—famous for her seventeen-inch waist and near forty-inch bust. He also dated Shirley Anne Field, who was truly beautiful in a more sophisticated way, and a serious actress who appeared opposite Laurence Olivier in *The Entertainer*.

Back in his Le Condor days, he'd met a model named Ann Davis who'd done commercials on TV and a print ad for Chanel. She'd been dating a buddy of his, a male model, whom she actually married, after which the bride and groom left the church through separate doors. The marriage was annulled by the time my dad met Ann Davis again. In 1965, they married at the registrar's office in Westminster. Two years later they had their first child—yours truly.

The young couple bought a house in Holland Park, near Notting Hill, and my father continued to make money renting out flats in Kensington. Then, through my mother's obsession with beauty, he became aware of a new product from Denmark called Carmen Rollers. This was an electric hair styling set that came in a red vanity case with a mirror. Despite the fact that the device sold for about sixteen pounds—half a week's wages at the time—all the models loved this "high tech" approach to hair care, which was perfect for creating the heavily lacquered bouffant styles that were de rigueur at the time for London's fashionable "birds."

My dad had a half sister, Jane Trent, who was a flight attendant, and she worked the London to New York route. He asked her to see if this contraption was available in the States. She reported back that it was not, so my dad went to speak with the man who had the UK rights. This fellow had no interest in expanding to North America himself, but he introduced Dad to the inventor of Carmen Rollers, Arne Bybjerg Pedersen. Dad bought the license, as well as five hundred roller kits, and with that he took off for New York.

Launching a new and expensive beauty device in the world capital of hustle was a daunting prospect, but then my father was the man whose greatest claim to fame was swatting away an angry husband's gun. Calling on the department stores proved more expensive and time-consuming than fending off angry rivals, but he scored with Saks and with Bonwit Teller, and the new venture was a success. In little more than a year he sold his North American concession to Clairol for $3 million, and he and my mother came back to England on a nice cushion of cash.

During his time in New York, my dad had pitched Carmen Rollers to the Glemby Company, which ran a string of hair salons. Now one of Glemby's owners, Seymour Finkelstein came to London with a pitch of his own. Glemby wanted to expand into the UK, and Finkelstein saw my father as just the man who could build them a business—which he did, starting at the department store J. J. Allen in Bournemouth.

A friend of my father's who ran his own salon on Bond Street noticed Glemby's sudden rise. His name was Vidal Sassoon. He was already a fixture in the world of fashion, but his small operation was not generating all that much money. So he looked at Glemby and said to my dad, "Can you do that for me?"

My dad invested £250,000 to come in as a partner while also helping Vidal buy out his existing partner, Charles of the Ritz. Suddenly, Vidal Sassoon was on its way to becoming a global brand. (The irony was that Vidal's greatest innovation, of course, was the five-point cut that made hair curlers—my father's previous venture—obsolete.)

Although one was Jewish and the other Irish, Vidal Sassoon and Tom Yeardye were cut from the same tattered cloth. Born in 1928 in the East End, then put into an orphanage when his father abandoned his mother, Vidal apprenticed as a hairdresser at fourteen, served in the Israeli army during the 1948 war to create a Jewish state, then came back to London to make his fortune. Nothing if not ambitious, he even went so far as to take elocution lessons to erase the cockney accent that was a nearly impenetrable class barrier in England those days. Suitably reborn and socially upgraded, he opened his first salon in 1954, on New Bond Street. Then in 1958, just as London was about to start "swinging," he moved to Old Bond Street, on the ground floor, just across from Cartier. Peter O'Toole had to have his hair trimmed in the basement to hide from the crowds who'd gather to watch. Roman Polanski filmed Catherine Deneuve from the salon's balcony for a scene in *Repulsion*. The glamour even followed Vidal home, where he shared a flat with Terence Stamp and Michael Caine.

Much like Vidal, my father always maintained an understated elegance. He always flew first class, wore bespoke suits, and had his shirts made by Frank Foster. In the late sixties, he was part of a group that included Roger Moore, Michael Caine, and Sean Connery, who frequented Doug Hayward's tailor shop on Savile Row, turning it into a kind of men's club, lounging about telling stories. And as was the case with those film stars, you could feel my father's presence the moment he walked into a room—he was that charismatic. When I was in my early teens and I went to some of the salons with him, the employees responded as if God had dropped by to say hello.

Vidal already had an office in L.A., but after my father came in, North American profits doubled in two years. Back in the UK the company expanded to Manchester and Leeds. Then they moved on to Germany and Hong Kong and built up a wig business and hair care products. When he saw how Japanese apprentices wanted to fly to London to observe Vidal cut hair, my dad suggested setting up a school.

After my dad moved to California to run the American operation, his vision expanded even further. He wanted to create a franchising system whereby individual entrepreneurs could pay for use of the Vidal name, get the appropriate training, and set up shop. But others on the management team argued that the brand name should be kept more exclusive, like Estée Lauder. Ultimately, the board took a vote and my dad lost. (Years later, Vidal told me that not following up on my dad's idea was the biggest mistake he ever made.)

In April 1983, while I was floating through Heathfield in a daze, the company was sold to Richardson-Vicks for £72 million, so my father did very well.

By then Dad was ready to shift into a lower gear, so he bought a small newspaper called *Beverly Hills People*, and he invested with Vidal in another very "L.A." product, MicroCool, which is a misting system for helping people stay comfortable outdoors in the heat. He was also on the board of Illingworth, Morris, an English textiles brand owned by the widow of actor James Mason.

Lucky for me, Dad's semiretirement left him available to become the elder statesman and spirit guide—not to mention investor—in my new venture. As chairman, he contributed enormously to the birth of Jimmy Choo. The legwork, however, was left to me.

. . . .

THE FIRST THING I SET out doing was to find space for a shop in my preferred habitat, a location convenient to Knightsbridge and to Mayfair, near where the ladies who lunch at Harry's Bar and San Lorenzo do their shopping. I had observed that Manolo Blahnik, our only real competition at the time, was on Old Church Street in a residential area in Chelsea, twenty minutes from the nearest tube station. God forbid that a customer has an actual job in an office and wants to pop over at lunchtime.

I wanted us to be more accessible, and I found the perfect spot on Motcomb Street, near Harvey Nichols, at the top of Sloane Street, between Belgrave Square and Harrods. If these points were the stations of the cross for a certain kind of woman, we were in the hot burning center.

The space was small, only 540 square feet, but I put down cream-colored carpet, and I found a furniture store somewhere in the Strand where I bought a sofa and had it covered in purple velvet. I installed some glass shelves, then went to an auction house on Lots Road and bought a cream marble table that I put in the back of the store with some flowers on it. It was all very basic, but it had the right look.

Behind the scenes we were even more frugal. We set up an office with two desks in the basement alongside the stockroom, and for quite a while that's where I worked, with no windows, and certainly no frills. When we started out I didn't even have a proper computer.

Jimmy's only concern was to have a famous feng shui master bless the enterprise. So we paid to fly this guy over from Malaysia and put him up in a smart hotel. Then we went with him to the shop at midnight and sat in a circle and went through some sort of chanting ritual. He put a Chinese symbol on the mirror, rearranged the cash register so that the money wouldn't "fly out of the store," and that was that.

For the longest time we had nothing to sell, so just for appearance's sake, we put a few Jimmy Choo couture shoes on display. We also bought some shoes from a factory and sewed in the Jimmy Choo label. But money flying "out" of the store was the least of our worries.

Jimmy kept his workshop in Hackney from which, supposedly, the designs for the collection were going to emanate. Assuming that I could leave this essential function in his very capable hands, I started looking for factories.

Jimmy had a manufacturing contact in Italy, so in the summer of 1996 he and I flew out, along with his niece Sandra, to visit their facility. We couldn't afford even the cheapest seats on a regular commercial flight, so we bought tickets on one of those charters that lands at some decommissioned military air base or other out-of-the-way landing strip you've never heard of. The whole trip was something of a bust, with Jimmy not really present mentally, and Sandra having to translate much of what was going on into Chinese for him. But it did help me begin to get a more realistic picture of my new business partner.

On the flight back, after the meal had been served, I noticed Jimmy packing up all the food and everything else on the plastic tray—including the tray itself—to take home. Later, when we went through customs, they asked him to open his bag, and rolls upon rolls of toilet paper came flying out. He'd taken all the free paper and soap and everything else free he could grab from the hotel and stuffed it into his bag. It wasn't even a nice hotel we'd been staying in. I pretended not to notice and simply walked on through.

In truth, my confidence in Jimmy was beginning to falter, not just because of his lack of sophistication but because of his lack of knowledge about shoe manufacturing. When his contacts came to nothing, Sandra and I found a book that simply listed all the factories in Italy and who they worked for. Book in hand, we left Jimmy at home and went back to Italy, cold-calling, knocking on doors to see if we could get an appointment. We were two young girls representing a brand they'd never heard of, with not so much as a single order to give them.

We made several of these exploratory trips, and when one of our flights to Florence was delayed, we started chatting with an English-woman, filling the downtime with a rambling account of what we were all about. She told us she had a friend in the shoe business named Barbara, and she offered to introduce us to her, which she did. When we went to meet this Barbara, she offered to make some introductions on our behalf—for $25,000. It was a bit of a con, but we paid, and she did get us through some of the right doors. In fact, she introduced us to the factory that would make our first collection for us. But the real value she provided came some months later, when she introduced us to Anna Conti.

Anna had done manufacturing for Bally, and when we met her she was working for a company called Custom Foot, which created made-to-measure shoes. Somehow we were able to lure her away to become our exclusive manufacturing agent, and she set up her own business called IF, with Jimmy Choo as her only client. She offered to source factories, place the orders, follow up, make sure all the leather and fabric samples came in on time, do quality control throughout the run, then oversee shipping to make sure everything was on time. So as soon as we could design our first collection, the rest of the production apparatus would be in place.

But first there was the challenge of designing the collection, and I was by now facing up to the harsh realization that Jimmy was not going to be the creative partner I'd hoped for. Producing shoes for his couture clients was his bread and butter, all he cared about, and all he did. At one point my father offered him £1,000 for each design he produced, but Jimmy simply never could wrap his head around the fact that we had gone into business with him on the expectation that he would actually help us create a global brand, which it was his job to design.

His reluctance to contribute had put us way behind, especially considering that we needed something to show at the Fashion Footwear Association of New York trade show in August and at another event later in the fall in Düsseldorf. To make the deadlines, we desperately needed sketches at the factory. Grudgingly, he worked up a few with Sandra, and we faxed them to Italy.

Ever the optimist, I spent the summer, when not scouting factories in Italy, phoning up Saks and Bergdorf, Nordstrom and Bloomingdale's, even Neiman Marcus, trying to line up buyers to come see us at the show in New York. I even rang up the specialty shops like Scoop NYC and Chuckies Brooklyn. Everyone recognized Jimmy's name from those credit lines in *Vogue* and from his association with Princess Diana, so at least he was earning his keep in that one respect.

But our selling samples barely made it to New York on time, and when we saw them we were horrified. The factory left them covered with black scuff marks, glue was visible along the seams, and the stitching was awful. They were so bad that we absolutely couldn't use them, so here we were at the Plaza Hotel with a stand for displaying product and, once again, no product to display. We felt like fools. We were so ashamed, in fact, that on the way out we actually walked down a half dozen flights of stairs to avoid the elevators for fear of running into anyone who might ask to see what we had to offer.

I tried to carry on, selling from sketches, but no one was interested. Well, almost no one. The lone ray of hope during this otherwise dismal expedition came from Michael Stachowski, who placed a modest order for Giorgio Beverly Hills. This was the legendary boutique that had launched Rodeo Drive in the early sixties, when movie stars like Natalie Wood and Liz Taylor used to come with an extra limo in tow for their packages. So if we had only one outlet, this was not a bad one to have.

The next shoe show was in Düsseldorf later that fall. We had no choice but to go with the same designs, but I asked Jimmy to remake all the samples by hand. "I'm only doing this for you," he said, and I was thinking, "What's your problem? You own half the company, you know." But he still acted as if doing anything on behalf of the brand was a major imposition on his time.

In Düsseldorf we at least had well-made shoes to display, but nothing sold, and now I had to face the fact that even with quality samples, the concepts Jimmy and Sandra had come up with were just not that exciting. This is when it dawned on me that Jimmy was a cobbler, and he really had no interest in becoming a designer. I had set up a business with a "creative head" who, in fact, had no creativity.

This was the point at which I moved Sandra to Motcomb Street. For the next collection, I would come up with the ideas and Sandra would sketch them out on paper.

Over the winter, Sandra and I started going to the weekend flea market on Portobello Road where I'd had my T-shirt stand with Barnzley, only now the objective was to pick out pieces that could inspire designs. But we were not alone. One day we were browsing, only to realize that we had Dolce on one side of us and Gabbana on the other, and we were all staring at the same shoe.

I would buy vintage things and put them into different groups that made up little stories. Sometimes I would find a focus on a single vintage shoe. At other times I would say, "Let's put the front of that sandal together with the back of that shoe." I was also collecting pieces of jewelry and bits of fabric. Later, we would go to the manufacturing trade show in Italy called Lineapelle, which was a huge eye-opener for me, with pavilion upon pavilion devoted to buckles, feathers, leather flowers, bits of fur, resin, studs, glass beads, lasts and heels, and, of course, the glitter fabric that became a Jimmy Choo staple. I had never known there were so many possibilities.

But that's how the Jimmy Choo DNA began to emerge. The first collections were based on things that had caught my eye. The lovely part of it was that the things that struck me, and that I related to emotionally, other women related to as well.

During this period Jimmy would drop by the shop nearly every day, but only to drink tea and to check in on his niece. She would be picked up every day precisely at six p.m. in a minicab driven by a friend of his so that she could then work "the night shift" back in Hackney, helping her uncle fill orders for his couture clientele.

The few times that Jimmy had anything to say about design, it was with a complaint that I was making the heels too high or in some other way violating the cordwainers' code. But what he saw as heresy, the rest of us saw as innovation, style, and fun.

. . . .

AT THIS VERY EARLY STAGE, a friend introduced me to two young publicists named Natalie Lewis and Tracey Brower, who had just set up their own firm, Brower Lewis PR. They, too, were just starting out, hungry and talented, and we were able to put them on a retainer of something like £500 a month.

Natalie and Tracey went with me to our first Paris show in the spring of 1997. This collection was our breakthrough moment, and it was the result of my inspirations and Sandra's skill as a sketch artist. We now had good samples as well, but we were still on the fringes.

We'd rented space at Tranoï, an exhibition for the edgier realms of fashion that was set up in tents and stalls in the Jardins des Tuileries, just down from the Crillon.

It was in this outdoor environment more suited to a craft show or a farmer's market that I first met Julie Townsend, the buyer from Saks. She stopped by, looked at our samples, and said, "These are good. These are great!" Then she backed up her enthusiasm by placing an order for three thousand pairs of shoes.

Just like that we were in. We'd cracked it.

My father had told me that if we could sell twenty pairs of shoes a week from our Motcomb Street shop, and priced them at roughly £250 a pair, we'd have a business. Now here we were with three thousand pairs en route to the leading retailer in North America. Suddenly, we had the rarest of good fortunes for a start-up company: positive cash flow. Our sales were £250,000 that first year, with the shop rental costing us £15,000, and only one employee other than Sandra and myself.

After that huge breakthrough with Julie's order we still had a show to run, and other customers to talk to, but already my mind was moving ahead. I was positioning Jimmy Choo as a luxury brand, so we were out of place with all the fringe designers and jewelry makers at Tranoï. As we closed up shop that day, I remember walking past the Crillon and thinking, "Someday, that's where I want us to be."

Brower Lewis was brilliant at getting our story out and setting up appointments with the editors to get them to come see the collection. That spring they also helped us throw a fabulous party at the Wellington Club for about three hundred guests that was a huge hit.

I remember somebody mentioning that if this business was as successful as that party, we'd do very nicely. So clearly we were getting the "style" and "image" part of the business down as well.

The fashion world is like a traveling circus—the same designers and the same editors showing up season after season on the same schedule in New York, London, Paris, and Milan. But I didn't like the idea of being seen in a crowd along with all the other shoe lines, isolated in the separate universe reserved for accessories. So in the fall of 1997, rather than go to FFANY once again and simply hire space in the exhibits at the Plaza, we came for Fashion Week instead and took a suite at the Carlyle, got rid of the bed, and filled the room with shoes.

For Fashion Week in London, we set up in my apartment, and Sandra and I would literally sit on the floor while the buyers told us what they wanted. I would write out the order by hand and then fax it to Anna.

Now that we had demand, Anna Conti was expanding our network of suppliers, adding the Ballin factory in Padua, outside Venice, and Paoletti near Florence. Her husband made gift boxes in Florence, and she sat in a tiny office in his factory while I was downstairs at Motcomb Street and we would fax each other back and forth.

When we came back to Paris for the spring 1998 show, I had another meeting with Julie Townsend, and what she had to say was just about as exciting as that first huge order she'd placed the year before. Our first year sell-through at Saks was an incredible 95 percent, and we were indeed exhibiting our wares in a suite at the Crillon.

The other recurring event for anyone in the shoe business is, of course, Lineapelle, which takes place twice a year in Bologna. Shoes are made from separate components that have to be assembled, and all the best components—uppers, heels, insoles, as well as the best leathers—come from Italy. All the tanneries and all the leather makers exhibit at the show, and you go around until you find the leather that you like, from the tanneries you like, and then you establish a relationship and these become your regular suppliers. You also see what new colors they're showing and the new technologies that have come along.

I was still trying to engage Jimmy—after all, my dad and I had signed over half the company to him—but when I invited him to come with us to Lineapelle, he spent all his time trying to find whatever freebies he could take home for his couture operation. He was fixated on picking up heels and scraps of leather, never on the big picture.

Now that we were up and running, my itinerary also included six trips a year just to keep tabs on the manufacturing end of things. So six times a year Sandra and I would fly to Italy, stay in a not particularly great hotel, and have Anna drive us around. We'd spend the day at Ballin near Venice, then drive three hours to Petra, stay the night, and get up at six in the morning and work with the next factory. Later, Anna brought her younger brother Massimo on board, and she would stay in the office, leaving it to Massimo to come with us and drive us around.

I also wanted to keep our investor in the loop, so I brought my father along on one of these trips to Paoletti and then up to Ballin. To make it a full team effort, Jimmy and Sandra came, too, so it was the four of us checking into some little pension just below the factory.

Each season, our first conference with each of the suppliers would be based on Sandra's sketches. By the time of the second meeting we saw every shoe in the collection, with Sandra marking the shoe with a silver pen, moving the strap a millimeter down or up to get the balance right. I was obsessed. I really wanted to make the perfect shoe.

I would stand next to Francesco, our last maker, and say, "No, I want the toe flatter" or "Shave it down by a millimeter." Then we'd go to the heel supplier and stand next to his machines. "No, thinner in the middle," or "Wider," or "More flared out at the base." I had very clear ideas about what I wanted.

Month by month, the DNA of Jimmy Choo was expressing itself more and more clearly. In terms of manufacturing, this meant only the best components and an obsessive attention to detail. In terms of design, it meant vintage ideas reconsidered, exotic fabrics and extras, and sex appeal that was also sophisticated, never cheap.

So what makes a shoe sexy? It's the balance of the foot, and where the straps are placed, and maybe being low cut at the front so you see toe cleavage. Then again, I've been told that the nerve endings for the genitals and the foot are adjacent in the brain, which is why a little cell migration is capable of giving people all too great a passion for feet and for shoes. We tried to stop just short of that point.

When we started out, the shoe industry offered plenty of opportunities to innovate on a purely practical level. Boots for women had always been too wide at the calf, for instance, and nobody had thought about improving that aspect of the fit. So I created a line of boots with the upper portion cut very tight. Say your foot was a size 39 or 40

(8.5–9). For boots that size we would use the same upper portion you'd find on a traditionally sized 38 (7.5–8), which led to some comical moments in the store. For the longest time our only dedicated sales-person was Hannah Colman, my brother Daniel's girlfriend. Hannah would have the customers lying on the sofa with their leg straight up in the air, struggling to pull the zipper down.

Vassi Chamberlain's 1996 story in *Tatler* about the launch of Jimmy Choo had confirmed my sense that it was incumbent on me to have a certain look, a certain lifestyle, and plenty of exposure in the media. I never set out to "live" the brand. It just so happened that I had specific interests and friends, and I lived a certain way, all of which contributed to the buzz around Jimmy Choo. After a while, maintaining that life-style became part of the job, with all the added stresses and strains of running a company, along with encroachment on what otherwise might be considered "free" time. I was still living at home, I had no car, and I had absolutely no social life other than entertaining related to the business. And all the while, Sandra and I were each making the same £15,000 a year, which meant that I was always overdrawn at the bank.

At the beginning, we made Jimmy available to the press as well as me, but at the events Brower Lewis set up, his only contribution was to complain that he was not designing the collection. This was entirely true, but not for want of our begging him to do so. Moreover, this was not a positive message we wanted conveyed to the public. But then even within the inner circle he remained a pall of negativity. When he came to monthly board meetings, he always brought his attorney, and then he'd have nothing to say. Adding insult to injury, he began to complain to his couture clients. "They stole my name. They're ripping me off." These were the phrases that got back to us. Somehow he failed to remember that we had licensed his name. In 2001, we bought it outright.

. . . .

OVER TIME, JIMMY'S ECCENTRICITIES BECAME even more personal, and more problematic.

A girlfriend of Sandra's invited her to go to a Sting concert, and Sandra adored Sting. Jimmy called the friend. Who knows exactly what he said, but that was that for the concert.

Then I was in the store one day, on the shop floor, when Jimmy came in. He went downstairs to see Sandra, and almost immediately she started shouting. I called my father and I said, "You better get here quick—something's going on downstairs with Jimmy and Sandra." Luckily, Dad was just around the corner at the Lowndes Hotel and it took him about two seconds to get there. My dad went racing down the stairs and told Jimmy to get out of the store. That would be the last time I'd see my business partner for many months.

Still another time, Sandra and Jimmy were supposed to be coming to Motcomb Street for a meeting. They showed up late, and when Sandra walked in I could see she'd been crying. I took her aside and asked her what had happened. She said that Jimmy had been raging at her in the car on the way over. It seems Sandra had ended up falling in love with Tony, the minicab driver her uncle had hired to spirit her away each evening, and Jimmy was worried about what that might mean for her commitment to his business.

A few days later my father and I took Sandra out to lunch at the restaurant across the street from the shop. We said, "Listen, something clearly is not right. If you need our help, we'll help you."

Shortly thereafter, Sandra showed up on my parents' doorstep in an absolute state. She said she'd been sleeping in a car all weekend because Jimmy had chased her out.

"That's it," I said. "You're not going home. You're going to move in with me."

So Sandra moved into my house on Chester Row, which gave her the opportunity to really open up and confide about the madness she'd been experiencing.

Jimmy stayed in his shop during that year, and his only contact with Sandra was through forwarding her mail. When it arrived I could see Chinese characters scrawled across the envelopes in pencil. I asked her, "What does this mean?"

"Traitor," she said.

Jimmy was upset not just because she'd told others what was going on, or because she'd moved out and was living with me, but obviously because she was taking time away from his shop to work for this new company. Sandra had been in his studio for years. I think he'd assumed he could get her to work all-out for the Jimmy Choo brand and that people would still see the design as having come from him.

Sandra had gone through a lot of stress, and we felt we needed to reward her for the good work she was doing. My father was chairman, and my title was managing director, so in December 1997 we gave her the title of creative director. This was another mistake born of my naïveté because I didn't really think about titles that much. But this one proved misleading to the industry, often creating confusion about my role and Sandra's.

A creative director does not necessarily make sketches, but instead formulates and impresses upon the designers the vision that informs the collection as a whole. The creative director establishes the kinds of designs that will be created, incorporating a sense of what will appeal to a target market. It's steering, not rowing. So even though my loftier title was managing director, I remained de facto creative director as well.

. . . .

IMMEDIATELY AFTER OUR FIRST BIG sale to Saks, my father had told me, "If you want to be a serious business, you have to break into America." This was probably the best advice he ever gave me, because without a strong North American presence, it seems to take British brands about twenty years to truly "arrive."

We had cracked Saks and Giorgio Beverly Hills, but now we wanted our own dedicated stores as well. So my dad called on his old friends from his Vidal Sassoon venture, Philip Rogers and Annie Humphries. Back in the eighties, Richardson-Vicks had sold the Vidal Sassoon product line to Procter and Gamble, and Rogers and Humphries, a stylist and a colorist, respectively, had acquired the shops.

My father took Philip to lunch at the Carlton Tower and proposed a deal that would allow us to expand exponentially, but on a shoestring budget. He offered Philip and Annie a 50 percent stake in a new subsidiary called Jimmy Choo USA. Their end of the bargain was to provide a fully functional, ready-made back office to handle our North American retail operation, that back office being Vidal Sassoon's staff and systems. In addition, we would be able to follow in the Vidal Sassoon slipstream in terms of real estate, where we could benefit from Vidal's established reputation as a guarantor for the leases. Philip and Annie agreed.

After thirty years on Rodeo Drive, Vidal had acquired two adjoining spaces on the corner of North Canon and Little Santa Monica Boulevard. We took the one on the corner because it had a big window with columns that you saw if you were driving up Santa Monica, so it was like having a billboard on this major thoroughfare. It also didn't hurt, when selling high-end women's shoes, to be next door to a high-end hair salon. I would have preferred to have been back at the center of the target, Rodeo Drive itself, but certainly I couldn't complain about the rent—our share would be slightly less than half the $15,000 a month.

Philip's choice to design the interior for the new store was an architect who'd worked with him at Sassoon. Philip and my dad wanted to use him to save money, but designing a hair salon is different from designing a retail space—much more functional—and I never felt that he was able to translate my vision. Trouble is, once the store was done, we were stuck with it for quite a while.

Aesthetic quibbles aside, we still needed to launch with a bang, and to do that we hired a wonderful woman from the wilds of Canada named Marilyn Heston. She had worked for BWR Public Relations but had recently set up her own shop, called GGI, for Get Good Ink. I liked Marilyn a lot, and, having just launched a new venture, she was really hungry. Rather than our going to a big firm and being handed off to some account manager, I knew Marilyn would be able to give us the attention that we wanted.

Marilyn had started out managing VIPs on cruise ships, where she happened to meet the actor Charlton Heston and his family. One thing led to another, and she wound up marrying Charlton's son, Fraser, by which time she was doing publicity for films like *Buffy the Vampire Slayer*. The first time she went to the Oscars, it was as Fraser Heston's date, and she wore a simple skirt and blouse—a fashion faux pas that imprinted deeply in her psyche and that led indirectly to her becoming the essential go-between for the world of fashion and the world of the Hollywood star.

Marilyn set up a joint Vidal Sassoon/Jimmy Choo launch event, with the proceeds from sales going to help the Children's Action Network. Stars like Rosanna Arquette and Rita Wilson came by to pick out shoes (while being photographed by us). My brother Daniel served as DJ and we got food from Maple Drive, the restaurant owned by Dudley Moore. Dad invited a lot of his friends from the beauty business and from the corporate side of Hollywood, and suddenly we "belonged."

Our entry into L.A. could not have been better timed because the cultural context of fashion was going through a sea change. Magazines had always put beautiful models on their covers, but over time they realized that featuring an actress instead sent their newsstand sales through the roof. We were entering the age of All Celebrities, All the Time.

If celebrity worship was the new world religion, then the holiest night of the year took place in the spring when all the glitterati gathered for the Academy Awards. A magazine feature could reach hundreds of thousands of potential customers for a fashion brand. The way to reach a billion was to dress the actresses who were competing with each other for attention at that one highly televised event. Designers had learned that getting their gown on the right body on the red carpet was a force second to none. We wanted to achieve the same éclat for shoes.

Women in Hollywood are hardly rubes when it comes to fashion. They have stylists to make sure they know what's good and what's happening even when they're simply buying for their personal wardrobe. Anyone who'd ever shopped in London knew about Jimmy Choo, so it was not all that difficult to find lovely young feet happy to be associated with our brand. Of course, even more aware of the cutting edge were the stylists to the stars, and because these people worked for multiple clients, contact with a single stylist gave us that many more shots at scoring a win.

In the spring of 1998, we made our first foray into the Oscars, and I was up all night on the phone from London trying to orchestrate the gifting of shoes to all the right women. Our payoff came through Kate Winslet, nominated for Best Actress for *Titanic*, when she mentioned her Jimmy Choos—a first for any shoe brand—on the red carpet. Going forward, Oscar night was to become a major event on the Jimmy Choo calendar.

I called around London after the show, describing this wonderful thing we'd just done, a breakthrough I thought all the features writers should write about, only to discover that no one in England watched the Oscars. Hilary Alexander at the *Telegraph* was the only one who took the bait, and she did a big piece with pictures of the actresses and pictures of the shoes. After that, interest in the Oscars exploded in the UK.

Then on July 5, 1998, we made our first appearance on *Sex and the City* and our visibility skyrocketed. The script had Carrie Bradshaw running for the Staten Island Ferry when she stumbles and screams out, "I lost my Choo!" The "Choo" she lost was in fact a style with tiny feathers we called the "Marlene."

That one mention helped turn us into a household name. Suddenly women who'd never heard of us, women who lived in small towns in the American heartland, thought about us in the same heady company as the other luxury brands being mentioned, brand names like Prada and Gucci and, admittedly, Manolo Blahnik. But the most amazing aspect of this turn of events was that, while manufacturers of everything from diapers to diet drinks pay fortunes for product placement in movies and TV, we got this huge call-out entirely for free. Years later I spoke with Candace Bushnell, the show's creator, and she said she put the reference in the script because she'd been in London and stopped by the store on Motcomb Street and fell in love with the product. Ultimately, Jimmy Choo would be mentioned on the show thirty-four times.

In London, when we did our first sale at our little shop, there was a line around the block. Women were literally fighting each other to get in, and I had to put my brother at the door to serve as bouncer, letting in just a few customers at a time. The shoes were sexy. They were fun. They had interesting detail and color, and our factories were producing real quality at a price point between £250 and £400.

Three thousand miles away in Manhattan, we found retail space in Olympic Tower, on Fifty-First just off Fifth Avenue. St. Patrick's Cathedral faces the entrance across Fifty-First, Saks is one block south, and all the luxury boutiques are clustered right there along the avenue, so Olympic Tower allowed us to be in the center of Manhattan's most exclusive retail district without having to pay for a Fifth Avenue address.

To run the new store, we brought in Michael Stachowski, who had been the Giorgio's buyer and the first (and only) one to buy off our sketches at that first, wretched FFANY. To launch our new East Coast location, we hired Harrison and Shriftman to do PR, and we threw a huge party hosted by Lucy Sykes, the fashion editor of *Marie Claire*, and her twin sister Plum from American *Vogue*, who'd been a features assistant alongside me at British *Vogue*.

Our plan for North American conquest did not initially include Las Vegas, but an unsolicited offer came in from the developers of the Venetian Resort Hotel Casino. They were creating a 500,000-square-foot shopping destination called the Grand Canal Shoppes, and supposedly Neiman Marcus was going to be their anchor. That never happened, and the other brands they said would be coming in never materialized. But we signed on and the location did okay, and then after a while we moved on to a spot inside Caesars Palace.

So now we had three North American stores—L.A., New York, and Las Vegas—and eight employees. I did all the buying for the US stores—the London company sold to the US subsidiary at 25 percent off wholesale—and Philip's people did all the billing, shipping, and accounting. Even so, it seemed that I was constantly shuttling back and forth across the Atlantic, and across the four North American time zones. Jet lag was to become a permanent condition.

. . . .

FOR THE 1999 ACADEMY AWARDS ceremony, Sandra and I flew to L.A. with sixty pairs of shoes in half a dozen different styles, but only in black and white. At that time, fashion was still all about matching, and my idea was to dye the shoes to match the dress. This was the servicing of celebrities at a whole new level, light-years beyond the gift bag.

We took a suite at L'Ermitage Beverly Hills on Burton Way and, to save money, shared it with Nadja Swarovski, a longtime purveyor of fine crystal. Marilyn arranged a tea, and we sent word to all the stylists, the agents, and the managers, inviting them to come to the suite. We showed them what we had to offer—shoes in every size and style—but all in white satin. Then we explained how we would go the extra mile, dying any pair on-site to match the color of any dress.

We flew over a woman from London who knew about dyes, but even so we were up all night, mixing the colors in the hotel bathtub, struggling to get the shades exactly right, then applying the color to the satin with a sponge. Julianne Moore changed her dress at the last minute, which meant that we had to re-dye her shoes, which meant that she went out on the red carpet with wet feet.

Phillip Bloch, who dressed stars like Nicole Kidman, Halle Berry, and Sandra Bullock, came to the tea and asked that we send over a box of shoes and bags for Salma Hayek. The fashion director of the awards themselves, L'Wren Scott, ordered shoes for all the pretty young things who would be assisting the stars on and offstage. The list of actresses who wore Jimmy Choo that year included Geena Davis, Rachel Griffiths, Kim Basinger, Jennifer Lopez, Minnie Driver, Julianne Moore, Hilary Swank, and Uma Thurman.

Cate Blanchett was up for Best Actress for *Elizabeth*, and her stylist, Jessica Paster, asked us to make her a pair of Jimmy Choos covered in diamonds. We contacted Craig Drake, a jeweler in Philadelphia, and asked him to make a diamond bracelet that could become the ankle strap of a shoe. Of course, once we'd arranged to apply forty carats of diamonds to Cate's eggplant-colored heels, her stylist called to say the shoes were too small.

Marilyn began phoning all over L.A., trying to find a store that carried our label where we could find a replacement for Cate. Saks in West Hollywood had a pair, but they were a half size too small and the wrong color—black. Marilyn drove over and bought them anyway. Then she called shoemaker Jack Zatikian. We drove over to his house in Los Feliz, near Griffith Park, and we stayed up all night as he rebuilt the shoe, then covered it in white satin so it could be dyed. Marilyn showed up the next morning with the diamonds. "Sew them on," she said.

The story attracted such massive worldwide coverage that the red carpet was almost beside the point. As it turned out, Cate never wore the shoes for fear of being upstaged by her feet. But after the ceremony she auctioned her Jimmy Choos—sans diamonds—as well as her dress, to raise money for the American AIDS Foundation. The outfit went for $15,000. The diamonds were returned to Craig Drake.

We'd been the first brand to set up shop in the L'Ermitage, but by the next year the hotel had become this sort of Moroccan bazaar with shoe designers from high end to Hush Puppies, as well as jewelry designers, makeup and hair products, and designers pushing racks of dresses through the corridors as if they were on Seventh Avenue.

I maintained my aversion to being part of the crowd, so I moved our suite to the Peninsula Beverly Hills on Santa Monica, just off Wilshire. But Jack Zatikian remained a regular component of our Oscar strategy, dying the shoes, fixing the straps, and even adding more of a platform—whatever it took to get it right.

The following year, Nadja Swarovski and I collaborated on a special collection, creating seven distinctive shoes embedded with her company's crystal. These "one of a kind" shoes were prototypes for our next fall line.

. . . .

MAYBE IT WAS THE HOLLYWOOD influence, but back in London I started getting a little splashier in how we presented the brand. When Ian Shrager opened one of his first hotels, I did a press day in his restaurant. I took the fish off the ice in his display cases in the main dining room and arranged the shoes there. Visitors got to see not only this glam new venue in London, but how many shoes could be displayed on a bed of ice.

This was also about the time we began working on our first Cruise Collection, resort wear meant to be sold in December, just in time for winter vacations. Sandra's inspiration was "nautical," an idea that left me underwhelmed. That's when I came up with the idea of glitter—in all colors. Pink. Yellow. Blue. And it was a huge hit.

In keeping with our edgier and more exclusive image, we asked Jimmy to move his shop from the dungeon in Hackney to a town house on Connaught Street in Bayswater. This space provided a workshop in the basement, a showroom for his couture clients on the ground floor, and living quarters for his family upstairs. At about the same time we moved our offices to Pont Street, above Jeroboams, the wine shop. I'd received a small bump in salary by now. I hired an assistant, Katherine Drummond, who comes from the Redgrave acting family. In addition, we acquired an actual computer for processing our orders, and I hired a friend, Adrian Harris, to write the code. Even so, it was still Sandra and I who were up all hours entering the orders into the system.

Around this time we also started producing shoes for men. My father wanted to put my brother Daniel in charge of this new line, because he thought Daniel needed a focus. But my brother's real passion is music, which did not translate so well to working in the fashion industry. So for a while I wound up managing the men's line in addition to everything else I was doing. Daniel would show up very dutifully at the shop—mostly to please my father—but he would be so hungover that he would go and lock himself in the bathroom to take a nap. Hannah, his girlfriend who sold for us, often had to get a ruler and poke him under the door to wake him up.

I'm afraid neither of my brothers inherited my father's drive. In the Yeardye family, as in so many others, the sons' level of worldly success seems inversely proportional to the father's. History shows that inherited wealth has rarely been the spur of great ambition or character development, but sometimes it can help generate extraordinarily colorful eccentricities. As I was about to discover, those eccentricities can sometimes be wonderfully entertaining, at least for a while.

.... 5 ....

In May 1998, I attended a Narcotics Anonymous meeting in London, where I ran into a bunch of old friends who were all going out for dinner afterward. The ringleader was Henry Dent-Brocklehurst, who'd booked a table at La Famiglia. I knew Henry only slightly, and he was very gracious but also full of regret. "I'm so sorry," he said to me, "but I don't think there's any more room."

I left it at that, and after the meeting I simply went home. Shortly thereafter, someone rang my bell. I opened the door, and there on my threshold I found a young man who looked as if he had taken the proverbial step out of the pages of *GQ*. He'd been at the NA meeting, where I'd quickly noted that, along with being incredibly handsome, he was an American, and very funny. His name was Matthew Mellon.

"You have to come," he said. "To the restaurant. We'll make room. I don't think you'll take up all that much room, will you?"

I liked the look of him, and I thought it was very chivalrous that he'd made this special effort to include me, and so I went. The restaurant was around the corner on Elizabeth Street, and as we walked over Matthew was talking a mile a minute, and I must have been laughing the whole time. Even so, there was nothing terribly romantic or "like a first date" about this encounter. It was a perfectly nice evening, and when we were done I simply walked home by myself.

But then a few weeks later, Henry Dent-Brocklehurst provided a second opportunity for Matthew and me to get together by getting married in grand style to a Hawaiian fashion model with the unlikely name of Lili Maltese. The ceremony was to take place at the Dent-Brocklehursts' family seat, Sudeley Castle, in Winchcombe, Gloucestershire, and with a guest list that included many of the well known, such as Liz Hurley and Hugh Grant, Mick Jagger and Jerry Hall, as well as many of the wellborn, which included the aforementioned Matthew Mellon.

Henry, as his double-barreled moniker (and the castle) might suggest, comes from a terribly aristocratic family, and he'd just come home from L.A. to help with the family estate. His mother is Lady Ashcombe, and his godmother is Camilla Parker Bowles. As a wedding venue, Sudeley dates back to the twelfth century, and though the current structure goes back only to the fifteenth, it is the burial place of Catherine Parr, the sixth wife of Henry VIII, which is not too shabby.

All of us stayed in the village, and the next morning there was a convoy of cars to take us the two-hour ride back to London. It turned out that Matthew and I were staying at the same small hotel, but when it came time to leave, we were being ushered toward two different vehicles. When he saw what was about to happen, he jumped out of his and ran back and got into mine, and that sort of sealed the deal.

At this time, Matthew was living in L.A. and I was incredibly busy with Jimmy Choo in London, but we began to date, after a fashion, with him flying back and forth across the Atlantic, staying with me whenever he was in the UK.

. . . .

MATTHEW CAME FROM THE HIGHER echelons of America's own version of aristocracy. In the nineteenth century, his great-great-great-grandfather, Judge Thomas Mellon, had placed shrewd bets on industrial expansion and thereby built a fortune to rival the Rockefellers and the Vanderbilts. He first founded Mellon Bank, then expanded into other enterprises, and when he died, he left one of these businesses to each of his five sons. Mellons turned a new process for making aluminum into Alcoa. They were also instrumental in building General Motors, U.S. Steel, and Heinz. Their investment in oil, the Spindletop field in Texas, became Gulf Oil, and that's the line from which Matthew is descended.

His mother, meanwhile, came from a long line of Drexels and Biddles, again very much to the American manor born. As a slightly darker distinction, Matthew claimed to have been the model for Julian, the drug-addicted rich boy in Bret Easton Ellis's *Less Than Zero*.

Matthew's parents had divorced when he was young, and he'd spent a large share of his earliest years sailing with his father out of Northeast Harbor in Maine, and in the Caribbean. But then when Matthew was five, Karl, his father, dropped out of sight, reappearing eleven years later with long hair, a beard, and rather lame apologies, as well as promises of being more of a father in the years to come. Unfortunately, Karl was seriously bipolar and in 1983, at the age of forty-five, he killed himself. As is usually the case, this parental suicide did nothing to make the teenage son a happier and more stable person.

Matthew grew up with his mother in Palm Beach and, according to the tale she told her son, he could not expect to inherit anything from his father's family but the Mellon name. He enrolled in the University of Pennsylvania and along the way had rather un-Mellonish summer jobs working as a ditchdigger, and in the kitchen of Danny's Seafood Connection in Boca Raton.

Then on his twenty-first birthday, he was summoned to Pittsburgh. His uncle Jay had served as something of a surrogate father, and now the older man brought his nephew into the boardroom of Mellon Bank and gave him the good news. Having reached his majority—surprise!—he would have access to thirteen expansive trust funds. As Matthew told the press, he immediately rang up the *Wall Street Journal* to start a subscription. He also bought the first BMW M5 in the United States.

Matthew was already a member of St. Anthony Hall, the Mellon family's traditional fraternity at Penn, but he bought a ten-bedroom mansion just a few blocks away as his own private Animal House. He did his first stint in rehab while still in college.

God knows how he managed to graduate, but thereupon he took a job with New York's then mayor Rudolf Giuliani, doing "opposition research" and writing what he called "mudslinging" press releases. The Ford modeling agency had approached him, but his family would have rather he join the Sandinistas than have him appear in advertisements. By the same token, they were none too pleased when he began to spend his evenings in downtown clubs, and at an uptown place called Au Bar, often dancing wildly without a partner (and without shoes), even entering break-dancing contests and—God forbid—winning. He used to hire limos with the drivers rotating shifts as, coked out of his mind, he kept the party going around the clock. Unfortunately, these binges represented more than high spirits and youthful energy. Matthew had inherited his father's bipolar illness.

Matthew Mellon was utterly beautiful and utterly goofy, which was a very endearing combination. He was also damaged goods, wounded and struggling, and that, I think, is where we made the real connection. My mistake was in assuming that, because I'd overcome my addictions, he could, too.

. . . .

IN 1993, MATTHEW MOVED TO L.A. to produce rap music for Grindstone. He then moved on to film, trying to put together a documentary, which, as I recall, had something to do with nuns. He collected Ferraris, leased one house in Beverly Hills and another on the beach in Malibu. But crack was becoming the era's drug of choice, and the smart set and gangland began to overlap, which added too many guns to the mix. Then in 1994 he overdosed, and a friend took him to his first 12-step meeting. He went on to a Malibu rehab center called Promises, where people with agents and managers are regulars. When he got out, he moved in with Henry, the two of them adrift without drugs, floating in their pool, waiting for their next NA meeting. He was still in that state of post-addictive limbo when we met.

After about six months of our peculiar, transatlantic romance, Matthew invited me to come to a charity dinner in Pittsburgh. He picked me up in a limousine strewn with rose petals, blindfolded me, took me to a waiting helicopter, recited a bit of verse he'd written, and proposed while circling the Mellon Bank building. It was a sweet poem, with "I want to marry you" expressed very lyrically. It all seemed rather sudden, but like the always plucky fictional character I'm supposed to resemble, perhaps I had "a special radar for inappropriate men." Of course I said yes.

Matthew moved to London to be with me on a live-in basis, and my brother Gregory, who was an estate agent at the time, working for a company called Foxtons, scoured Belgravia to find us a house, eventually locating a duplex on Eaton Place, not far from Chester Row. Matthew bought it, and I paid for the decorating, which led to a photo spread in W.

Matthew didn't take to London at first. Our famously English weather was a problem, as was the somewhat arcane and highly structured social system, which is difficult for anyone from the outside to navigate. Certainly the people aren't quite as gregarious as they are in L.A. But Henry had moved back as well, so at least Matthew had one close friend, and he did his best to acclimate.

. . . .

THE NEXT BIG SCENE IN our script was, of course, a wedding, and, initially, we thought we'd get married in Venice, just because it seemed the most romantic place on earth. We actually took a trip there with my parents to look at churches. My mother was sober at the time, and she behaved, and over a three-day period we must have looked at fifty possible venues. The wrinkle, of course, was that all the beautiful and atmospheric chapels in Italy are Catholic, and we were not, and the priests there take this matter of religious affiliation very seriously. For a while we thought about converting. We even went to see the priest at a Catholic church in Knightsbridge, but he declined the assignment, expressing doubts about our religious fervor.

My father had his own doubts, not just about having a Catholic wedding in Venice, but about having a wedding anywhere with Matthew Mellon as the groom. According to tradition, it's the bride's father who pays for the wedding feast, and that led to some discussion about just how grand a ceremony we were going to have. Dad offered a budget of £100,000. Anything beyond that was up to us.

Even during this prenuptial phase of high romance and heavy distraction, I still had a business to run, and I still had the same troublesome business partner. In April, I received an unwanted wedding present from Jimmy in the form of an article published in the *Mail on Sunday*. He had spoken all too openly with the reporter, going on about the growing rift between us. He even went so far as to say that we were harming him by using his name (for which, you may recall, he was being compensated with half ownership in a company that was going to make him rich). As for the fact that Sandra and I were, in fact, designing the collection, he responded, "Anyone can sketch a shoe."

The father of the bride, who was also chairman of the company, stepped in and wrote him a cease and desist letter. Jimmy responded by saying that I was the one who should be restricted from speaking to the press. We offered to buy him out. He refused.

Matthew and I continued our path to the altar, but to get married in England you have to fill out forms and sign documents in front of the superintendent registrar within the village or town where you reside, so we actually took care of the formalities with a simple civil ceremony at the registry office on Kings Road. We were still planning the "big church wedding," of course, and we were so focused on that larger event that the moment of officially becoming man and wife really was not a big deal for us. We had a few friends along as witnesses, and then my dad took us to lunch at La Famiglia. Afterward, we had tea at Claridge's.

By this time we had settled on the perfect setting for a proper English wedding: Blenheim Palace, the home of the dukes of Marlborough and birthplace of Winston Churchill. It's a gorgeous example of English baroque set in a two-thousand-acre park to the west of London, and *Vogue* wanted to do a feature. But of course that meant that the dress had to be perfect.

Six weeks before the big day I still didn't know what I was going to wear. Matthew and I were out at the Oscars when I ran into Carlos Sousa, head of PR worldwide for Valentino. He said, "Darling, you must come to us. Don't worry! We will work it out for you."

Trouble is, at that time I really didn't have any money. My salary from Jimmy Choo was still not much beyond £15,000 a year, which just happened to be the cost of a couture dress from Valentino.

Matthew's brother, Henry, graciously stepped in to loan me the money, so when we got back to London I set up an appointment and booked a ticket to Rome, whereupon Valentino himself did three sketches for me to choose from. *Vogue* covered the story, with photographs of me being fitted. It was the only couture clothing I've ever had made, and it was amazing. But the lasting value-added was that Valentino and I became great friends. He began to call whenever he was in London, and later he would invite us to spend time with him on his boat.

At this point, it was still unclear how the rather grand scale of this event was going to be financed. My mother was back to being her normal, difficult self, and so for a while my parents weren't going to come at all, and then they were going to come and were inviting ten friends, and then they ended up bringing thirty guests. Every step of the way was fraught with the kind of family drama I'd known all my life, with my mother continually causing scenes behind the scenes. As per usual with my mother, you could never anticipate what nonsensical thing was going to set her off, and thus you could not avoid the trip wires. Harry Winston was loaning me a fifty-carat diamond to wear, and when I went to Paris to pick it up, I took my mother with me, hoping that letting her borrow something really lovely, too, might placate her, but to no avail. I was the bride but, as usual, our interaction wound up being all about her.

Adding to the stress was the persistent question of who was footing the ever-growing bill. The invitations said "Mr. and Mrs. Yeardye invite you . . ." but, as it turned out, Matthew kicked in $400,000 in addition to my father's £100,000, and then when I received my first large cash proceeds from Jimmy Choo, I reimbursed him. This slightly unusual arrangement added a huge element of friction I really didn't need because Matthew's uncle Jay, the kind of multimillionaire who always flies coach, was sensitive about the Mellons being taken advantage of for their wealth. I think he also had an inflated sense of just how much money my father had.

We did the American thing of having a rehearsal dinner the night before, but with an English twist. Henry was best man, and he allowed us to stage the event at Sudeley Castle. Maria Grachvogel made my dress for the evening, a bias-cut cream slit dress with a crocheted lace tail. We brought over a clear plastic marquee from Paris under which the 170 attendees could sit and enjoy the sight of the illuminated castle while listening to an Irish folk band.

The ceremony the next day was in a church near the estate, small but still large enough to accommodate our three hundred guests, which included, once again, Hugh Grant and Liz Hurley, even though they'd announced their split one week earlier. We weren't part of the congregation or property owners in the area, so technically all the minister could offer us was a "blessing." But we went through all the normal vows, and it looked like a proper enough wedding, especially for a couple who'd already been married for several months.

My maid of honor was Anouska Hempel, daughter-in-law of Anouska Hempel the hotelier, and she wore an Elie Saab dress that complimented my Valentino gown. We had young boys in morning coats as ushers, and Matt Clifford, who plays keyboard for the Stones, composed a special processional. It was held late in the afternoon so that the light would be perfect as we stepped out of the chapel and the *Vogue* photographer caught us releasing a flock of doves.

I think all brides are worn out by the time the big day arrives, and true to form I was utterly exhausted. In truth, the wedding was one long stretch of misery for me, and I felt like crying the whole time. I'd been working incredibly hard for Jimmy Choo, planning this huge event alone while trying to keep everyone happy, and I'd just about reached the end of my tether.

The dinner was held in the library at Blenheim, with catering by Admirable Crichton, flowers by Kenneth Turner, and a five-foot-tall cake made of profiteroles. My face hurt from maintaining a beauty contestant's frozen smile, and I was counting the hours. I had one more costume change, an amazing gray silk cocktail dress from Chloé for going away. Then I'd throw the bouquet and go back to the hotel and cry.

When it came time for the toasts, Uncle Jay ended his by thanking Matthew for graciously hosting the festivities, and I felt like I'd just been kicked in the stomach. On top of everything else, I now felt utterly humiliated (insult added to injury when you consider that I would pay for everything in the end), and I felt terrible for my dad.

Matthew had flown over an American disco cover band called Boogie Knights to play at the reception. I drifted around the floor for a moment or two, faking merriment, but very soon I found my way to the small room just off the main hall that had been set up as a lounge. I sat there in my wedding dress, staring off into space, as vacant as I'd ever been at Heathfield, unable to connect with anyone.

We had to be out of the palace by two a.m., and by then it had begun to rain, and Matthew and I left in a blue Bentley, driving down the very long drive as sparklers and Roman candles shot up into the night sky.

There were two small hotels in the nearby village of Woodstock, and we were staying at the one called the Bear, a Tudor bed-and-breakfast with the musty bar and the shabby green carpet. I went up to the room alone, and Matthew partied until dawn with his American friends, all of whom were staying at the place next door. It was not an auspicious beginning.

. . . .

OUR WEDDING PRESENT FROM UNCLE JAY was a honeymoon trip to Bali, and on the eighteen-hour flight from London I was a zombie, getting a good head start on a serious commitment to rest and relax-ation. We were in the South Pacific for two weeks, and for the first time in years I had some genuine time off, with no faxes coming in at all hours.

Some might wonder about two reformed addicts being in such a faraway place on their honeymoon, but we didn't need NA meetings to keep us on the straight and narrow path. We stayed very busy with tons of scuba diving, and I even picked up my advanced certification.

One day we were out in a boat, anchored above a reef just off one of the smaller islands where the currents draw you around in a big circle. This was the last part of the advanced course where you have to swim around a patch of treacherous water, and we employed the buddy system. I was in the water with my partner when I saw Matthew signal that he was going up. My buddy and I followed, and luckily we all popped up just alongside the hull. We climbed aboard and waited for the other people to come along—a couple from Hong Kong and the dive instructor. And then we waited some more.

When we'd been waiting about forty-five minutes, Matthew said to me, "This isn't good." He had calculated the current and the wind, and he said, "They're being swept out to sea. I can tell you exactly where they're going to pop up."

He explained to the mate what must have happened, but the man wouldn't take the initiative. Then another hour went by and I said, "Matthew, you're going to have to do something. They're going to drown."

Having spent months every year in Maine and in the Caribbean sailing, Matthew had his captain's license and knew how to handle big boats. In the end, he had to push the mate away from the controls and commandeer the wheel. He started the engine and headed out to where he figured the wind and the current would be taking the three missing people, and he nailed it.

He did such an amazing job—he pretty much made a beeline right to where they were treading water, still being carried out by the current. I had never seen three more terrified people, or a more grateful trio. The instructor was so shaken that he quit his job and gave up diving. The couple from Hong Kong continued to send Matthew a Christmas card for years afterward.

Matthew had so many talents and admirable qualities—it's unfortunate that emotional stability was not among them. When you go into rehab, they tell you that the first five years are the most difficult because that's when your emotions are still very raw. That's where the saying "one day at a time" comes in. They also advise you not to take up with a newcomer to sobriety because that person may relapse and drag you down with them. When I met Matthew we were both sober, but sobriety is so much more difficult for people who are bipolar. So I knew he was vulnerable, with his mood swings, his dancing all night, and his rages. But, eyes wide open, I still thought I'd hang in there, and I tried to have confidence in my husband's character and resolve, and not just in his skill with boats.

Still, it was not an easy time for either of us.

London is like New York in that it's all about work, and not fitting in made Matthew restless. At parties he had trouble talking to the other men, and so his default was to follow me around. My father was not impressed by how his new son-in-law was shouldering his responsibilities as a married man.

Then on a trip to Lineapelle with me, Matthew happened upon the exhibit from the Vibram company, where he saw a sole for a wind-surfing shoe, and it gave him an idea. Why not take the new structural innovations in athletic shoes and adapt them for dress and casual shoes? He decided to launch his own line for men based on this new concept—a traditional upper, but a lightweight, shock-absorbing sole that incorporated rubber, polyurethane, liquid silicone, and similar materials. He would call his brand Harry's of London, named after his grandfather, Harry Stokes, who had been quite the dandy. The logo would be the heron from the Mellon family crest.

Matthew set up the company, and Anna Conti's brother Massimo connected him with some men's factories, and I have to hand it to him— the shoe was really innovative, and Matthew made a fantastic product. The only problem was that he hired a woman as chief executive officer who didn't fully appreciate the competitive advantage of their distinctive niche. She tried to expand into traditional leather-soled shoes, when they should have focused on the dress shoe with running shoe technology, which Cole Haan managed to pick up on and exploit very nicely.

Even so, the company is still around. Matthew sold a majority stake to La Compagnie Financière Richemont SA, and today they have their own shops and are represented in twenty countries.

For our first winter vacation as an old married couple, Matthew chartered a yacht with a captain, and we invited a number of people to come sailing with us in the Bahamas. The guests included Vassi Chamberlain and her husband, Adrian Harris; Kate Reardon, who is now the editor in chief of *Tatler*; Christian Hammer; and Yazmen Olclay.

We started off in Nassau and were supposed to be crossing over to

Harbour Island when a huge storm came up. After the incident on our honeymoon, I knew we could count on Matthew's seamanship. Also, this boat was at least seventy-five feet, so we were perfectly safe, but the waves seemed to be about ten feet and the swell was pounding and knocking us around, and some of our guests freaked out. Meanwhile, Matthew was up on the deck, entranced by the whole thing. Then everyone began to get seasick, so down below we had all these London socialites sitting in the lounge vomiting into plastic bags.

By the time we made it into port, our guests were understandably eager to stretch their legs. I'm not sure anyone uttered the fatal words, "We need a drink," but if someone had, I'm sure Matthew would have seconded the motion. The long and the short of it is that all the guys went into town, and when Matthew came back he seemed utterly paranoid, so much so that he hid in the ship's head for two hours.

It turned out that he'd picked up some cocaine on the island, and next thing you know he was convinced that the FBI was installed on the next boat over, watching us with night vision goggles.

Sad to say, but for us, this was already the beginning of the end.

Once we were back in London, life did not become any easier because I was in the office every day, working very hard, and Matthew had nothing but free time on his hands, and I'd come home and find him freebasing in the kitchen. Then his mania would take over, and he might step out to buy a paper and not come back for days. I was constantly trying to track him down, calling family members, calling car services, knowing that he was capable of turning up anywhere in the world. He would check into hotels, start getting the paranoid delusions of cocaine psychosis, then leave without paying his bill. And then, of course, the hotel managers would call me to clean up after him and to settle his accounts.

At times I had to track him down relying on his limo company. Once Henry and I found him in a crack house in Notting Hill, and we went in and found some gangster type sitting in the kitchen, with Matthew's wallet on the table in front of him. For a moment I was worried that my husband had been murdered. Then Henry said to the drug dealer, "You better tell us where he is, otherwise you're going to be looking down the wrong end of a shotgun." It was all bluster, and the dealer was not terribly impressed. Later, we found out that Matthew had been hiding under the bed.

I still thought I could help him and turn it around. I always tried to keep him sober, and I tried to be helpful without "enabling" his addiction, but one never knows.

Matthew and I went to Saint Tropez for the summer, staying on Valentino's boat, and I discovered that I was pregnant. Despite everything we were going through I was thrilled. I was thirty-three, and having a child was definitely on my to-do list, even if the father was clearly not going to be much help.

So now I had a baby in the works, as well as a husband who was sometimes endearing and wonderfully funny, and sometimes completely mad. I was still trying to manage a global brand with a business partner who was working against me every step of the way. The pot-boiler plot was coming to a nice simmer, and yet the villains who would send it boiling over had yet to appear.

····· 6 ·····

As 2000 came to a close, Jimmy Choo was turning a profit of around £3 million a year. We had our own London boutique and we were represented at 450 other stores, including Harrods and Selfridges. To top it all off, we'd won a British Fashion Council Award, which Jimmy insisted on accepting on our behalf, even though his design contribution had been nil. Jimmy's personal publicist was running the awards and was more than happy for him to go through with the sham. "I leave the ready-to-wear to my partner and team," he told the press, rather missing the point of the accomplishment (i.e., the ready-to-wear) for which the award was being given.

In the United States, *Sex and the City* and the Oscars had ensconced us solidly in the pantheon of pop culture. With a new administration coming to Washington in January 2001, both presidential daughters wore Jimmy Choo to their father's inauguration. We were poised for explosive growth well beyond our own three stores, Saks, and Giorgio's.

Every quarter we held a board meeting in St. Helier on Jersey, the Channel Island where the company was chartered. Jimmy rarely showed up, but when he did, he almost always voted against whatever proposal was on the table. Voting strength was proportionate to ownership, so having a half owner with such negativity could definitely throw a wrench in the works. Despite all the evidence that the time was right to expand in the United States, Jimmy was dead set against it. My father tried time and time again to make him understand how he was going to benefit as the company grew and increased in value. My father would lay it all out, and Jimmy would smile and say, "Yes, yes, yes." But after a while our relationship deteriorated to the point that any conversation, rational or otherwise, was out of the question. Not only had we "taken Sandra away from him," we'd blown his cover by letting the press in on the fact that he had nothing to do with designing our collections.

Eventually, the breakdown got to the point that my father said, "Would you consider an offer for your shares?"

Jimmy's response was to sue us on twenty-two counts of breach of contract.

I don't know how Jimmy found the cash to hire the lawyers, but I do know that he'd taken on an adviser named Ivan Sheer, who was not an attorney but an executive at Warner Music. When Jimmy and his team showed up at a meeting at the Sheraton in Belgravia, the main complaint was the way in which we'd set up the separate US company with Philip Rogers, but the claim was deemed to be without merit and the case never went to court. We assumed it was a ploy to try to intimidate us into paying more for Jimmy's shares. And Sheer, who was taking a hefty percentage of Jimmy's proceeds, seemed highly motivated to sell.

But this feuding was not good for business. We'd put enormous effort into building the brand, and internal fighting could tarnish the image of a product that was meant to be glamorous, sexy, and fun. As

I would eventually discover much to my regret, and only with the passage of time, where Jimmy really hurt the company that carried his name was in refusing to sell his shares to my father and me. He was simply too filled with resentment to follow that otherwise very natural and very logical course.

Until this time we had been entirely self-funding. My father had put up the initial £150,000 of seed money, and after that first sale to Saks we were self-funding. When we needed a bank loan to set up shop in North America, my father took out a £600,000 mortgage on his house to provide the additional capital. If only Jimmy had been willing to sell to us, we would have been in the incredibly enviable position of owning the company outright. We simply could have gone to the bank, taken out another loan, and retained complete control. But as a sandal-wearing Greek first observed a couple of thousand years ago, *Pathei mathos*. We suffer into knowledge.

After Jimmy finally agreed to sell—but not to us—we entered into a very tense six-month period as we tried to find a new partner to buy his shares. During this time, of course, I was also growing larger by the day with my pregnancy and with all the attendant discomforts. It was not to be the peaceful period of gestation I'd hoped for.

Matthew put us in touch with a friend of his who was an investment banker in New York, who in turn put us in touch with Javan Bunch from Merrill Lynch. Javan introduced us to the Gucci Group, to the people who represented the Wertheimer family, and to Chanel, who declined to make an offer. (After researching our operations, however, Chanel did decide to start working with Anna Conti for their own shoe line.)

We went through various proposals from the other companies, but the pieces never seemed to fit. And then a friend of mine named Alexandra Montazzi called and said, "I just met a guy named Robert Bensoussan, and he's interested in your business. Would you like to meet him?"

I said, "Sure," which is how we were so blithely introduced to the world of private equity. If only I had known.

. . . .

ROBERT BENSOUSSAN WORKED WITH A financial group called Phoenix Equity Partners, who were said to have nearly three-quarters of a billion dollars to play with. They had a consumer, leisure, and retail division, run by a man named David Burns, but the company as a whole was more inclined to invest in cement factories than fashion.

David seemed very keen, but he was concerned that his partners might not be as interested as he was, so he asked them to go home and discuss the acquisition with the women in their lives. This bit of informal market research brought back a resounding endorsement of the brand, as well as the acquisition.

For his part, Robert had a long history with luxury brands. He'd worked in finance for Lainière de Roubaix, then ran a ready-to-wear line for Charles Jourdan. He then worked for the French fashion house Sonia Rykiel, then for Christian Lacroix in Paris, Gianfranco Ferré in Milan, then joined the board of Inter Parfums, Inc., in New York, and was retained by Rose Marie Bravo as her personal adviser to work on the repositioning of the Burberry brand in Europe and Asia. In 1999, he put together the leveraged buyout of Joseph, bringing in Albert Frère and LV Capital as partners.

At first blush, then, here was a man who knew the fashion business inside and out. Upon reflection, of course, one begins to wonder: That's a great many jobs in a very short period of time, and each job is of surprisingly short tenure. Is there an issue here?

Robert Bensoussan didn't want to simply acquire Jimmy Choo. He wanted to create a separate entity for Phoenix called Equinox Luxury Holdings, with himself as chairman and chief executive.

We negotiated through the second half of the summer, and the Phoenix Equity investment committee was to meet on September 11, 2001, to decide whether or not to invest in Jimmy Choo. Robert was traveling to Pont Street to meet with Raj Patel, our accountant, and Lou Rodwell, the company secretary, when the terrorist attacks hit New York and Washington and seemed to put the whole world on hold.

David Burns rang up to say that everything would now have to be reconsidered because all around us the share prices for luxury goods were crashing to earth. Dad and I were not overly concerned because we would be keeping our investment in the business, rolling over the vast majority of our shares. The only person selling equity was Jimmy, which was, of course, the whole point of the transaction.

A few weeks later David rang up to get our results. Post-9/11, our sales had actually increased by 40 percent, even in New York. We had no explanation, except for the maxim, "When the going gets tough, the tough go shopping."

Meanwhile, we weren't just sitting on our hands while Phoenix deliberated. We moved from Pont Street to a 3,000-square-foot office on Ixworth Place. We were hiring more people, including more design talent and more product development people, as well as more help in finance. In keeping with our history of penny pinching, though, the offices were quite simple and the furniture was from IKEA.

In October we moved the store from Motcomb Street to 169 Draycott Avenue in South Kensington, just around the corner from Joseph. Retailers like Ralph Lauren were moving into the neighborhood, making it more of a shopping mecca. To celebrate the new store, heavily pregnant or not, I held a lunch at Drones to benefit the Twin Towers Fund.

Ultimately, David Burns and Phoenix overcame their anxieties and agreed to buy, and Dad managed to roll in the rights to the US market that had been acquired by Philip Rogers and Annie Humphries. In terms of personal gain, it made more sense for Philip and Annie to hold on and grow their equity, but they agreed to sell out of loyalty to my dad and to protect the deal with Phoenix.

We discussed various options at first, and we knew that Phoenix had done deals with varying equity positions—minority, majority. Robert, however, pushed them to acquire a controlling interest.

The offer that emerged was for Phoenix to pay £9 million for Jimmy's shares, with their stake to be valued as 51 percent of Jimmy Choo Limited. At first Dad said, "No, we're not doing it." He was never one to surrender control of anything. But I was so desperate to get rid of Jimmy that I talked him into taking the deal.

"How bad could it be?" I said.

Later, I could only blame myself.

The £9 million for Jimmy was certainly not a bad payout for his allowing us to use his name. But even with this windfall, Jimmy pushed Robert to invest in his couture business. Phoenix balked at that, although they did allow Jimmy to license his own name for seven years, in exchange for a royalty of one pound a year. He had to brand his product Jimmy Choo Couture, and his shoes always had to cost more than our ready-to-wear product. He was also enjoined from ever speaking to the press about the business without approval from us.

For an additional $4 million, Phoenix would simultaneously acquire the US business, including our three US stores as well as distribution rights. That part of the deal would yield $2 million for Philip Rogers and $2 million for my dad, a sum that he shared with me. This was the first real fruit of my labors with Jimmy Choo, and I used $400,000 of it to repay Matthew for the wedding.

All of Jimmy Choo, both European and US, would now be combined under a new entity, Yearnoxe Limited, of which Dad and I together would own 49 percent. The fact that someone else would now have the final say in how we ran the company was going to take some getting used to. Little did I know just how much lay ahead.

Even before the deal closed, we began to have meetings in order to get to know our new partners and to try to educate them about our business. At the first of these, which took place at the Sheraton in London, I suggested that we buy a factory. We were having issues with people copying our shoes, and I thought we could improve our margins by having our own dedicated facility to produce at least a part of the collection. Robert didn't like the idea, though, so I let it drop. A few years later we did a deal with Petra in which we acquired one-half of one factory, and sure enough, it produced all the savings and efficiencies I'd predicted. But this time around it was "Robert's idea."

This was my first, painful lesson in private equity: The founder is no longer in charge, and the battle of ideas is always subordinate to the battle of egos.

But back at that first meeting at the Sheraton, the other players from the Phoenix Group began to ask follow-up questions about the intricacies of production. I was the only one who could answer because I was the only one intricately involved in operations. In fact, I'd been up to my elbows in leather and lasts for five years, so the conversation wound up being a mini-seminar in shoe design and production, as well as the ins and outs of doing business in Italy.

Later, when the meeting was over and we were walking out of the hotel, my father turned to me with a smile and said, "You know, you and I are going to split our 49 percent right down the middle."

I had never really given much thought to my father's share versus my share, but coming from him, this declaration of parity was a welcome acknowledgment of my contribution. Of course it felt good, but the way my mind works, the relief I feel at avoiding failure or abuse is always more pronounced than any real pleasure in achievement or recognition. I knew all along what I'd been contributing. I knew that this split was the way it should be and that it would have been grossly unfair if it had been otherwise. Now it was simply being confirmed.

The more powerful validation, though, came after Phoenix completed their due diligence. After David Burns had spoken to all the staff, he asked my dad to sign a document formally establishing that the Yeardye shares were to be equally divided between the two of us. Clearly what he'd learned was that I was the one making all the day-to-day decisions, and he wanted my ownership stake to be explicit for fear that otherwise I might leave.

It was at this point that Dad set up a couple of trusts in Jersey to hold the family's 49 percent of Jimmy Choo, with one-half earmarked for me. Matthew pushed me to gain the utmost clarity between what was to benefit me and what was to benefit the rest of the family. He'd met my mother, and he'd heard my stories.

"If anything happens to your dad," he said, "you're screwed."

The upshot was a main family trust to be called Marqueta, and then a second trust to hold my shares called Araminta, which was the name we'd chosen for our baby, who we knew was going to be a little girl. As I reviewed the documents I looked for the word "irrevocable." Some people view "a mother's love" as the absolute bedrock of certainty. I did not. And as I would discover a few years later, my mother had been pushing for a split of 70/30 even then.

Although our 49 percent stake represented a sizable asset, it was not terribly liquid. Our ownership stake in the company would be locked up until Phoenix decided to exit. In private equity, this is usually a period of three years.

Robert met with Dad and me at my house for the signing on November 19, 2001. Dad would be chairman of the board of the new company and I would be president. Robert was named CEO, but this was supposed to be an interim arrangement for only six months or so. But then he decided that he liked being the head of a company with our kind of name recognition, especially, I think, among stylish women. So he stayed on.

Even though Phoenix was now the majority partner, none of their money ever went into actual operations. To finance expansion, we arranged a £2 million line of credit with Barclays Bank.

The Holy Grail of private equity is an accounting metric known as EBITDA, which stands for "earnings before interest, taxes, depreciation, and amortization." It would become a daily obsession for us all, because EBITDA multiplied by a certain number—usually around 10–12 in the fashion business—is the basis for valuation upon exit. And in private equity, it's all about the exit.

Our EBITDA going in was £2.9 million, which was quite a lot for a company with only nine employees. We closed that year with revenues of £12 million, based on fifteen thousand pairs of shoes. So it wasn't as if Jimmy Choo was a distressed asset that had to be turned around by high-priced financial engineers. We were a household name with a product that was flying out of the stores.

The challenge was to create more stores.

Expanding our retail presence, especially in the United States, had been the impetus for parting ways with Jimmy, which led to the Phoenix deal in the first place. At least with Robert on board he could manage that expansion, which freed me up to work on the collection. More outlets might increase our volume of sales, but to maintain the vitality of the brand, we needed creative vigor and constant innovation.

One of the ideas I pushed through at the time was to have a House Collection, which is to say a selection of basics—a plain pump, a slingback, a plain boot—that would always be available, year in and year out. They would come in the most basic colors—black, red, and camel—and they would never go on sale. That way, any woman who entered our store, no matter what she was looking for, would always have something to buy. Over the next few years, the House Collection became 30 percent of the Jimmy Choo business.

Between 2001 and 2006 we grew at roughly 30 percent a year over-all, opening about forty stores in all the major American cities you might expect, including Miami, Washington, Chicago, Dallas, and Houston. If we went to a prime location or a shopping mall and said we wanted to open a Jimmy Choo store, they'd roll out the red carpet. The path had already been cleared with the brand awareness and the prestige we'd established long before Phoenix ever entered the picture.

To manage this kind of growth, we needed to move beyond the space we'd shared with Vidal Sassoon in Philip Rogers's offices, so we established our US headquarters in New York at Fifty-Ninth Street and Lexington Avenue. We hired a president of US operations, a head of US public relations, and a manager for the US wholesale business. Finance was overseen from the UK.

We still had Anna Conti as our agent to oversee production in Italy, and of course I was still flying back and forth relentlessly. Dad had a small office at the Ixworth Place location, but he kept in touch mostly by phone, and by having lunch with Robert at the Lowndes Hotel.

Until now we'd been relying on a part-time accountant and an off-the-shelf accounting program for personal computers. Robert hired Deloitte & Touche to bring us up to speed on our systems and record keeping. They sent Alison Egan, head of their retail division, who came in on a three-month contract, but Robert was so impressed that he offered her the position of chief financial officer.

We also had a distribution agreement for international wholesale with Body Lines, a German company that had been an early retail customer of ours. We renegotiated the agreement such that Body Lines would retain Germany and Austria, but we could regain the rest of

Europe and deal direct. A couple of years later we brought all rights back in-house.

We were ready to launch our in-store boutiques in places like Saks and Harvey Nichols, but there was also much to be done to continue to build the brand's visibility well upstream from the point of purchase. I felt that it was important not only to have a collection at press week, but also to do charity projects and collaborations, events that crossed fashion with art and gave us opportunities to reach out to the community and to expand our share of buzz.

I thought that Jimmy Choo as a luxury brand should own an event the way that Cartier owns polo—Cartier sponsors the Cartier International Polo Tournament at the Guards Polo Club in Windsor.

I also felt that the perfect brand fit for us would have something to do with the glamour of film. Charles Finch, formerly with William Morris, had set up his own business linking fashion brands with Hollywood, and in January 2002 we teamed with him to sponsor his first dinner at San Lorenzo to celebrate the British Academy of Film and Television Awards. This was the Saturday night of awards week when all the actors and actresses, even those who live in Australia or California, are in town, and so it was a great way to welcome them back to London. The turnout was extraordinary, but Robert looked at the numbers and canceled our participation.

After more than a decade, this dinner is still one of the hottest invitations in town, and Charles has added a second event in L.A. during the Oscars, and a third at Cannes. Robert's decision was incredibly foolish, and a wasted opportunity comparable to the loss of exposure we would have suffered had we been too timid to take the risk and make our commitment to outfitting stars on Oscar night. You could chalk it up to a bean counter's mentality, but he would go on to make similarly disastrous choices that were far more revealing of his character.

Robert is a large, somewhat burly man, with a grizzled beard and a dodgy eye, and, as I was soon to learn, he is also someone who likes to shout and to throw his weight around.

Each summer the Serpentine Gallery in Kensington Gardens gets an artist to come in and build a special pavilion for a party that's sort of a "circus night" out in the park. Yves Saint Laurent and many other fashion houses had sponsored it with great success in the past, and Jimmy Choo being a British brand and London being our home turf, I thought we should support the event, even though it was expensive, on the order of £100,000. This was a couple of years later, after we had a different private-equity partner, and when Robert saw the invitation I'd commissioned, he took a copy over to the partner's office in Hyde Park Circle and threw it on his desk.

"What do you see wrong here?"

The partner looked at it and shrugged.

"My name is not on it!" Robert complained.

He refused to attend.

Being treated like an employee at the company I'd founded took some getting used to.

. . . .

AT OSCAR TIME DURING THAT first year of our new relationship with Phoenix I was eight months pregnant, so I didn't make it to California.

Instead, I stayed home at Eaton Place to enjoy a baby shower, the typical afternoon tea and girl talk with Brenda Tafler, Claudia Schiffer, Emily Oppenheimer, Vassi Chamberlain, Jessica de Rothschild, and Daphne Guinness.

Matthew liked his parties a little more revved up, so he went on to the festivities in L.A. alone, taking with him thirty pairs of shoes from his Harry's of London brand for men. He took a suite next to Jimmy Choo's in the Peninsula and retained our publicist, Marilyn Heston, to make sure that anyone coming round to see the Jimmy Choos also checked out Harry's of London. He followed our procedure of giving away shoes to agents, managers—even lawyers—and he managed to put Harry's shoes on the feet of Sting, Elton John, the ubiquitous Hugh Grant, John Travolta, and Denzel Washington. Ultimately, Robert found the implied co-branding too close for comfort and, at his suggestion, Matthew backed off.

My husband seemed normal enough when he'd left London, but during his stay in California he went on a rampage and disappeared for eight days. I was frantic as I tried to locate him.

It so happened that my parents were also in L.A.—they loved to be there at Oscar time—and also staying at the Peninsula. My mother was actually standing in the lobby one evening, talking to the manager, when she saw Matthew walk by. She knew I was looking for him, and so she said to the manager, "God, that's my son-in-law! He's been missing for days." The manager told her, "No, madam, you must be mistaken. That's Mr. Goldstein." Matthew had checked back into the hotel under an assumed name—his standard MO. He'd use his real credit card to book the room, but if anybody wanted to reach him, there was no Mr. Mellon on the guest list. They'd have to know to ask for Mr. Goldstein.

He also changed his cell phone number on a regular basis, but my dad managed to track him down. When my dad told me that he was going to try to speak to Matthew, I said, "Be nice. Just try to get him to come home for the birth."

Just to be safe, I also called Matthew's brother, Henry, who got in touch with the limo company Matthew always hired, then tracked down the car. Henry said he found the limo idling at the curb outside a club, opened the door, and slid in. Matthew didn't bat an eye, Henry told me later. My errant husband said simply, "Hey, bud," and took another sip of his scotch. Eventually, Henry got him on a plane to London.

Eager as I was to have Matthew home, when he showed up he was more than anything just one more problem to take care of. He hadn't slept in days, and he's always very disconnected when he's been in mania. I'd become accustomed to these limitations, but at this particular moment, his disconnect from the larger agenda was hard to take.

On April 10, I worked through the morning, waddling around in all my enormity, and then I started to have cramps. I went home and lay down for a bit, Matthew and I had lunch, and then he drove me to the Portland Hospital in his Porsche. I knew it was going to be a long evening, especially for me, even more so when the epidural kicked in on only one side. I was sweating profusely by the time they took me to the delivery suite, and Matthew went back up to my room to get some sleep.

At six the next morning, April 11, 2002, I gave birth to a six-pound baby girl, and Matthew was on hand to cut the umbilical cord. He was sufficiently cogent and engaged to send texts all around announcing the baby. But then he started jabbering about buying a Bentley. There I was on my first morning as a mother, blissed-out, a little woozy, with this little baby girl in my arms, and all my errant husband could talk about was a car. Clearly he was still coming off his manic episode.

The name we'd chosen—Araminta—means "collector of thoughts." I had been doing some research and stumbled upon this cross between Arabella and Aminta, which is all very English. I liked it all the more for being the name of a character in the play *The Confederacy*, written by the same John Vanbrugh who had been the architect of Blenheim Palace, where Matthew had our wedding. Mostly, I just thought Minty Mellon would be a wonderful name.

I'd always told him I'd leave him immediately if he relapsed, and maybe it was the hormonal rush of motherhood, but I relented. I pressed him to try harder and to do what I'd done, which was to go to the meetings and to find a new group of people to be with. He needed to change the patterns of his life but, maybe by not exercising more tough love, I enabled him.

All I know for sure is that his relapse into drugs only got worse. He was doing coke and alcohol to the point of psychosis, which would lead him to very matter-of-fact statements like, "There's somebody on the roof. I know they're coming to get me."

We had a board meeting at my house a week after I gave birth, and all the while I was worried my husband might be freebasing in the kitchen.

After a few weeks I took some time off, and Matthew and I took little Minty to Capri to visit Uncle Jay and his wife, Vivian.

Robert called while I was there and said, "When are you going to stop vacationing and get back to the office?"

I realized now the full irony of my huge mistake. I had rid myself of the man who had vexed me most—namely Jimmy Choo—only to saddle myself with an incredibly difficult CEO. In addition to which, I now had a bipolar, drug-addicted husband who was spiraling out of control.

I really couldn't trust Matthew to handle the baby, so in May, I left Minty and the nanny with my parents while I went to Italy for Lineapelle, the leather goods show. The plane was filled with people from the shoe business, and I couldn't repair to the bathroom to express milk because it was so disgusting, so I simply had a jacket thrown over myself and I was pumping milk like mad. After that, Minty usually went with me on all my business trips until she was old enough to start school. I would do the opening, or the meeting, then go back to the hotel, where she and her nanny would be waiting. Of course, some caretakers were better than others. That summer we rented a house in St. Tropez, and we went down to the beach for lunch with our friends Jonathan and Hayley Sieff.

When we came back we found the nanny out on the lawn covered with blood, screaming, "The baby's been kidnapped." I was so terrified that I threw up. We began searching all over, and happily we found Minty asleep in her crib. That's when we realized that the woman was simply drunk. We were having a party that night, so we had some liquor in the house, and she'd gotten into it, so much so that she fell down and bloodied her face. When Matthew took her outside to try to talk to her, she keeled over on the grass.

As soon as this alcoholic nanny revived, I put her in a cab and shipped her off to the airport, but when I called to report the incident to the agency they said, "Well, there's always more than one side to every story." But evidently there was not, because years later this same woman was brought to trial, accused of shaking a baby to death, only to get off on a technicality.

These are the kinds of things that terrify a young mother, but I had my own special fears. Once, when Minty was about eight months, I had to leave her with my parents while I went to the office. It was a joy to see my father's interaction with his granddaughter. He would spend hours drawing with her and teaching her things.

Once when I came back to their flat, Dad was sitting in the drawing room, and I asked him, "Where's Minty?"

"In the back with your mother," he said, scarcely looking up. I walked down the hallway to the bedroom, which was fairly dark, and I remember having this utterly creepy feeling that almost made me sick. It was the feeling of fear I'd always associated with my mother, as if she were entirely capable of causing me harm. Now I was feeling that sense of menace on behalf of my daughter.

. . . .

THE DEMANDS OF THE BUSINESS didn't grow any less just because I'd taken on new responsibilities in my personal life, and as I charged through my days I began to feel more and more like a prizefighter. I was lucky to get a few seconds to sit in my corner, but after a splash from the water bucket and some styptic for the cuts, the bell would ring and it was on to the next round. I always seemed to be counterpunching, responding to whatever craziness was being thrown at me. I was desperate to get out ahead, struggling to break into the open air.

In the UK, most department stores lease the space for their shoe departments and let a third party manage it, but Harvey Nichols was different. They ran their own shoe department, but it never had been a great success. Manolo Blahnik still refused to sell through any of the London retailers, so the US brand Joan & David predominated, but then in 2000 they filed for bankruptcy. This left Harvey Nichols with space to fill, and so they gave us 700 square feet in the front of the shoe department to create a Jimmy Choo in-store boutique.

The night before we launched our concession, in September 2002, I held a dinner at San Lorenzo. I had a poem printed on T-shirts to give away to guests:

I think I'm in love with my shoe
I was sure that it felt the same, too
'til it happened to mention
With heartless intention
"I'm dating a gold Jimmy Choo."

I had wanted to make these boutiques such a nonintimidating environment that a woman would feel so comfortable coming in that she'd simply want to stay. I thought these spaces should be very feminine, like a 1940s boudoir designed by Jean-Michel Frank or Jean Royère. In 2002 that meant using David Collins, a luxury interior designer and architect who could masterfully create this look. But once again Robert had his own ideas. David came in for a meeting, but Robert argued that he wouldn't be able to manage the rollout and insisted that we use a company called Vudafieri, who had designed for Pucci.

I met with Vudafieri and laid out my vision, and then we went back and forth looking at sketches. Usually you'll get a warehouse somewhere and you'll do a mock-up, but we were so rushed for time that my first glimpse was actually at the store, and only a few hours before opening. I was mortified. It was so tacky—more like a bordello than a boudoir, and a Barbie bordello at that. The sofas were badly designed, there were little mirrored stools with lilac crystal balls, and the chandeliers had horrible multi-crystal beads. And there was no hiding this monstrosity because you went up the escalator and—bam!—there it was. The humiliation was all the more because it was personal. I was the one in charge of the brand's image, so naturally everyone was going to assume I'd done this. But this was another instance of Robert's need to exercise control and power, even when he lacked the appropriate experience and sensibility. For him, it was all about winning the point—my person, not yours—rather than acting in the best interest of the company. It was a huge mistake that I didn't push harder for what I knew to be right. But every time I'd complain about something, I'd be told, "You're not a team player." I came to realize that this is what a man says to a woman in business any time she isn't willing to do what he wants.

We didn't have the time or the money to hire another designer, so we were stuck with Vudafieri's fiasco, not only for Harvey Nichols, but for all of our other boutiques. The best we could do was to tone it down, and at least by the time we moved into our new location in Manhattan I could stand to look at it without wanting to retch.

Between 2001 and 2002 our business at Saks had exploded from $200,000 to $2 million. We had to raise our prices to hedge against the decline of the dollar, but the growth was real. We had amazing product, and our sell-through rate was so good that Saks increased the number of stores they put us in to thirty-nine. They were committing to us the way Neiman Marcus had invested in Manolo.

The in-store boutiques and the department stores were great for volume, but in terms of profit, our own stores would always deliver more. This was the financial reality that had prompted the talk of expansion that led to Jimmy's departure and to our being saddled with Phoenix and Robert in the first place. As far as I was concerned, there was no turning back now.

The greatest opportunity for expansion was the seemingly limitless commercial real estate lined up along the seemingly endless corridors of America's shopping malls. The first of these that we penetrated was South Coast Plaza in Orange County, California. It was perfectly located at the confluence of major freeways and a short drive from the wealth of Newport Beach. I was on hand when we opened next door to Armani in 2002. I then went on to Florida to open a store in Coral Gables, south of Miami, and both of these locations did brilliantly.

I did not, however, attend our opening at the Mall at Millenia in Orlando. This store was entirely Robert's idea, and I knew it wasn't going to work. Even Matthew said to me, "Nobody in Orlando is going to buy your shoes," and his instincts were right. The store was a dud.

The rivalry between Robert and me became even more toxic as it extended beyond issues of expenditures or real estate and began to eat away at the creativity of our brand.

I'd been collaborating on a series of ads with Raymond Meier, one of the great accessories photographers. He works mostly for American

Vogue, and there's not a big location fee because he usually shoots at his studio in New York. But I began to experience a surprising headwind of resistance from within the company, which I would later discover to be deliberately inspired by Robert.

The immediate upshot was that I turned to my second choice, Helmut Newton, to do a shoot along a seedy dockside in Monaco. It showed a serene-looking woman in black stockings and stilettos leaning against a chain-link fence. Of course you could see up her skirt.

The trouble was that, while Helmut had done brilliant work in the seventies, and what he produced for us was technically brilliant, we still needed an art director. I was forced into that role, but this was not long after I'd given birth to Minty. I still had all this belly fat, and I felt ugly and stupid and exhausted, and it was hard to influence him. This was the fashion business after all. Given the way I looked, what could I know? So what we came out with was static and flat, when what we needed was a compelling narrative to tell our story.

Most fundamentally, our problem was that for anything creative we were caught in the squeeze of needing A-list box office on a B-list movie budget, and the pressure fell on me to create wonders on a shoestring. Fortunately, when you're forced to work outside the box, sometimes you stumble upon something that's absolutely brilliant.

Brett Ratner was an old friend, and one day I was at his house in California looking at an album of his photographs. He'd directed the film *Rush Hour*, among others, and I thought his still work was fantastic. I said, "Why don't you do a campaign for us?"

Brett had "narrative" coming out his ears, and he came up with a concept and storyboards for a series of ads that looked like stills from a Quentin Tarantino movie. The first one had Nicole Richie and Shawn Hatosy in a glamorous night scene, fighting their way through paparazzi, and of course her Jimmy Choo bag was front and center. Then we put Heather Marks out on a landing strip at night, holding a flare to signal the plane. Smuggling? Espionage? Who knows? In another, a gorgeous model and Quincy Jones are driving across the desert to dispose of a body. In one shot they've dug a hole and are leaning on the shovel, another model's feet (in Jimmy Choos, of course) sticking up from the open trunk of the car. In another, Quincy sits in the backseat of the old Lincoln, glowering, while the beautiful blonde in her Jimmy Choos and a killer dress changes the tire. Another takes the cinematic reference all the way back to *Sunset Boulevard*, with the gorgeous model in the gold lamé swimsuit standing outside a modernist house in the Hollywood Hills. In the swimming pool beside her floats the body of a man in a *Reservoir Dogs* black suit and skinny tie.

The campaign only lasted three seasons because it became more and more difficult as we went along, and then it began to deteriorate. We'd started out with something that was too expensive and we didn't have a proper art director. We wanted it to run in all the high-end glossies, which was incredibly expensive, so, given our skeletal budget, we had to run it very cleverly—one month in *Vogue*, the next month in *Harper's Bazaar*, and so on. I had so much on my plate that eventually I just threw up my hands in despair and let Sandra give it a try. But that didn't work out any better.

Our next strategy for dramatic growth was in handbags. The Fendi Baguette had become a "must have" in the late nineties. Prada introduced their Bowling Bag, and then came the Chloé Paddington and the Yves Saint Laurent Mombasa. We'd sold about six hundred Jimmy Choo bags in 2001, mostly evening bags that went with the shoes, but now we wanted to move more aggressively. Being known as an "accessories brand" was far superior to being known as just a shoe company, and bags were the natural next step.

We needed a strong design link to the shoe, but we didn't want to limit ourselves to evening bags, so we brought in the Spanish designer Alvaro Gonzales. He had a studio in Florence, and his usual role was as a consultant, but we hired him to do the actual design. Later, we put him on staff in charge of bags.

We held design meetings to look at the prototypes as they began to arrive from Italy. The idea was that you'd have your main bag—the signature piece—and then you'd do variations—smaller, larger, with different options. The favorite was the Tulita. The leather was soft and sensual, but it carried external pockets and buckles that gave it an edge.

In March 2003, I hosted a lunch at the Plaza Athénée in New York for a small circle of well-connected women, including Cornelia Guest and Lillian von Stauffenberg. Caroline Berthet had replaced Harrison and Shriftman in handling our events and publicity, and after dessert we gave each of these women "the bag." It wouldn't be available in stores for another five months, but I wanted it to be seen and coveted, which it was. We developed long waiting lists for it in a range of styles, from a small evening bag to a large tote. In the seasons that followed, we always gifted the fashion editors just before each major show, hoping to ignite the same kind of buzz.

That summer, our next big innovation was "The Flash," an item dropped into the collection at midseason to draw customers into the store and to keep the press buzzing. The first of these was a $330 foam, high-heel wedge with a "flip-flop" top, made of terry cloth. It was the perfect shoe for getting a pedicure, and it sold like mad.

In 2003, we also opened four new stores in the United States: Dallas in March; Manhasset, Long Island, in May; Short Hills, New Jersey, in September; and 716 Madison Avenue in Manhattan in August. These were in the range of 1,000 to 1,500 square feet, and rents were cheaper than they'd been before 9/11 turned the economy on its head. We opened in Moscow the same year.

· · · ·

MATTHEW WAS TRYING HARD AND doing better, and Jennifer Moores, daughter of the San Diego Padres owner, invested $2.2 million in Harry's of London, so things were looking up. Still, he bristled at being referred to as "the husband of . . ." Mostly, his biochemical demons were still very much an issue.

That summer he and I got the notion that we should go to Deepak Chopra's institute in San Diego so that Matthew could get some help, as he put it, "with the critters in my head" We flew all the way there, only to discover that the institute was closed. (The assistant who'd booked the flights hadn't checked.) We pleaded and cajoled, and eventually we got Deepak to come and spend a few hours with us, but to no great effect.

This was the same summer that Matthew and I went to Ibiza, where we rented the house of French fashion designer Jacqueline de Ribes. Ibiza has its lovely, quiet side where you can swim in your own little cove. Then again, it's also known for its huge party scene at places like Pacha and Amnesia, so it was a bit of a risk.

Our neighbors were Elle Macpherson, and Simon and Yasmin Le Bon, as well as a large contingent of friends from Narc Anonymous, who I hoped would help keep Matthew on the straight and narrow. Max and Jane Gottschalk joined us on the island, as did Arabella Bodie, former girlfriend of Prince Andrew, now married to Glenn Spiro, the jewelry designer. We threw a big dinner for Valentino and other guests that included Jade Jagger, as well as a fair-haired boy named Oscar Humphries, the son of Barry Humphries, the comedian who plays the role of Dame Edna. Unfortunately somebody wanted to go out clubbing, and inevitably Matthew volunteered to take him.

I should have known better. I should have tied him to a chair. The best I could do was to ask Glenn to "keep an eye" on him. Matthew insisted on trying out a club called Space, and all seemed to go swimmingly. Everyone had a nice time, Matthew drove them home, and then it was off to bed. But not for my husband. No one realized it at the time, but he turned around, went back to the club, and launched into his preferred state of suborbital mania.

When I woke up the next morning he still wasn't home. In fact, he didn't come home for another three days. When at last he came staggering up the drive with a bottle of vodka in his hands, that was it for me. I had my own daughter and two of our friends' children present and this was simply not acceptable.

I let him sleep it off, but then the next day I told him, "You simply have to leave."

He grabbed a wad of cash from a drawer and disappeared, and I was incredibly sad for all of us, especially Minty. But I had to follow through for her sake.

I called my dad and said, "Go to my place and get all my things. Just rent something for me and Minty so I can move when I get back."

"What should I take?" he asked.

"Half," I said.

Matthew was due in New York for a Harry's event, and Max Gottschalk, who was an investor in the company, got him there and through all his commitments. Matthew is remarkable in that he always manages to "get through it." He has a bravado that's hard to challenge, and a winning smile, and a great sense of humor that seems to compensate for his many sins.

After New York he chartered a plane and flew to Corfu, where he took up with the daughter of a Russian plutocrat. When he came back to London, I got him into a clinic.

To this day I've never had any ill feeling toward Matthew. He was never out to deliberately inflict pain the way my mother had. He was just unwell, with a disease that was poisonous for me to be around. Even today, I still feel terrible about what happened between us. In truth, he missed his calling, which was to be a chat show host, most of whom suffer from depression, or mania, or both. He is funny as hell and very bright, but at the time of our marriage he was also a raging addict, and that was just too frightening to be around, for me and for my daughter.

. . . .

WHEN I RETURNED TO LONDON I moved into a shabby little terrace house on Draycott Avenue. With the Phoenix deal, my salary had risen to £60,000, which was still far below the norm for the kind of responsibility I had, and woefully inadequate to support the kind of lifestyle I had to maintain as the public face of the company. I had to have a nanny so I could work, so money was tight. It reached the point that I had to ask my father for help with my rent.

Our year had been very profitable, though, so I went to lunch with David Burns and said, "Look, I need to increase my salary."

"A dollar now will cost you fourteen dollars on exit," he said, invoking the formula (EBITDA multiplied by 14), which private equity uses to calculate a company's value.

"That's all well and good," I said, "but I still need money to live on."

So the company agreed to loan me money to be paid back against my shares on exit. Essentially, I was borrowing money from myself so that I could afford to go to work.

That autumn, to ease my frustrations, and to cleanse my palette, I suppose, I began a rather ill-considered affair with Oscar Humphries, the fair-haired boy who had been with us in Spain. In my mind, once I'd said to Matthew, "It's over!" it was over. I had been through hell, and I considered myself single, and I was determined to bounce back and have some fun, and on my own terms, thank you very much.

Oscar was new and smart and only twenty-two, a boy toy. And even though I was still officially married, I didn't care who saw us together. Truth be told, being seen was all part of the point. I felt I was pioneering new realms of equality for women, a bit like Demi Moore with Ashton Kutcher. I was a self-made woman, and on my own now, so why shouldn't I be able to do what I wanted?

Oscar was very bright, and he was passionate about art, and the difference in our ages wasn't all *that* great. As I was leaving on a business trip, he asked if I'd mind if he wrote an article about what it was like to have a relationship with an older woman. I must have been very distracted because I said, "Fine." But it's also true that in my distanced way, a self-protective residue from childhood, I often agreed to things merely to escape an awkward confrontation. I know I complied many times in business meetings under that duress, as well as in my personal life.

When I returned from my trip his piece was in the *Daily Telegraph* and London was buzzing. The article named no names, but that slender fig leaf only stirred up more of a guessing game. I think the whole business just showed how naive we both were about the prospect of anonymity because of course it came out that his "older woman" was me. Matthew was upset, but I didn't really care, even when the *Mail* referred to me as "Mrs. Robinson." After all, Anne Bancroft, who played the part in *The Graduate*, was barely thirty-six when the film came out, six years older than Dustin Hoffman, who played the "boy" she was seducing. (When Oscar and I were together, I was thirty-five.)

Oscar went to Milan with me, but by November our relationship had run its course, and my boy toy went home to Australia. Still, the gossip about the affair and about my fractured marriage all but overshadowed the opening of our boutique on Bond Street. To mark the occasion, we threw a party for the women working in the City, England's version of Wall Street. This was a more subdued group than the ladies who lunched in Knightsbridge, but they had money, and they spent it on clothing, and they were very much part of the audience I wanted to reach.

Meanwhile, Matthew needed help, so Uncle Jay flew over to take him to rehab at Promises, the refuge for addicted actors and rock stars in Malibu. Matthew insisted on chartering a plane, Jay prevailed on him to fly commercial, but then Matthew got the last laugh by ditching his uncle when they arrived at LAX.

Somehow my husband surfaced at L'Ermitage, and Nat Rothschild found him and suggested that he go to the Meadows in Arizona. Nat even fronted the money. So the inimitable Mr. Mellon took a limo, doing coke all through the six-hour drive across the desert, and when he arrived he was in such bad shape that they put him on a suicide watch.

When I visited him there for Family Week, he asked for one more chance. In fact, he offered me $2 million if I'd try again, but I couldn't take the offer seriously. I still cared deeply about him, and I wished him well. In December, I even went with him to a party for Harry's of London, but I made it very clear: As a couple we were done.

In a typically farcical footnote to the relationship, shortly after our breakup I started getting calls at the office from someone saying that Matthew owed him money. Not only that, the caller said, but Matthew owed some nasty gangsters money and they were going to murder him unless I paid all the debts.

It so happened that a friend of mine was in my office at the time, a friend who, on his mother's side, has family connections in the world of people who make other people disappear. He took the phone, and he had a very pointed conversation with the would-be debt collector/extortionist on the line.

An hour later the man called back. "I've paid off the debts myself," he said. "You'll never hear from me again."

7

I f only I could have achieved that kind of closure with Robert Bensoussan.

Our CEO tormented me relentlessly, and yet I could never find the extenuating circumstances that might make me feel more charitable and forgiving about his boorish behavior.

I became a particular target not only because I was a rival as a figure of authority but because of my role as the public face of Jimmy Choo. In most private-equity ventures the CEO is the star, but in fashion it's the creative head that people want to see and hear. Still, Robert should have made his peace with this by now. He'd been in the business a long time.

Especially in the early days, I was unique in being able to speak about everything, from the design of the collection to the nitty-gritty of operations, so of course I did the press interviews. And it was not as if I were trying to hog the limelight. I would have been happy to share the responsibility of living in the media's glare. In fact, I tried to, but in Sandra's first exposure to the press she was quoted as saying that no one could possibly wear our shoes for more than four hours. Another time, when she was asked why we were at the Oscars, her carefully crafted answer was, "I have no idea."

As the brand grew and the press attention became global, I found myself doing one or two interviews a week, and any time I was to be photographed, it was on me as the representative of a fashion brand to engage fashion industry professionals to assist with hair and makeup.

After a while I was being asked the same questions so many times in so many different languages that I dreamed of being able to give them a recording that addressed the top dozen or so issues that journalists always wanted to ask me about. I tried to find more creative ways to describe what we were doing, if only so that in every interview I wouldn't have to listen to myself repeat the same tired lines.

Robert just never seemed to accept the fashion industry's requirement that the person in charge of creating the brand serves as the face of the brand. My father had warned me that by being out front I would become a target.

After a while he decided to bring all Jimmy Choo PR in-house and to hire Tara ffrench-Mullen, who'd worked at Gianfranco Ferré. Not long after, Robert called Caroline Berthet, in charge of marketing in New York, and asked her to take me out of a promotional video.

Not long after, the singer Pharrell Williams approached me about doing a collaboration. Pharrell loves fashion, and we agreed that he'd design a shoe, we'd put it in our collection, and we'd split the profits fifty-fifty. Robert went ballistic. Lawyers got involved. Obviously the idea couldn't go forward with Jimmy Choo, but Pharrell went on to design sunglasses for Louis Vuitton, and to be featured in American *Vogue*.

That was when the penny truly dropped for me regarding the character of this man who now had executive authority over the business my father and I had built. It was also the moment when the full burden of regret descended on me for agreeing to go down this path. In retrospect, the evidence for Robert's character had been there all along.

Months earlier, when we were opening the store in Beverly Hills on North Canon, my father and I did an interview—a sort of father-and-daughter relationship piece. Robert didn't like something my father said, and so he rang him up and screamed at him. That was the first time my father said to me, "This man is no good."

Hope springs eternal, and three or four years is the normal term for a private-equity firm to hold a company they've invested in. So by the time I had Robert's number, we were expecting Phoenix to exit and I thought we could simply wait him out.

Truth be told, my father was ready to cash out himself. He was only seventy-four, but his mind was as keen as ever and he kept very fit, going for an hour walk in the park every day. But he'd begun to talk more and more about liquidating his shares, buying a house in Beverly Hills, and settling in for a nice retirement in the sunshine surrounded by lemon trees.

So with impetus from both sides of the Jimmy Choo ownership equation, "Exit Strategy" became an item for discussion at our monthly board meetings.

For an entrepreneur, this kind of transaction is the moment of truth. You've worked like a dog to build something from the ground up, often laboring for years without much compensation because, rather than pay yourself the going rate, you're pouring every cent back into the business. And no matter how successful the venture, extracting the value of the equity you've built up is dependent on multiple factors, most of which are beyond your control: the general state of the economy, the health of your particular industry, the short-term profitability of potential buyers.

In the fashion world, extracting value is trickier still because there has never been a natural fit between fashion and the world of the Dow and the UK *Financial Times* and Stock Exchange. A successful brand has to juggle art and commerce every day, and Wall Street and the City are interested only in the latter.

In the nineteenth century, when most of the grand old fashion houses were founded—Hermès, Bulgari, Burberry, Louis Vuitton—they were owned by an individual or by a family. The same was true for Chanel, Prada, Gucci, and Fendi in the early twentieth century, Dior just after the war, and Valentino, Yves Saint Laurent, Armani, and Versace more recently. Serious investors paid attention to businesses with smokestacks, and they viewed fashion as something of interest to their wives, a marginal realm of artisans holding pins between their lips, plying their trade in tiny ateliers.

But about the time I was having my first cigarette at Heathfield, the engine of the economy was shifting from heavy industry to high technology. Ideas, protected by copyrights and trademarks, were being valued more highly as assets than big brick buildings and clunky machines. The potential for growth seemed inversely proportional to tangibility.

Eventually, the big financial players took note that luxury goods were embedded with "intellectual property" in the same sense that software and biotechnology were, and thus had some of the same advantages. A luxury brand offered the owner the opportunity to profit from ideas and image, with almost limitless prospects for scaling up through licensing, and through the halo effect of brand image that could travel all around the world, even migrating to other products.

One of the first to see the opportunities here was Bernard Arnault, and it made him the richest man in France. His family had already made one fortune in construction, developing vacation homes on both sides of the Atlantic. Then, in 1984, he gained control of Société foncière et financière du groupe Agache-Willot, which owned the Boussac textile group, which in turn owned Christian Dior.

In 1987, Arnault hired Christian Lacroix away from Patou, a couture house, to establish their first brand from scratch. He then acquired Céline, the leather goods company, and bought a controlling interest in LVMH.

Meanwhile, a Bahrain-based private-equity firm called Investcorp bought Tiffany & Co. and took it public. They invested in Saks Fifth Avenue, the watchmakers Ebel and Breguet, and the exclusive jeweler Chaumet. In 1993, they bought Gucci and revitalized it by hiring Dawn Mello as creative director. She, in turn, hired Richard Lambertson, as well as a young fellow named Tom Ford.

By the mid-nineties, Hermès, Tiffany, and LVMH were already publicly traded companies. Then Bulgari did an initial public offering to finance global expansion, and the stock more than doubled within the first year. Morgan Stanley, who had done the public offering for Bulgari, began to encourage Investcorp to put Gucci on the same track. In October 1995, Gucci appeared on the exchanges in New York and Amsterdam, as well as in Milan. The stock doubled in value in only six months.

Suddenly, there was a strong "luxury goods sector" in the world of global finance, with additional IPOs by Donna Karan, Ralph Lauren, and Burberry. Coverage of the fashion world expanded beyond *Women's Wear Daily* to the *Wall Street Journal* and the *Financial Times*.

But as the suits failed to acknowledge to the detriment of all concerned, fashion is not a "rational" business that can be brought to heel by an MBA wielding a spreadsheet. You don't necessarily spur success by tightening the supply chain or by cheapening the quality of the materials. Winners and losers are subject to the ineffable forces of creativity, inspiration, and very fickle trends. You can have a $12 billion business, but each decision to purchase each individual item of inventory still depends on the customer's fantasies, her self-image, and her own awareness of what makes her feel more attractive. Making such an intimate connection with the customer relies on a different set of skills entirely.

Our growth had been stellar, and all indications were that we would continue on that trajectory. We had manufactured 7,300 pairs of shoes in 1997. In 2001 that figure increased to 15,000. In 2004, our number had shot up exponentially to 180,000, which exceeded the volume of Manolo Blahnik. We also expected to sell 23,000 bags in 2004, up from about 1,000 three years earlier. Revenues had nearly doubled from £12 million in 2001 to £22 million in 2003, with £34 million projected for 2004. Profits were on the same track: £3 million in 2001, £4 million in 2003, and £7.5 million projected for the year ahead. In terms of retail outlets, the potential for growth was similarly exponential. Gucci had nearly two hundred stores. We had barely twenty.

Even so, we were probably too small to capture the interest of the big institutional investors. And the mergers and acquisitions craze of the 1990s had already passed us by. In fact, it had recently reversed, with "de-merging" on the rise. So this was the context in which we began to have talks with bankers.

Goldman Sachs sent over an all-female team—each of the women wearing Jimmy Choos—and they proposed a very public auction. But their valuation came out low—at £60 million.

Rothschild agreed with us that it should be at least £100 million, and they said they could achieve that mark, so we went with them. Their point man, Akeel Sachak, an Indian born in Tanzania and educated at Oxford, pushed for a stealth approach, which he dubbed Project Jewel, a code name to keep the transaction under the radar.

A valuation of £100 million was still comparatively small for Rothschild, but at the same time our public profile was huge. It didn't hurt that *Legally Blonde* was in the theaters, with multiple plugs for Jimmy Choo, or that Reese Witherspoon, the star, insisted on keeping all the Jimmy Choos she'd worn on-screen. In their prospectus for potential investors, the bankers could include clips not only from that movie but also from *Sex and the City*, as well as song lyrics by Beyoncé, P. Diddy, and Pharrell Williams. Jimmy Choo, though always tasteful, was the embodiment of "bling."

The Swiss firm Richemont was on an acquiring spree, but their profile was hard luxury (Montblanc, Cartier, Van Cleef and Arpels, Piaget, Alfred Dunhill) rather than luxury fashion per se. On the other hand, they had owned Chloé since 1985.

Gucci Group would have been a natural partner, but they'd been thrown for a loop by their purchase by Pinault-Printemps-Redoute, and now Tom Ford and Domenico De Sole were leaving. Moreover, they had just run up a long string of acquisitions—not just Alexander McQueen and Stella McCartney, but also Yves Saint Laurent, and a direct competitor in the market for luxury women's shoes, Sergio Rossi. So Gucci passed.

LVMH seemed a logical player because they did not have a luxury brand of women's shoes. Berluti was part of their portfolio, but they made footwear only for men. Still, LVMH was under pressure to develop the strength of their existing brands, rather than to grow by acquiring new ones.

For months we went through pitch meetings and intense discussions with strategic buyers, and with millions of dollars riding on the outcome, it was all incredibly stressful and disruptive for everyone in the organization. Anytime there's a merger or an acquisition, everyone wonders how it will affect him or her personally, that is, will they still have a job? At times the stress is palpable. Tempers flare.

. . . .

MEANWHILE, MY OWN PERSONAL LIFE was not exactly an island of serenity, with de-merging on the agenda there as well.

I'd been living apart from Matthew, still not ready to face the added stress of a divorce, but my father told me that staying in marital limbo was madness, and after a while I was ready to make the break official. He called around on my behalf, and on his recommendation I engaged Sandra Davis, the divorce attorney who had worked for Princess Diana and Jerry Hall.

Even thusly armed, however, I was still far more interested in mediation than confrontation. I told Matthew, "I don't want anything from you. I'll look after Minty, and you can set something aside for her when she turns twenty-one."

I was offering to take full responsibility for her life, health, and happiness, and I asked for nothing in return. In my naïveté I imagined that Matthew would say, "That's great. Thanks," and we'd split amicably.

Instead, my husband responded by suing me for £10 million, claiming that his name and money had been instrumental in building Jimmy Choo.

For his lawyer, Matthew hired Raymond Tooth, also known as "Jaws," the man who had represented Sadie Frost against Jude Law, and Pattie Boyd against Eric Clapton. Before Irina Abramovich settled out of court for a pedestrian £155 million, Jaws had been on his way to the largest divorce settlement in history, with Roman Abramovich's £18 billion fortune in the crosshairs.

Suing me was bad enough, but their line of argument was especially galling, primarily because I'd changed my name to Mellon only at Matthew's insistence. I had been Tamara Yeardye at work, and that's what I continued calling myself until Matthew actually got very, very upset, saying, "We're married! You should be using my name."

On April 19, 2004, I was at my London home in South Kensington when I got a call from my girlfriend Elika Gibbs at about two in the morning. My father was ill, and my mother had called Elika because her boyfriend was a doctor. Elika had listened briefly and told my mother to call an ambulance. Then Elika called me.

I went over immediately, arriving just as the emergency medics got to my parents' house. My father was being carried out on a stretcher and my mother was in a state. She was so agitated that she couldn't go in the ambulance, so I climbed in and I rode with my dad to the Chelsea and Westminster Hospital on Fulham Road.

When we arrived at the ER, they looked him over and their assessment was devastating. They said he'd suffered an aneurysm and that the hemorrhage on the brain was so big that they couldn't do anything about it. They said flatly that he wouldn't last very long and that I should simply sit with him and talk with him. They said he probably wouldn't be able to respond but that he'd be able to hear me all the same.

I was in shock, of course. I couldn't believe this was happening, and I was utterly torn apart. He was my dad, and I loved him, but he was also my mentor and my business partner. He was the one solid rock I'd ever known in my life, and now he was leaving me behind. I held him and tried to say good-bye, and he was so strong that it took him eighteen hours to die. I don't think I stopped crying once the whole time. All the while my mother was sitting in a chair in the corner of the room, not crying, not touching him, not responding in any way. I have no idea what she was or was not feeling.

Hannah Colman, who had started working for us on the shop floor on Motcomb Street when she was only seventeen and was now head of all European sales, came around to help us call people and make the arrangements. Robert, overflowing with humanity, rang up and said, "What are you doing over there?"

She said, "They need my help."

He said, "We need you in the office. You need to get back here."

She wasn't even scheduled to be working—she was supposed to be on holiday.

We held the funeral in a church in Knightsbridge, on a bright, sunny day. I was the only one who spoke. My mother was too stunned, and my brothers deferred to me. After the service, we went back to my mother's apartment in Eaton Place for a tea with a small group of friends.

This was the end of an era. My father had been such a force in my life—my primary emotional attachment, as well as my partner and guide in business. His passing left a power vacuum like the death of an ancient king. From now on I was going to have to fend for myself, without his protection or advice, and it remained to be seen if I was up for the challenge.

. . . .

MY PARENTS HAD BEEN PLANNING to move back to California, so after Dad's death my mother flew out to L.A., checked into the Peninsula, and began looking for a house in Beverly Hills. My brothers went with her, and my work took me out there often enough, so I would check in on her from time to time.

Minty and the nanny traveled with me, and while in L.A. we stayed at the Peninsula as well, and I tried very hard to set aside my anger toward my mother and help her get through this difficult transition. Matthew was gone, and I wanted Minty to have a grandmother, and I thought that maybe in the midst of our grief or some such we could all bond as a family. I was a grown-up now, and no matter how much she'd hurt me as a child, I knew that I should at least try to forgive her, if only for Minty's sake. For a couple of weeks I even left Minty and her nanny at the Peninsula with my mother.

Meanwhile, I was the one working, continuing to build the engine of wealth that my mother and brothers were living on.

The business that kept me coming to L.A. that season was something I'd set in motion months before with the Elton John AIDS Foundation, a project aimed at raising money to build rape shelters across South Africa.

I'd met Elton and his husband, David Furnish, at the event they do in Windsor every year to raise money for the foundation. Theirs is one of the most highly regarded charities because it's very efficiently run, with the money going to help, not to pay inflated administrative costs. I went up to David and I told him about this horrific article I'd read in the *Times* about a three-year-old girl who had been raped in Africa. This kind of thing happens all the time because the men there believe they can rid themselves of AIDS by sleeping with virgins.

I said, "If I raise money, can we put it through your charity? Can we set it apart for rape shelters?"

He said, "Absolutely."

I didn't want to do a predictable fund-raiser, just another black-tie dinner. So I rang up Pilar Boxford, the head of all regional brands at Cartier, and I proposed that they go in with us on a book of photographs of women, by women, for women. But we had to make it fun, and we had to offer a chance to be creative, because the people you want associated with your project get a lot of requests from charities.

Then it occurred to us: With jewelry and shoes sponsoring, why have anything else in the pictures? Why give press to brands that weren't contributing? So let's have everyone pose in the nude.

Each celebrity model would be wearing nothing but her Cartier jewelry and her Jimmy Choos. The creative part was that she could be as covered or as uncovered as she cared to be. She could stand behind a door with her foot and her hand sticking out with a ring on it, or she could be in bed with a sheet covering everything but her hand and her foot, or she could be stark naked—it was entirely up to her.

The whole affair turned out to be an enormous administrative chore, so eventually I asked Arabella Bodie to manage the project, riding herd on our celebrities, arranging schedules for photographers like Mary McCartney, Pamela Hanson, Sam Taylor-Wood, and Ellen von Unwerth, and organizing hair and makeup.

. . . .

MEANWHILE, I WAS FLYING BACK and forth between L.A. and London, continuing to attend secretive pitch meetings for Project Jewel as Akeel tried to drum up interest from among his select group of potential buyers. We would do presentations at Rothschild's conference room with lots of bullet points and pie charts, and with Robert, the CFO, and me all trying to create the illusion of one big happy family—just like during my childhood. Robert would speak to the financial issues, and I would speak to the creative, which didn't interest them all that much, though they did like hearing about the celebrities.

My father's death had added new impetus to the idea of a sale because his equity needed to be sorted out for the benefit of my mother. So all during this period I sent her faxes to keep her abreast of the situation and to explain her options. If she were allowed to leave money in, it would very likely increase in value. On the other hand, continued investment most likely would not be an option because new owners usually want nonactive partners to cash out, just to simplify decision making. This seemed to be a nonissue as far as my mother was concerned because she made it quite clear that she wanted to receive her ownership stake entirely in cash that could be reinvested to generate monthly income.

On October 31, 2004, the *Mail on Sunday* blew the cover on Project Jewel by announcing we were for sale. They got it wrong, of course, saying that Burberry was the leading contender, which was all a bit awkward, given that Akeel had just introduced us to Lyndon Lea, a thirty-four-year-old financial whiz known as the "boy banker." The head of European operations for Hicks, Muse, Tate & Furst, a private-equity firm based in Texas, he was in the process of leaving to set up his own firm, to be called Lion Capital.

Lyndon was very charming and obviously a driven, self-made man. His mother had been a hairdresser, and now he was a devoted polo player with a private jet. When we had our first conference with him at Rothschild, I liked what he had to say because he seemed to have a strategic vision for the brand. He seemed to be interested in more than the typical private-equity game plan of leveraging, pumping up the EBITDA for three years, and then getting out. Then again, I was still new to this game.

We continued our discussion over dinner at Harry's Bar, and during the cocktail chatter I actually heard Robert say that when he came into the business "it was like being given the keys to a Ferrari." This was the one time he ever acknowledged—at least in my hearing—the value of what my father and I had created.

Ultimately we had three offers. Lambert Howarth, a huge shoe company that supplied Marks and Spencer, wanted to do a reverse takeover, meaning that they would buy a controlling interest, rename the entire entity Jimmy Choo, then take it public. Soros Private Equity Partners also made a proposal, but one that left them with wiggle room for an extended period of due diligence. Given his head start, Lyndon was able to make us an offer within a week, with no contingencies.

It was in November 2004 when the owners of Jimmy Choo sat down in the conference room at Ixworth Place to decide which offer to take. Representing Phoenix were David Burns and Robert. On the family's side were myself; my mother; Nick Morgan, who managed the trusts in Jersey; the accountant for the trusts, Raj Patel; and Timothy Gere, who managed the trusts' investments.

Lambert Howarth's valuation was £125 million, but part of their offer was in stock rather than cash. Lyndon's offer for Lion Capital was based on a value of £101 million, all cash. We decided to go with Lion, which was a very good thing because Lambert Howarth soon went into bankruptcy.

As anticipated, Lion didn't want any extraneous shareholders hanging around to complicate decision making, but again, my mother was happy to cash out, taking her relatively illiquid private-equity shares and reinvesting elsewhere.

I was doubly delighted. Not only would this deal rid me of Robert, it would rid me of my mother. For all my efforts to please her, take care

My father, Tom Yeardye, at his desk at the Vidal Sassoon offices in the early eighties. We relocated to California for my father to run the business from the United States.

y mother, father, and I posed in the garden behind our Tudor cottage in Wingfield, Berkshire, where I grew up.

My father and me as a young child.

A friend and me at summer camp on Catalina Island in the seventies.

Here I am sneaking out of the basement boiler room of the chalet at the Institut Alpin Videmanette, in Rougemont, Switzerland, in 1984. Madame Yersin, the headmistress, moved me to her chalet after too many late nights at the neighboring boys' school.

Photograph by Geoffrey Shakerley

This is the gorgeous library at Blenheim where our wedding dinner was held with catering by Admirable Crichton, flowers by Kenneth Turner, and a five-foot-tall cake made of profiteroles.

After six months of dating, Matthew and I became engaged. We were married at Blenheim Palace, the home of the dukes of Marlborough and the birthplace of Winston Churchill.

Photograph by Geoffrey Shakerley

My mother and father celebrating at my wedding.

Matthew posing for a picture at the wedding reception with our friends
Hugh Grant and Liz Hurley.

Matthew holding Minty on his shoulders during our trip to Lyford Cay, Bahamas, in 2004.

Matthew and me at a boar shoot on a friend's estate in Germany around 1999.

Minty and me in Ibiza in 2003. This was the summer that Matthew disappeared for three days after clubbing all night. It was the last straw in our marriage.

Minty, age two, posing with me for a picture in my house in London.

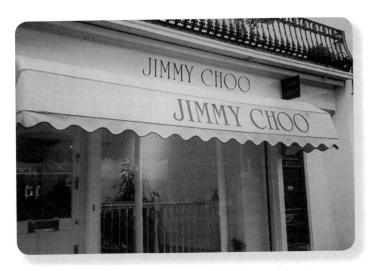

Our first-ever store on Motcomb Street, in London, a perfect location for attracting a mix of professional women and the ladies who lunch. It was a small space, but we gave it the right look.

The interior of our first London store.

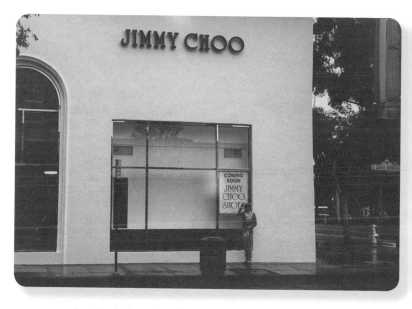

Standing in front of our first U.S. store in Beverly Hills in 1998.

Sandra Choi, Hannah Colman, and me out to lunch.

Working in the factory in Italy where we produced our first collection. I spent many long hours there perfecting every design.

The early years at Jimmy Choo with some of our first designs from the 2001 collection.

Robert Bensoussan and I attended a Jimmy Choo dinner in Miami during Art Basel to open our Miami store. I put on a brave face for the event, which took place in December 2006 during the hostile takeover.

Jimmy Choo, the Chinese cobbler who became my cofounder.

Josh Schulman, former CEO of Jimmy Choo and current president of Bergdorf Goodman, and I visited China in 2007, where we opened our first store in Beijing.

At Jimmy Choo's tenth anniversary party, Sandra and I held a cake decorated with the iconic feathery shoe worn by Carrie Bradshaw that made the Jimmy Choo brand a fixture on *Sex and the City*.

One of our more distinctive designs in which we collaborated with Richard Phillips to feature his Nuclear print on a clutch bag in 2007.

One of the last shoes I worked on before leaving Jimmy Choo in 2011.

The "Loop" shoe from our spring/summer 2009 collection.

Posing at a Jimmy Choo ad campaign shoot with Charlotte Pilcher (far right), my longtime friend and Vogue stylist and consultant at Jimmy Choo, and Angela Lindvall, an American supermodel and actress.

ending an afternoon on the boat with Giancarlo Giammetti and Valentino 2001—shortly before discovering I was pregnant with Minty.

Christian Slater and me at
Cannes Film Festival in 2C

Harvey Weinstein and his then girlfriend, now wife, Georgina Chapman of Marchesa.

Elle Macpherson and Liz Hurley joined me at an intimate OBE reception dinner that I threw for a few close friends.

In 2010, I received the Order of the British Empire honor for my services to the fashion industry. The beautiful ceremony was presided over by the Queen at Buckingham Palace.

Minty, Michael Ovitz, and I celebrated Christmas on Michael's yacht in 2012.

Minty, eleven years o
with her horse.

of her, and reconcile with her, I was coming to the conclusion that the best I could hope for was to remove myself from her in order to protect myself.

But just as my mother needed investments that were more liquid, I, too, needed to generate a monthly income to live on. So I cashed out roughly half of my half of the family's share. The rest I reinvested in Jimmy Choo, in return for which I received 64,000 shares of stock in this entity that I would partly own in partnership with Lyndon's Lion Capital.

At last my dream of financial independence was being realized. But no sooner had we given Lion the good news than it seemed as if the gods wanted to have a laugh at my expense.

Concerned about continuity in management, Lyndon announced that he wanted Robert to stay on. In fact, he insisted that both Robert and I be contractually locked in. He actually went so far as to demand assurances that my nemesis and I would be able to continue working together "harmoniously."

If my father had been alive, I'm sure we would have resisted. Robert was an employee, an obstructive, pain-in-the-ass employee who could be replaced. But I still hadn't found my voice. I was still complying with the unreasonable in order to evade and avoid.

I also felt trapped. I needed this deal to go through because it's only during these exit transactions that a partner in a private-equity deal can cash out, and I was counting on realizing the capital I needed to live on. If I resigned the deal would most likely collapse—I was actually part of what was being purchased, creativity as a form of chattel.

Beyond that fact, and while I had a huge emotional investment in the brand, Jimmy Choo was by far the best financial investment I could make. I would be leaving in a large stake, so to ensure the increase in the value of that investment, I had to stay on and be on top of my game, in order to keep the brand creative and fresh. Under those circumstances, continuing to work with Robert was a bitter pill I was simply going to have to swallow.

Before he died, my dad told me, "We'll probably sell this company for £100 million, and it will be right around November." On November 14, a memo went around listing a price of £101 million. I only wish my dad could have been there to relish the moment and to receive this one last confirmation of his business acumen. But tribute enough—after transaction fees and what little debt we had, the Yeardye family's share was a return on his initial investment of three hundredfold.

The legalities remained to be worked out, and after the announcement, Robert came to me and said, "I think we should use the same lawyers, Travers Smith. We can save on costs."

I had used Andrew Roberts in the past, and he had been at Travers, so this seemed to make sense.

I said, "Sure." Sharing lawyers was another rookie mistake.

What hadn't occurred to me was the extent to which I was swimming with sharks and that I needed personal representation. Once again, Robert was only one shark among many. The one who would give me the most grief was the one I'd had to deal with all my life. As I would soon learn, despite my fond hopes of distancing myself, my mother still had her teeth embedded in my flesh.

The allocation of shares between our two trusts would become a morass of confusion, at least in her mind, which would lead to a legal battle that would consume years of my life and millions of dollars, and bring me to the edge of despair.

8

The signing of the Lion deal was scheduled for November 18, 2004, and we had a conference call line open twenty-four hours a day to iron out last-minute complexities. Among these pesky details was the requirement that the agreement be approved and signed before magistrates on the island of Jersey, where the family trusts had been set up. Our operations centers were in the UK and the United States, but Jimmy Choo Jersey Limited, in Jersey, actually owned the brand and licensed it to Jimmy Choo Limited. JCL ran operations, and JCJ received royalties. There were no taxes on the income received by JCJ in Jersey so long as it was not repatriated to the UK.

Jersey, officially known as the Bailiwick of Jersey, is a strange little place that might have been dreamed up for a Monty Python routine, somewhere between *Spamalot* and the "Ministry of Silly Walks." Lying only twelve miles off the coast of France, it is a British Crown dependency. In Viking times it had been kicked back and forth between the dukes of Normandy and the dukes of Brittany, but it's been more or less English since William and all that in 1066. It's famous for its cows, but its real economy is devoted to financial services, making it rather like the Caymans, only with foul weather.

To accommodate the signing requirements, David Burns and Robert booked seats on the forty-five-minute flight to Saint Helier, Jersey's capital, and they were on their way to Gatwick when Akeel called to discuss how Lyndon was going to be financing the acquisition—which was by taking on massive debt.

Robert was livid that, by being acquired, we were putting the company £50 million in the hole. (I, on the other hand, wasn't even informed of this development.)

To calm the waters, Lyndon called Robert and asked him to come to their offices on Grosvenor Place, just opposite Buckingham Palace, where he explained how the debt was being structured in a way that would allow Robert to leverage his own equity stake. Our CEO was reassured, but by now they'd missed the last flight to Jersey.

Lyndon graciously offered his own NetJet, and when they landed, they went straight to the lawyer's office in Saint Helier, and the signing dragged on and on. At quarter past eight the pilot called to remind them that Jersey's airport closed at nine, but there was still plenty of fine print to read, and it wasn't until ten that the deal was done.

I'd spent the evening waiting by the phone at my lawyer's office, and after the call came through I took a deep breath and went over to my mother's house to "share the good news." I found her sitting by herself in her living room, her knees pulled up to her chest, rocking back and forth. I knelt down and said, "Mom, they've signed it. Everything's done. You're going to have plenty of money. You're going to be okay."

I think this may have been the one instance when I found it possible to set aside her lifelong cruelty to me and feel real compassion for her. At the same time, I still felt like a wounded child, not only angry but still hoping against hope for a crumb of recognition. I would have given the world for a single word of kindness from her, a simple, "Well done." But she simply kept rocking and staring off into space. It was frightening and very sad. And as usual, there was nothing for me.

Back in Jersey, the Jimmy Choo financial team was forced to stay over, neither having packed so much as a toothbrush. They flew out again at six in the morning, but no one thought to send a car to Luton Airport north of London, and these high-rolling gentlemen enjoyed the novelty of taking the commuter rail back into town.

When I received my copies of all the final documents, I reviewed all the details, including the distribution of "sweet equity," the small number of shares set aside as an added incentive for management. According to a preexisting agreement, Robert and I were to have parity on all remuneration. And yet I noticed right away that Robert had received 5 percent and that I had received only 3 percent sweet equity.

So at the first board meeting I spoke up. "This isn't right," I said. "Our agreement was to have parity on this."

Lyndon acknowledged my point, and he told Robert to put the extra 2 percent back into the pot so that it could be distributed on exit.

This was a directive from the chairman of the board, stipulated at a board meeting and entered into the minutes, so I went on about my business, feeling certain that the error would be corrected.

My lawyer, Andrew Roberts, called and said, "Do you want me to follow up?"

I said, "No. I trust Lyndon on this. Besides, it's in the minutes of a board meeting."

Another rookie mistake. I should never have been so naive.

Over the next two years, Lyndon came to perhaps two board

meetings, and when he did, none of his earlier talk of strategic vision could be found. As usual, EBITDA was all that mattered. Lyndon sent over his bean counter, Robert Darwent, to count all the beans, and as long as the numbers were looking good, that was that.

. . . .

THEN, AS IF MY PERSONAL soap opera weren't sudsy enough, it spilled over into farce when Matthew got arrested for hacking into my computers.

As we'd been working our way toward the sale of Jimmy Choo, he must have worried that I'd be siphoning off cash to numbered accounts in Switzerland or the Caymans. He had Jaws request financial details that we thought were intrusive, so we refused. Not long after, I began to receive e-mails claiming to have "things on your soon-to-be-ex-husband." I thought this sounded not only sleazy but creepy. I'd also noticed that Matthew seemed to think he had quite a bit of privileged information about our business, even though his information was incorrect.

The Metropolitan Police soon showed up and asked to examine my computer. They explained that the e-mails I'd been receiving were Trojan horse messages containing viruses. If opened, this "malware" could record every keystroke on my keyboard.

As it turned out, Matthew had hired a company called Active Investigation Services to explore any and all electronic transactions. This company was run by a couple of former policemen who were already under surveillance for running a lucrative sideline in illegal wiretapping and computer hacking. To keep Matthew on the hook, they'd even sent him a bogus e-mail, supposedly from my lawyer, alluding to several million I'd supposedly secreted away in Malaysia.

The climax of this series of events occurred when London's finest raided Matthew's apartment at six a.m. and took him away in hand-cuffs.

My husband was charged with criminal conspiracy and faced the possibility of five years in prison. Eventually, I would be subpoenaed to testify. For now, in addition to everything else, I had to deal not only with my daughter's father being indicted and out on bail but also with the paparazzi and detectives snooping around in the bushes outside my house.

. . . .

ON JANUARY 24, 2005, THE Yeardye family met at the Pelham Hotel in South Kensington for one of the meetings we had several times a year to go over the trusts. My mother was there with my brother Gregory, along with Timothy Gere, a financial adviser, and I could feel the tension immediately when I walked in the room. They were already deep into a tête-à-tête with Raj Patel, the accountant, and Nick Morgan, the trustee from CI Law on the island of Jersey. I wondered what the hell was going on.

When the meeting came to order, Nick began with a celebratory tone, noting the recent surge in the assets under his guardianship and acknowledging my role in helping to create that wealth and to bring it into the family fold. The two trusts collectively were being enriched by roughly £44 million, which, after transaction fees and other expenses, represented our 49 percent share of a company valued at £101 million.

There was discussion about the tax implications of my mother's move to the United States, and then it came time to review the allocation of the Lion proceeds to the two separate trusts. My mother had taken her half of the £44 million entirely in cash to set her up in retirement. Thus the Marqueta Trust, the one established for her benefit, had received a direct infusion of roughly £22 million in cash.

My situation was a bit more complicated. I had taken my half of the Yeardye holdings partly in cash, but then I'd rolled the rest back into the company. As I mentioned earlier, this large reinvestment of many millions had actually been a requirement of the deal with Lion.

Nick passed around the summary of the accounts, and I saw immediately that, in the Araminta Trust, half the cash was missing. You don't have to be a financial genius to note a discrepancy of several million pounds.

"What the hell is this?" I said. "You're only showing half the money I cashed out."

Nick mumbled for a moment, then explained that, with my divorce still in process, he thought it best to hide some of my money, so he'd decided on his own to transfer half my cash from my trust to my mother's. He freely admitted that the money was mine—he was just trying to "reduce my exposure."

So he'd assigned my money to a trust that benefits the one person who had always seemed to question my basic right to exist. He'd handed over my money to the one person I trusted least in the world.

I said, "Nick, you need to put this back." Then I repeated, with rising emphasis, just below a scream: "Put it back."

As I investigated further, I saw that the cash left in my trust, the cash that at least had been properly accounted, was not properly invested. People at the time were making a 10 percent return on equities, and I wasn't even getting the standard bank interest. Even at 5 percent, which was the going bank rate at the time, I was missing out on tens of thousands of pounds in interest every month.

Then, just to top it all off, my mother slid a piece of paper across the table. I was already so angry that I could hardly focus, so it took me a moment to realize that what I was looking at was a list of debits she had been running against me. While I'd been working myself silly trying to build the brand that had just delivered £22 million into her account (not to mention several million more that was not rightly hers), she'd been drawing up a list of my infractions, which included the rent money I'd borrowed from my dad, which, as I was quick to point out, I had already paid back.

And then it got genuinely creepy. She wanted reimbursement for clothing she'd bought for Minty while I was away on business. Thanks to me she'd just come into £22 million, and she wanted me to pay her back for a few hundred pounds I'd asked her to spend on her own granddaughter?

But then I saw the entry that really chilled me because I could already see where it might lead. Back when we were first expanding into North America, Dad had mortgaged their house for £600,000 and loaned the company the money. She now wanted me to pay back the amount in full, even though it was clearly documented—and verified by Nick Morgan the trustee and Raj Patel the accountant—that before my father died he had been fully reimbursed by the company. The most frustrating, and frightening, part of it all was her failure to understand even the most basic arithmetic as it pertained to the business and how it was structured.

It was the American company, half owned by Philip Rogers, that had received the loan. At most, I was half owner of the other half, which was owned by my father, thus obligating me for one-quarter of the loan, which, again, had already been paid back. But in my mother's eyes, anything that was not as she thought it should be was my responsibility. Thus somehow I needed to pay back the entire amount. It was her lifelong fixation: Anything that was wrong was Tamara's fault. It had been that way for as long as I could remember. But how can a person incur that kind of wrath and resentment as an infant or a toddler? What had I ever done to deserve this?

Marqueta was making certain distributions of money to banks outside the trust to provide monthly income for my mother. The trust was also buying her a new house in Beverly Hills and arranging for the insurance. But my mother persisted in her tone of injury, complaining about me and saying how sad it was that she was going to be all alone and having to take care of a big house all by herself, at which point I simply lost it.

"I bought you that fucking house!" I screamed.

You might say that after that, our relationship began to deteriorate.

Elsewhere on the domestic front, my divorce was still proceeding to trial. This separate legal matter required a financial hearing to determine all the assets of both parties. By this time, I was both emotionally and physically exhausted, barely able to stay conscious as I sat in the courtroom listening to the judge's recitation of the facts. Suddenly I was wide awake—given a jolt of adrenaline far stronger, and far less

TAMARA MELLON

pleasant, than any illegal high I'd ever taken on—as I heard the judge say ". . . primary asset is in the form of 32,000 shares in Jimmy Choo Limited, which is . . . blah blah blah."

I was apoplectic, but as was my custom at the time, I kept the rage inside. Here, for once, my lifelong predilection for hiding my feelings served me well, at least in that it allowed me to exit the courtroom before I screamed out, "What the fuck!!!?"

Straightaway I called Nick Morgan.

"What the hell is going on?" I said. "Half my shares are missing."

He fumbled and mumbled, appearing not to understand.

"I own sixty-four thousand shares in Jimmy Choo," I went on. "The Araminta Trust shows thirty-two thousand."

He was useless, so I called Raj Patel, the accountant for the trusts.

"Where are my shares?" I said.

He, too, seemed confused at first, and then evasive, and then as he began what I suppose was meant as an explanation, I remembered a conversation we'd had at the Jimmy Choo offices just after the closing. I'd been going over documents related to the family's allocations when Raj very casually called me aside and said, "You know, there are some extra shares. How do you want to deal with them, vis-à-vis your mother, I mean? Do you want to split them?"

And I said, "Sure."

Once again, I was naive. Perhaps evasive. Distracted. Maybe simply stupid. But I thought he was talking about the sweet equity, which was three points, and while that was a serious amount of money, I was willing to be generous. There was no reason we should have split it, but this was still at the time that I was bending over backward to be nice to my mother.

Now it dawned on me that the "extra" shares he'd mentioned so casually weren't the sweet, and they certainly weren't "extra." They were the main course. They were the shares I'd acquired by reinvesting millions of my hard-earned dollars in Jimmy Choo. They were half the wealth I'd built up by nearly killing myself for the better part of a decade.

The trustee and the accountant came to the office on Ixworth Place and we had a face-to-face meeting with my lawyer, Andrew Roberts. Both Nick and Raj were talking double talk, blaming each other for the "mistake," and at the same time trying to justify the misaccounting according to "my father's wishes." "My father's wishes" according to whom? My father had made his wishes quite explicit in the legal documents setting up the trusts and giving half his equity in Jimmy Choo to me. And yet these two kept referring to my 64,000 shares in Jimmy Choo as "the extra shares" or "the shares that appeared after the sale."

In a private-equity deal you don't just "buy" shares. Any investment you make is accounted as a loan. By reinvesting and putting my money at risk, I had "loaned" Jimmy Choo Limited many millions.

As a record of this transaction, I had been given a "deep discount bond," or loan note, for the amount of money represented by the 64,000 shares. And just to make perfectly clear what that loan was all about— a standard procedure in these deals—the note had been stapled to the document representing the shares, a financial instrument known as an institutional strip.

Nick listened to this remedial lesson in private-equity finance and assured us that everything would be put right, but we still seemed to be talking past each other.

As the meeting was coming to an end, another vague but disturbing recollection filtered up to haunt my consciousness. My father had once described how, when the trusts were first being organized, Raj had come to him with some documents, proposing a new structure that would transfer debts between the trusts. The new structure would have left me hugely financially exposed.

My father told me that he said, "You better take that and rip it up and get rid of it."

But, in fact, this proposition made absolutely no sense except in the twisted worldview of one person: my mother. I think my father had been happy to work with dopes like Nick and Raj because their weakness ensured that he could retain control. But if these functionaries were amenable to outside control, God knows my mother would find a way to control them. With the old king now gone, all the monsters in the realm had indeed been let loose.

. . . .

I CONTINUED TO FLY ALL over the world, living in a state of perpetual jet lag while trying to appear bright and smiling and cheerful at public events, but as the court date for the divorce drew near, the pressure became so intense that I just couldn't take it anymore. Matthew and I met for coffee, and I said, "Look, I will give you £1.5M and we won't go to court."

He agreed, and so at least one gut-wrenching conflict was downgraded from a crisis to a mere unpleasant set of details.

Even so, I was still juggling a small baby, an impaired ex-husband, and an asshole of a CEO that I couldn't get rid of. I'd been killing myself to build a global brand, still being paid well below market rate, only to discover that I'd been robbed not only of half my shares but also half the money I'd taken out to live on.

For what exactly, then, was I working so hard? For a while it was so overwhelming, not to mention depressing, that I found it hard to go on.

And then Robert's true inner self came to the fore. More and more he seemed to want Jimmy Choo to be his own little fiefdom. It did nothing to help our relationship when, shortly after the sale to Lion, I was featured on the cover of the British edition of *Newsweek*. Robert hated the attention I received, but until now he could dismiss it as my being a "glamour girl." Now he had to read the news weekly's kind words about my business acumen and leadership skills.

I had tried to accept this unpleasant rivalry as the cost of doing business and move on. And then I was astounded to learn that he was running a director's account on me, keeping tabs on my expenses as if I were a junior sales representative. It was all so mad that even to this day I have no idea how they compiled it, but Robert had hired Alison Egan as the CFO, so it was no surprise that she would do his bidding.

Afterward, I had my own accountants try to work it out line by line, but it was impossible. Robert and Alison had charged me for express shipping of production samples from Italy to London, as if this were a personal expenditure. It was just like the list of the debts my mother said I owed her. Robert had compiled so many debits against my account that my £50,000 Christmas bonus was held back. "You owe the company money," I was told.

After this, my primal nemesis came back to add one more note to my humiliation, and, I suppose, to the sense of farce. The new bean counters from Lion came in one day and said, "You know, we've noticed that your mother's taking so much stock from the Beverly Hills store that it's affecting turnover. If she wants to come in and order up front, that's fine. And if she wants to take something from the store, we can give her a 50 percent discount."

This new policy brought out the worst in my mother. No sooner had word of the new policy reached the West Coast than she was at the store on a spree, lining up thousands of dollars of product on the counter, ready to go. The manager came over and said, "Mrs. Yeardye, I'm sorry, but you know we've been instructed that we have to charge you for these. We're happy to give you a 50 percent discount." Apparently, she grabbed all the bags and, in her perfect coif and her Chanel suit, went running down the street toward her Bentley.

This was the way Bernard Arnault had started out, acquiring Louis Vuitton, then taking it public, then acquiring other brands. Robert had worked for Arnault, had watched what he'd done, and evidently was now trying to follow in those footsteps.

He and Jim looked at Holland and Holland, A. Testoni, Stephane Kélian, the French shoemaker, Geoffrey Beene, and Bill Blass, but none of it worked.

Of far more serious concern was the damage Robert's meddling was doing to the brand, going behind my back to speak about me with the staff at Jimmy Choo, and then, worst of all, interfering with the design team.

For Robert, exercising control appeared more important than what was good for the business, but then, the battle between "the suits" and "the creatives" has been going on for as long as there have been suits. There's a wonderful moment in *Mad Men*, when a conflict erupts between the account execs and the copywriters and Don Draper, the mysterious and charismatic creative director, deadpans the much deeper truth: "They can't do what we do and they hate us for it." And yet with Robert there seemed to be far more to it. With Robert it seemed personal.

In designing, I never think about what women want—just about what looks great. And I can find inspiration almost anywhere, from watching Lauren Hutton in *American Gigolo* or Michelle Pfeiffer in *Scarface* to seeing African tribal masks in a museum. I might take a notion and start pulling Blondie album covers, or buying coffee-table books on punk rock or vintage bowling shirts from Wisconsin. It's not an intellectual process that you think through—it's simply an emotional experience—creating in the moment, on the spot, with "lightbulb" moments. There's a creative flow and sometimes you work on something and it gets better and better and other times you have to throw it out. But a successful product is when you have an emotional reaction to it—when you walk in a room and think, "I've got to have that, it's amazing!"

So we would go through this back-and-forth process two or three times, with me throwing out ideas, then the team making sketches, and then me editing them. I'd say this is the right direction, this is the wrong direction, this is a good one. We should develop this one more and not that one. Then we'd send the sketches to the factory where the first samples would be made up.

But each year I would also take the team on an inspiration trip, shopping in flea markets and collecting vintage pieces that spoke to me. Then we would come back and put into groups everything we'd picked up.

I took the team once to Jaipur in India, and then to shop in the hippie market in Goa. I also took them to Morocco, and we shopped in the bazaar and stayed in these cute little riads and got inspiration from the lanterns around the courtyards.

Istanbul was next on my list, but no one else wanted to go, which I didn't understand at all. Later I found out that it was a Robert-inspired mutiny. Be that as it may, I took the trip by myself, absorbing the souk and the rugs, the jewelry and the spice market with its amazing colors. I took hundreds of photographs there, including shots of the architecture with the patterns of the tiles and the paintings on them.

But Robert's most costly power play came at a very pivotal moment in fashion, when we were poised to capture the next wave.

At the Lineapelle show in Bologna, I'd been sitting with one of the suppliers when I picked some components off the shelf—a very stiletto heel and a platform with a very thick sole—and I said, "I want it just like this." Right there on the spot I was designing, and actually assembling, a very different kind of shoe, the heavy platform sandal. We and everyone else had been making shoes that were single soled and very strappy, and now I was proposing to increase the volume of the shoe, making it considerably heavier, even clunky, but with a thin heel.

I set this new idea in motion, and then I went on a business trip.

When I came back, the shoe I had designed had been taken out of the collection. I was astounded that they would be so presumptuous. It wasn't until later that I appreciated that the propaganda campaign Robert had launched against me in-house had led to the creative team essentially disregarding my input.

To make matters infinitely worse, just at this moment, Christian Louboutin came out with his peep toe platform, and women flocked to him. The platform stiletto became the hot shoe, Louboutin became the hot brand, and for a while our customers transferred their loyalty to him. Then Yves Saint Laurent came out with almost exactly the same design—and that was that. We couldn't go ahead without looking like copycats.

It may seem absurd to make so much over one missed opportunity. But until that moment, Louboutin had only one platform style, and this new shoe he brought out truly made him a household name. It's like that in fashion—make or break on one roll of the dice. It was truly a watershed moment, and not our finest hour.

We continued to grow the business, but only by opening new retail stores. Robert was able to tout this increase in dollar volume, which is certainly better than flat sales or a decline, but the proper measure for the health of a brand should be "like for like" growth in the same universe of stores. That kind of growth would require the continuous creativity I was trying to keep alive, but which my jealous CEO was undercutting at every turn.

My father was dead, my marriage was over, and now with Robert firmly installed, it looked as if I was going to be stuck in a never-ending custody battle over the company that I'd conceived and carried to term.

Not only that, but I was still fighting for "custody" of half the shares I'd already earned.

. . . .

THAT NEXT SUMMER I RENTED a house in Malibu, which was pleasant, but everything shut down at night, and there was only one good restaurant and just this empty stretch of sand and surf, and I felt isolated.

While I was there my friend Diana Jenkins introduced me to her neighbor, Robert Ritchie, also known as Kid Rock, and we all hung out together on the beach. I liked him a lot, and in fact we're still good friends, but the media made it out to be far more than it was. They did the same with Flavio Briatore, the head of the Renault Formula One racing team, with Pharrell Williams, even George Clooney. Every friendship I struck up with a well-known bachelor became, in the pages of the tabloids, my next reckless affair. The fact is, I was far too busy, and far too exhausted, to get too worked up about anyone.

I was also still trying to reach out to my mother, so while I was in California I put together a housewarming party for her. Older people don't get out much, so I gathered my brothers and a bunch of friends and some Hollywood people around a long table outside by the pool.

Later, in an affidavit pertaining to our dispute over the shares, she said I'd thrown a wild party and destroyed her house. My mother made the evening I'd put together for her sound like a major debauch, so much so that she described it as the "defining moment in the breakdown in our relationship." What I remember most vividly is my wonderful cook from that summer standing in the kitchen in tears because my mother was being so vile to her.

Shortly after the California dinner, Nick Morgan, the trustee, forwarded a handwritten letter my mother had sent to him. It was so degrading to me, and she talked about me in such a disparaging and dismissive way, that I've never spoken to her since. But then she'd always had a way of taking any detail of my life experience and making it sound utterly shameful, if not criminal. She seemed to relish using phrases like "she was BROKE!" when, in fact, the financial pinch that had me borrowing money from my dad was the result of the ridiculously low salary I took in order to help grow the company. What hurt most is that I was at her house, with my daughter, when she was putting these thoughts to paper.

Our book of celebrity photographs to raise money for Elton's AIDS Foundation continued to occupy a great deal of my time, and our list of models was pretty amazing: Christina Aguilera, Rebecca Banks, Tony Briar, Rachel Hunter, Lara Flynn Boyle, Rebecca Romijn-Stamos, Jodie Kidd, Victoria Beckham, Kate Moss, Macy Gray, Paris Hilton, Geri Halliwell, Serena Williams, Minnie and Kate Driver, Elle Macpherson, Sophie Dahl, Anne Heche, Mimi Rogers, Pamela Anderson, Yasmin Le Bon, Sarah Ferguson, among others. Of course I had to take a turn as well, lying on my belly on a bar with a huge Cartier diamond, my feet in the air.

A friend of mine, Beatrice Vincenzini, agreed to publish the volume. Her family owns newspapers, cable TV channels in Spain, the Italian national lottery, as well as the book company De Agostini. We called our photo collection "4 Inches." The innuendo in the title did cross my mind, but the fact is that "4 inches" was the maximum height for stilettos at the time. Now, of course, heels have gone on and up through the roof.

The book sold for $75, and it brought in a ton of publicity, and then we did an auction of photographs at Christie's in London, in New York, and in L.A. All in all we raised $3.5 million, which at the time was the single largest donation ever to the Elton John charity. We built rape shelters across South Africa that could provide every service that a woman would need under one roof: medical treatment, legal advice, and counseling. It's said that the money provided treatment for more than five hundred thousand women.

.... 9 ....

When Phoenix acquired us in 2001, we had only three stores; by the time Lion Capital came on the scene in 2004, we had nineteen. Now we were adding new stores on Bond Street and on Sloane Street, and on Via San Pietro all'Orto in Milan. Rents were going up all over Europe, which meant that you could pay millions for a top location, which also required a lump-sum payment to buy out the lease held by the old tenant.

In Paris the shopping mecca is Avenue Montaigne, and Robert found a space there that had been the concierge's flat for an apartment building. It was empty, and next to an alley, so the rent was cheap, but it took two years in court to gain permission from the prefecture. It was only 538 square feet, but it had 14 feet of window looking out on the avenue. I will give credit (even to Robert) where credit is due—this tiny location racked up nearly $3.7 million the first year.

On the product front, after shoes and bags, fragrance was our next objective. We talked to Clarins, to Procter and Gamble, and then to Interparfum. Primarily a distribution company, Interparfum had launched the fragrance brand for Agent Provocateur, as well as the fragrance for John Galliano. They were doing about $190 million a year, but with nine international subsidiaries, their global reach matched that of billion-dollar companies.

We also did an eyewear deal with Safilo, the huge Italian company that manufactured and distributed for Armani and all the Gucci Group brands. They had the capacity to merge plastic and metal, which seemed essential for capturing our design aesthetic.

I began to push our boundaries in other ways. In 2006, I initiated our first collaboration with an artist, Richard Phillips. He does large, hyperrealistic paintings that recall the pictorial style of fashion magazines from the fifties and sixties. We began working to reappropriate his images and put them on bags. Robert never understood what I was doing, and the board dithered over whether or not this was a good investment of resources, so the whole process dragged on and on.

I met the same kind of resistance when it came time to create a Web presence for us. Back in 2000, I had been one of the first to support Natalie Massenet when she founded the fashion site Net-A-Porter. Natalie didn't have the cash to pay up front for the shoes she wanted to sell, so I let her have them on consignment. As a result of that early boost to her business, Natalie and I had always enjoyed a great relationship. So when I wanted to launch a Web site for Jimmy Choo, I called her and asked her to run the back office—the bookkeeping and order fulfillment. It wasn't part of her business model to offer these kinds of services to outside clients, but for us, she said yes.

Net-a-Porter is still thriving. In 2010, Natalie did a deal that valued her company at £350 million.

By 2006, we were selling shoes and bags in over forty Saks outlets, and even Neiman Marcus was selling our bags (Manolo doesn't make bags). We followed the Tulita with the Tahula, with round handles inspired by the hula hoop. Bags were now 40 percent of sales, and bags deliver profit margins roughly 10 percent higher than those of shoes.

The general economy was soaring, fully recovered from the dot-com bust of 2000, and we still had immense room for growth, especially in Asia. We were opening stores in Mumbai, Dubai, and Kuwait, as well as in South Korea, Hong Kong, and Japan, and our revenues were approaching $120 million. With a growth rate of 45 percent, Jimmy Choo had already exceeded Lion's financial goals for the acquisition. So it seemed natural enough that we would begin to talk about an exit.

Even so, I was more than a little taken aback in November when Lyndon called me quite out of the blue and asked me to drop by his house in South Kensington. I went over and we sat down, and he said, "I have an offer for the company at £185M, and we're closing the deal in two weeks."

I thought, "My God, I'm being squeezed out. They're selling my company out from under me."

He said, "Here's the deal. You're going to cash out. You can retain 3 percent, and you can stay on as a sort of ambassador, but with no executive position."

I was still trying to absorb the implications, too stunned to say anything. You don't reach this point in a transaction overnight. This whole thing must have been going on behind my back for months, and it was no great challenge to figure out who would have been at the heart of it.

Robert's guerrilla campaign against me finally came into perspective. For whatever animosity or jealously he may have felt toward me, his ultimate goal was to have complete control of the company. In his mind, this meant that the company's founder could no longer be tolerated on the premises.

Apparently, Lyndon had been testing the waters with potential buyers when Robert asked flat-out what it would cost for him to acquire the company. Lyndon had come back with a price of £185 million. Robert then brought in Ramez Sousou from TowerBrook Capital Partners, who'd worked for George Soros and been the "underbidder" during the sale to Lion. A Palestinian with a Harvard MBA, Ramez had also worked for Goldman Sachs in New York and London, even headed the Goldman Mezzanine Partners fund. When Soros retired, Ramez and his partners bought the private-equity division of Soros Fund Management and created TowerBrook. Soros remained a significant investor, and lots of other family funds and institutional investors came on board.

TowerBrook were quite flush, with $2.5 billion to work with, all aimed at acquisitions. They were also making money hand over fist, even winning the European Fund of the Year by the European Private Equity and Venture Capital Association—none of which bode well for my chances of coming up with a more promising backer to team with in making a counteroffer.

With TowerBrook's bid on the table, Ramez and his colleagues would have exclusive access to our data and staff for their due diligence over the next four weeks, and during that time Lyndon had agreed not to solicit any other offers.

I called Lyndon and proposed a lunch at Harry's Bar. As soon as I sat down across from him I said, "I'll bring you £200M in two weeks. If I do, will you take it?"

He said he would.

In fact, he had nothing to lose. My offer, should I be able to deliver, would be a bump up of £15 million. But then, I'm also sure he never thought I'd be able to deliver.

I started talking to other private-equity funds, as well as to people who knew people, and one of my friends put me in touch with the Kuwaiti billionaire Maan Al-Sanea. We had a meeting and Maan expressed interest. He hired Lazard to begin putting together the deal, and another friend of mine, Ricardo Pavoncelli, to prepare the due diligence.

Things were looking up, but I couldn't let it get around that I was trying to raise money, so now, on top of everything else, I was forced to run a cloak-and-dagger operation à la John Le Carré.

The holidays were coming on, and I was at Matthew Freud's Christmas party when one of his partners, Kris Thykier, came up to me and said, "I know what's going on. Seems you're alone in this." Then he pointed to Bonnie Takhar, Robert's right-hand person who negotiated all the licensing deals. "Why don't you get Bonnie on your side."

I went over and spoke to her, and she was immediately receptive. From that moment on she became my well-placed eyes and ears, with her office directly next door to Robert's.

I'd already rented a house in St. Bart's for the holidays, and I'd even sent Minty ahead with the nanny to stay with my friends Vassi Chamberlain and Adrian Harris. I told the office that I was away on vacation when in fact I was in London, working from home. My assistant could tell from my e-mails that I hadn't really left, and so she called Sandra to see what was going on. This assistant also happened to be dating Sandra's boyfriend's brother, so it was all getting a bit too close for comfort.

It was also getting down to the wire, and I was not without anxiety as I waited in my lawyer's office on the evening of December 17, the day after TowerBrook's exclusivity expired. Then, at about ten p.m., my new friend from Kuwait, Maan Al-Sanea, came through with a non-binding offer at the level I'd requested: £200 million.

Robert's deal was to be signed at nine the next morning, so I called Lyndon and I said, "Don't sign with Ramez. I have a firm bid of £200 million. You can call Lazard to verify it."

He said to me, "Okay, Tamara, I'm a greedy capitalist. I'll take your deal." But then he said, "You better call Ramez."

Lyndon wanted me to dampen Ramez's ardor until he'd had time to speak with Robert.

So I called Ramez and I told him, "I'm not in favor of this deal. If you sign tomorrow, I promise you I won't publicly support this. And I will damage all your future acquisitions."

He was furious, and he knew that Lyndon had said he would not sell without my support.

But then with a touch of braggadocio that would become all too familiar, he said, "You know what, Tamara? I'm going to sign, and then I'm going to sign you up post-deal."

In other words, he didn't care what I thought. And he knew that I was captive to whoever owned a majority stake in Jimmy Choo.

By the next morning Lyndon had told Robert the whole story, including the fact that I was the one who'd topped his offer, and when he got to the office he was throwing thunderbolts.

His deadline had passed without closure, but nothing had been signed for my deal, either, and he was not about to give up so easily.

He quickly banged out a letter for everyone in management to sign, saying that they all wanted to go with his deal. In Star Chamber fashion, he then set himself up in the conference room and had all the senior executives come in one by one for their individual dose of intimidation. But none of them would sign. Except Sandra.

She had never expressed to me that she was unhappy with her position, but then again, everyone wants to be recognized, and just because someone doesn't assert her ego doesn't mean she doesn't have it. But mostly, Robert had worked her over, fueling the idea that she should have been recognized more and that I had been the one unjustly blocking her path. If I could be gotten out of the way, her path to recognition would be cleared. During TowerBrook's due diligence, Ramez had asked her what would happen if I left. Later, he told me she'd said, "I'm a big girl now. I can handle Tamara's job."

Robert's palace revolt failed, but now the problem was that the Kuwaitis were stalling. They weren't signing, and they had a Muslim holiday and they weren't contactable. So everyone was getting really nervous, especially me.

Lyndon had gone skiing in Whistler, but he agreed to fly to New York to talk. We met at Soho House in the Meatpacking District, and we discussed the situation, but in the end there wasn't all that much to say. He told me, "If the Kuwaitis don't sign within a couple of days, I'm going back to TowerBrook."

With that he walked out, and I was left sitting at the bar in tears. Private-equity deals include a provision for "drag along, tag along," meaning that minority owners can't withhold their shares to obstruct a sale. So unless something rather miraculous turned up, this was the end of my career at Jimmy Choo. That's when it occurred to me that this was Christmas Eve. If Danielle Steel had written the scene, I think her editor might have asked for a change. "Danielle, darling . . . a bit over the top, don't you think?"

The best I could do was to go on to St. Bart's as planned and be with Minty and wait, but I couldn't book a flight. The Kuwaitis said, "Don't worry. We'll pay for you to charter." I called Nat Rothschild, and his plane was available, so I took it. The expense was $40,000, for which, by the way, I was never paid back, but at least I was able to get to the islands.

. . . .

FOR THE NEXT WEEK I was in this beautiful vacation spot with my daughter, but it was the most stressful seven days of my life. I couldn't go out. I couldn't do anything. It was just awful. I sat inside, working the phone, trying to get Maan and his people to come through. They kept saying they couldn't take any calls because of their holiday. But that didn't affect Lyndon. He was on the phone day in and day out, warning me that time was up and that he was going to sell to Tower-Brook.

Ron Perelman from Revlon was on the island, as well as Harvey Weinstein from Miramax, and they tried to provide some moral support. Later, Harvey actually got on the phone with Ramez and said to him, "If you lose Tamara Mellon, I'm going to invest with her and we'll set up shop and eat your lunch."

At the end of the week, Minty and I flew back to London, and immediately upon my arrival I received a text from Maan saying they were backing out. A text?! That's how eighth graders break up with their girlfriends.

"It's all over and that's that," I thought. "I've lost my business."

I was too exhausted and too numb to feel the weight of it. But then it occurred to me that if I weren't going to be there to shape the collection, then it was good that they were forcing me to cash out. The same sort of palace intrigues had befallen Helmut Lang and Jil Sander, and both brands had suffered and plummeted in value.

Then again, there was a bolt left in my quiver. What if I could find some way to go back to Ramez, reengage with him, and win him over to my side?

The one thing Maan had done for me was to buy time—and, perhaps, to cast confusion among my enemies.

As a last-ditch effort, and with help from Adrian Harris, who by now was not only a friend but my financial adviser, I wrote an e-mail to Ramez explaining the design process and explaining all that Robert had done to undermine me and to interfere with my efforts to steer the brand creatively. I had to make him see my side of it and not Robert's. Essentially, I had to make him see that I'd been slandered and that he'd been gamed.

We got together in the coffee bar of the little hotel next to our offices on Ixworth Place.

"You've done your financial due diligence," I said. "You've examined the books and appraised the real estate. But now you need to do your creative due diligence. You need to go ask around. Talk to management beyond Robert's little clique. Talk to the design team. Find out who's really creating the value."

I guess I was convincing because he continued to listen. As my parting shot I said, "Buying this company without me would be like buying the *Titanic*."

Ramez was still being coy. "Don't you have issues with your mother's shares?" he said.

Clearly, Robert had filled him in on every detail that might undermine my position or sully my image.

Then he took a more philosophical tack. "Are you more interested in making money," he asked, "or in being a celebrity?" This was a line straight out of Robert's phrase book. Robert had tried to paint me as the Devil Diva, a spend-thrift glamour queen who contributed nothing, waltzing from store opening to celebrity gala to board meeting with no concern but to garner all the credit and to feather her own nest. All in all, it was a lovely package.

I will give Ramez considerable credit that he went back in and he interviewed a wider circle beyond the people like Jim Sharp and Alison Egan. He talked to Hannah, and to Bonnie, and to the design room.

A couple of hours went by, and I was in a state, but then he called me at home.

"Okay, Tamara. We're not doing this deal without you."

I could breathe again. After I'd inhaled, the first words out of my mouth were, "Then Robert has to go."

This was a big concession for them, not only because Robert had engineered the sale in the first place but because he knew the financial side of things inside and out, and the CFO was in his pocket. But they accepted my terms.

TowerBrook's lawyers were located at 30 St. Mary Axe, the forty-one-story tower in the City also known as the Gherkin, so called because of its resemblance to a curved-glass-and-steel pickle. We met there to sign on Sunday, February 4, 2007.

I had just flown back from New York, and I had the flu, but damned if I'd let them see me worn down. I pulled out all the stops in a black velvet pencil skirt and a leopard print fur jacket, and when I entered you could cut the atmosphere with a knife.

We had six different conference rooms for six different teams, and looking out through the glass walls to the sofas beyond, I could see the different factions waiting separately. Alison looked particularly nervous, and for good reason. Robert and I avoided eye contact. I did not want to speak to him. I couldn't even bring myself to look at him.

Ramez said to me, "You've won. You can let it go. You've won."

My victory lay in the fact that Ramez had accepted my assessment of my value to the company rather than Robert's. Moreover, my employment contract going forward would stipulate that if Robert came back to active management at Jimmy Choo in any way, they would have to buy my shares at a predetermined price, and I would be able to walk within twenty-four hours.

Even so, Ramez continued to admonish me like a teenager. "You know," he said, "you're not allowed to throw parties at home and charge it against the company."

I had never, ever thrown a private party and charged it to Jimmy Choo. Quite the opposite, I often did Jimmy Choo entertaining at my home and paid for it myself. I'd also made my home available for innumerable photo shoots, but obviously Robert's image of me had sunk in.

The sale, valued at £185 million, made the front page of the *Financial Times*. TowerBrook paid £170 million right away, with £15 million due if we met our targets for the year ahead. This was a multiple of 2.2 times sales, and nearly 10 times profits. Lion Capital had doubled their money in little more than two years. Of course, to finance the acquisition, TowerBrook was encumbering Jimmy Choo with another £80 million in debt, underwritten by UBS.

TowerBrook was acquiring a 60 percent stake, but as the second-largest shareholder, I continued as president. To save face, and to give us time to find a replacement, Ramez allowed Robert to stay on as CEO for six months. You'd think he wouldn't have wanted to hang around, pretending that he hadn't been pushed out, but he did. Robert was also allowed to keep his sweet equity, a little skin in the game to keep him from doing or saying anything more to damage the business. As another face-saving gesture, Ramez kept him on the board, but then, of course, TowerBrook cut back on board meetings, making them quarterly rather than monthly.

Once TowerBrook was able to do more forensics on the accounts, they found that it was actually Robert who had stretched the limits of corporate expenses. He'd spent £30,000 in Jimmy Choo funds at a charity auction in Paris to buy a table that had nothing to do with Jimmy Choo. (The fact that it was at a Jewish charity must have truly made this a memorable detail for Ramez, who is Palestinian.)

Hannah and Maggie White, head of store development, put together a big party for Robert at Home House, a private club on Portman Square, and everyone wore masks of his face. They also gave him a gift of a giant red pair of Jimmy Choos in his size. I did not attend.

Once again, TowerBrook had wooed us with talk of long-term horizons, as in, "We're not like the other guys—we have a real interest in the company." Then at our very first board meeting, they were already talking about their exit. The goal they set forth was £50 million in EBITDA in 2009. So, in fact, they were thinking only two years out.

As the dust settled, Lyndon was furious to discover that the EBITDA had been underplayed, which resulted in a lower purchase of the company. Lyndon said he'd lost £10 million. But he was gone now, and I was still around.

Alison came into my office, trying to mend fences. "I really wasn't a part of all that," she said. "I didn't know what was going on. I just gave them the numbers. I was just doing my job."

Obviously, I didn't believe a word she was saying, but her betrayal was small potatoes. I did mention to her something Robert had said that I thought was very revealing of his character: "The only reason we sold the company was because your father died." I asked her, "How can you think that anyone who would say that is a decent human being?" She left a few months later.

I didn't have the energy to pursue a more thorough housecleaning. I had been in the ring for a decade now, and my legs were getting wobbly.

For her part, Sandra tried to act like nothing had happened, but she overcompensated, saying such things as "You're like my big sister."

I just looked at her and thought, "What planet are you on?"

Jimmy Choo was the only real job she'd ever had, so she was still such an innocent, and I think she simply hadn't been strong enough to stand up to Robert. Getting rid of her would have made TowerBrook nervous because she'd been part of the design team from the beginning. But she was finished as far as I was concerned, and it was a big disappointment because we'd worked so closely together for so many years.

If she'd only stepped up and been open and direct and apologized for her disloyalty, I think I could have gotten over it. And in terms of our design work going forward, the rift between us became terribly awkward because, with my faith and trust in her destroyed, she really wasn't able to contribute. I'm sure I dismissed her ideas, not on purpose but because I was connecting so much more with other contributors. So I wound up just going through the motions and then working around her, which was not at all optimal, and all very sad.

What didn't become apparent to me until later was just how much Robert's bad-mouthing and undermining had trickled down to affect the other members of the team.

I still had faith in what we were doing, so I wanted to let my investment ride. I cashed out as little as possible, which was £4 million, but then I couldn't put my hands on it. Owing to the legal dispute with my mother and her claims on my assets, the money was immediately frozen.

At least the new pay package they were offering was £500,000, but in exchange for the raise I would have to give up many of the perks that are standard in the fashion industry, and necessary for the kind of public appearances I was doing. I would have to provide my own hair and makeup for events, lose my clothing allowance, and also forfeit my car and driver. So I said, "I'll take £290,000 as a salary, and you pay for hair, makeup, clothes, and the driver directly."

Andrew Rolfe from TowerBrook took the lead in finding a new CEO, and he put us in touch with Joshua Schulman, then the president of Kenneth Cole. The two of them had worked together at the Gap, where Josh had been vice president for merchandising in Japan and senior vice president of international strategic alliances. He'd also done merchandising for Gucci during the Tom Ford years, and been executive vice president of worldwide merchandising and distribution for Yves Saint Laurent.

Three days after the sale was announced we met in London, and I thought he was a good fit. He knew fashion, and I didn't sense any of the ego competition that was so transparent with Robert. He seemed not only happy with my being the public face of the brand, he knew how to leverage it. Oddly enough, he'd grown up partly in Beverly Hills, and even gone to El Rodeo School! It felt like a breath of fresh air, the beginning of a new chapter.

···· 10 ····

With the TowerBrook drama fresh in my memory, it wasn't as if I was looking for new adventures or for more work to add to my list. But one day I was on the phone with Harvey Weinstein, who was then dating the woman he would later marry, Georgina Chapman of Marchesa.

Harvey knew about all the Sturm und Drang I'd just been through and he asked me, "So, what do you want to do in the next five years?"

Out of the blue I said, "I want to bring back Halston. I think it's the biggest missed opportunity in the luxury business. The designs he did in the seventies are still relevant today. All you need to do is put some modern proportions on them."

Harvey said, "Oh my God, you're right! What a great idea!"

I was incredibly busy and I didn't think anything more about our conversation until a month or so later, when I was at the Oscars and one of Harvey's colleagues came up to me and said, "This is so great about Halston. We're closing in a week!"

Once again I was stunned. Utterly speechless.

"Of course we want you in on it," he said.

Of course.

By now you might think that I'd no longer be taken aback by a friend picking up my idea and running with it. Maybe I had been hopelessly naive to speak so openly. Or was there some cumulative effect to all I'd been through that marked me as an easy target for the next betrayal or stab in the back?

These kinds of negotiations take weeks, so Harvey must have made a call to the investment bankers the moment he got off the phone with me.

I said, "Send me the terms of the deal."

They were working with Hilco Equity Partners and with Financo to buy the Halston license from the current owner, James Ammeen of Neema Clothing. They were offering me 1.5 percent sweet equity to be on the board and to be a creative consultant.

I responded with, "That's beyond insulting. Good luck with . . ." Then they panicked.

I'm sure Harvey had been tossing my name around from day one as he'd tried to put the financing together. It turned out that he'd already negotiated himself 10 percent sweet equity for his genius in coming up with the idea and for having access to fashion insiders. Now one of the names he'd dropped was walking away.

But they kept calling me back, and I should have just kept going, but I was like a dog with a bone, infuriated that Harvey had developed my idea and now was presenting himself as the prime mover in all of this. It's also true that I really loved Halston, and if they did this deal, that would be it for a while. I didn't want to miss the boat, even though I knew instinctively that everything about this setup was all wrong.

To try to make it right, or at least better, I called my friend Rachel Zoe, the Hollywood stylist, and told her what was going on. More than a year earlier, she and I had talked over lunch about reviving the brand. She had a huge collection of vintage Halston, and in her work she took much of her inspiration from him.

I told her, "This deal is moving. You should come on board."

Then it was time to talk to Harvey. I told him he'd have to give up 1 percent of his sweet equity for each of us. And I also told him I wanted to invest $2 million. This became a fight because they'd already closed the deal, and letting anyone else in meant having to dilute their shares.

The purchase price was $27 million, with Hilco owning a majority stake. Harvey had put in $1 million, his brother Bob had put in a million, and their company had put in a million. Jim Ammeen, the seller, came back in and reinvested some of his proceeds.

To announce the acquisition Harvey sent around a draft of a press release that was supposed to list me as an investor, but it didn't. Upon my complaint he changed it to say that he'd brought me on as a consultant. He still referred to himself as the buyer, even when he'd put in half of what I was trying to invest and ultimately was a very minor shareholder.

Still, my love for the brand was unabated.

Halston's greatest innovation had been the one-shoulder jersey dress, cut from one piece, which was so easy to wear. I wanted to bring it back in spirit, recast for today. And God knows you didn't have to reinvent the wheel, especially not when the history of the brand is so glamorous, and with such a great story to tell, from Jackie Kennedy's pillbox hat to Studio 54. All you have to do is summon up that iconic image of Bianca Jagger drifting through the door on a white horse in a white Halston dress, and the whole scene with Andy Warhol, and Halston's Paul Rudolph–designed apartment on East Sixty-Third, where the boys wore Liza Minnelli's dresses at the drag parties and dinner consisted of caviar, a baked potato, and cocaine.

A lot of people take inspiration from previous decades. The kids everywhere are wearing vintage clothing now, but there's a difference between retro and renewal. That's part of the creative process. You go vintage shopping and it's the hunt for the one great piece that inspires you, and then you come back and you turn it into something modern. It may not even look like that original piece, but it's what the original piece inspires.

Raf Simons did this beautifully when he went into the archives at Dior and put a modern twist on it. So did Diane von Furstenberg, who relaunched her business with the wrap dress, only with modern proportions. She made the collar smaller and the width not so A-line.

For Halston, it would be no great stretch of the imagination to take the Bianca Jagger white trouser suit and re-create it with modern proportions. Before Halston, everything was very tight and fitted coming out of the sixties. It was very difficult to buy something off the rack, so women of means often had their clothes made. With jersey, the loose fabric he used, you could roll up the dress and put it in your suitcase, get somewhere, hang it up, and it was fine. His clothes were modern, sporty, easy, and convenient. If we brought back the asymmetrical jersey dress, I knew that every woman vacationing on the Med or in the Hamptons would buy them in multiple colors.

At my recommendation we hired Bonnie Takhar as CEO, and it

didn't take long before she and I came to the same conclusion that Hilco's people were all wrong. They were debt collectors, not fashion people, and most of all they weren't treating us right.

Bonnie and I met at the Mercer Hotel and I suggested that we push for a management buyout. So we spoke to D. E. Shaw, the hedge fund managers, about getting help with the financing. Then I went back to London and set up a conference call with Harvey and Bonnie.

"Harvey, I want you to know that we're not happy," I said. "I have a backing in D. E. Shaw, and the whole management team is going to walk in twenty-four hours if we don't get what we want. You're in my industry now."

. . . .

IN APRIL, JIMMY CHOO ANNOUNCED that Josh Schulman was our choice for CEO.

The same month I received a subpoena to testify at Matthew's trial. I knew the press would be all over this, so I asked Mark Bolland, a major figure in UK public relations, to go with me.

The proceedings were at Southwark Crown Court, a clinical-looking, contemporary brick building near Tower Bridge, just south of the river. The trial was a huge affair, with a total of eighteen defendants, and I appeared on May 3, the seventh day of testimony.

The issue, at least insofar as Matthew was concerned, was whether or not he should be held criminally responsible for authorizing the illegal hacking of my computer during our divorce. There was no question that he'd given the indicted investigators £12,000 and that he'd signed the contract and authorization they had asked him to sign. But that still left the issue of *criminal* responsibility, as in knowing what was going on, knowing that it was illegal, and then doing it anyway.

When I saw him on trial, my heart went out to him. I thought, "Oh boy. You're really in over your head this time." In fact, he was facing five years.

As the victim of Matthew's supposed crime, I was actually called as a witness for the prosecution. The prosecutor had me relate all that had happened, including the appearance of the Trojan horse e-mail on my computer, the one that promised to provide me with "things on your soon-to-be ex-husband."

But then when Matthew's defense counsel, Nicholas Purnell, began to question me, the discussion took a marked detour into Matthew's habits of mind. This was no time to gild the lily, so I simply told the truth. I said that being married to Matthew was like having another child. I said that he couldn't keep up with his bills or bank accounts and that he missed planes the way other people miss buses. When Purnell asked about Matthew's reading habits and powers of concentration, I simply said that my husband couldn't manage a comic book, much less a legal document.

The courtroom erupted.

I left the building mobbed by paparazzi, and the next day, the story was on page one of literally every newspaper in London, most of them quoting my comment about Matthew's inability to cope with a comic book.

The whole trial took six weeks, with the jury deliberating for five days. Two of the detectives were convicted, but happily Matthew was not.

Josh began work as Jimmy Choo CEO in June. In one of our first conversations I told him, "My title is president. But clearly I'm leading the creative process, so I think it's misleading and confusing for the industry." So we changed my title to chief creative officer. I liked what I saw of Josh at our first board meeting. Given all the delays, I was still working on the collaboration with Richard Phillips, appropriating one of his images for a "magazine" clutch bag, and the board was still uncertain about it. They asked Josh, "Is this a good thing?"

He said, "This is brilliant. This is the kind of thing we should put money behind."

And so we did, launching the line at Art Basel Miami in 2007. The Phillips bags were among our top ten best sellers, and now you see everyone doing this kind of collaboration with artists.

Josh also "got" the inspiration trips. He understood how important it was for the design team to be together and do these trips together to create the right kind of flow. When you're traveling and seeing things, you don't know what you're looking for until it hits you. Then, if you're lucky, the floodgates open.

For the first time since the initial Phoenix deal, it looked like we were going to have someone in charge who understood the business.

I took Josh on a tour of the stores and we talked about market niches where I saw the greatest untapped potential. One of these was ballet flats, which were a big business, and we weren't doing them well enough at all. I'd also wanted to do a biker boot for years, and a moccasin boot with fringe. I met with huge resistance on the biker boot—mostly from Sandra, oddly enough, who kept telling me we couldn't afford it—but at last I prevailed, and it became our third-best seller ever, moving five hundred thousand units.

Josh was also keen on orchestrating product, PR, advertising, and marketing. Raul Martinez, founder and chief creative officer of the ad agency AR, as well as creative consultant to American *Vogue*, was brought in to help shape the look of each campaign. He hired Terry Richardson to do the shoot at the Plaza, and it was Charlotte Pilcher's inspiration to have Angela Lindvall in the boots.

Ed Filipowski of the PR firm KCD was brought in to help with global strategy, even as we were opening stores in Cannes, Barcelona, Rome, São Paulo, Kuala Lumpur, and Tokyo.

On June 25, Josh and I went to L.A. to open a new store on Rodeo Drive. We threw a bash that was such a great success that the fire marshal showed up and shut us down. Luckily, we'd already planned to segue to a dinner for a selected few at the home of Wendi Murdoch.

Meanwhile, Halston's board ratified enough of our demands that Bonnie and I stayed on. She invested half a million, and I put in two.

After we'd reached our agreement and comity returned, one of the Hilco guys turned to me and said, "So now. . . . are you girls going to behave?"

Here was another moment when I should have simply walked out. In certain circles, it appears the only options for dealing with a woman are either to control her or to belittle her. But I still hadn't found my voice.

Halston needed the right designer, so we went on an extensive search. We talked to Peter Dundas, who's now at Pucci, and to Hedi Slimane, who's now at Yves Saint Laurent. He'd only designed menswear, but I thought he'd be great. Even though I had concerns about how well he could work with the investors, I would have given up huge equity to have him.

American *Vogue* recommended Marco Zanini, who at the time was working directly with Donatella Versace. We met up in London and he showed me his sketches, and then he invited me to his last show for them in Milan, which was very Halston inspired. "I just wanted you to see this. I did this for you," he said.

We hired him and set up offices downtown.

. . . .

IN FEBRUARY 2007, WE MOVED the Jimmy Choo offices from Ixworth Place to Lancer Square. We went from 3,000 square feet to 10,000 square feet of office space, and, as in the stores, the design was all very clean, with the same beige and lilac. Our back office was much larger now, with a much bigger PR department, finance department, and merchandising department.

Despite my role in representing the brand to the public, my focus was still very much on the product. We were hiring more designers and more assistants, but we were also introducing more collections—fall/winter and spring/summer, and now also a Cruise or Resort Collection, which hit the stores in November, and a pre-fall, which appeared in June. Considering the amount of work we were doing, it was still a very small design team.

Even a small team requires management, though, and we all know the well-worn descriptor for managing creatives: herding cats.

The hoariest management cliché, though, is that it's lonely at the top, which persists because the typical CEO manages through fear, remaining a distant authority figure, capable of screaming and throwing fits, firing you in a heartbeat, or bestowing undreamed-of privileges. It's very clear that you're not working *with* him; you're working *for* him.

My role was much more ambiguous. I was in and out, going to the Oscars and to meetings with bankers, then coming back to the design room and rubbing elbows. I certainly was not a remote and a fear-inducing authority figure. At times, I appeared to be simply "one of them," and yet I also got special attention and special privileges—all of which could lead to resentment, which, of course, Robert had encouraged and tried to exploit in his attempt to divide and conquer.

Some of the time, certain people on the team were still deliberately dismissive, as if they were saying, "We've got the word on you." This made trying to come back out from under Robert's slander campaign like fighting a clique of "mean girls." Then again, I know that my remoteness, that residue of "vacant" Tamara from my actual school days, can be misinterpreted and perhaps off-putting.

Fortunately, we also had some grown-ups on the team, like Elisabeth Guers, our head shoe designer, an amazing Frenchwoman who never fell for the Robert bullshit. Neither did Alvaro, the bag designer. He told me that Robert had called him once and asked if the company could survive without Tamara. He'd said, "No."

I also had Charlotte Pilcher, the stylist I'd worked for in the early days, and whom I'd brought on board as my creative right hand during the end of the Robert era, when I really needed a friend. She was also another pair of very experienced and savvy eyes that I trusted completely, and she became a part of all of our design meetings.

During this period, Minty would occasionally sit in as well. She'd sketch shoes, and then we'd pin her designs up on the wall. Her favorite movie from this era was *The Devil Wears Prada*, and it may have gone to her head. She'd come in and collect employees' phone extensions and write up a list of their names and numbers. Then she'd ring them up and tell them they were fired. Thank God the staff saw the humor in it.

. . . .

IN THE FALL OF 2007, Amanda Kyme, who was working for us one day a week on celebrity gifting, called to say that there was a man she wanted me to meet. Christian Slater was in town doing a play called *Swimming with Sharks*. She said he didn't know anyone, and she wanted to introduce us.

I knew the name from the movies *Heathers* and *True Romance* and the like, but I said, "Oh God, Amanda, no actors. No rock stars, please."

She said, "Oh come on, come on. Just have dinner with him. I think you'll actually get on."

I looked at my diary and I said, "I have something every night for the next two weeks. Except Wednesday, I guess. A friend of mine is having a dinner. Matthew Vaughn, he's a producer. I guess Christian could come to that."

So I met him at his hotel and he came to the dinner, and actually, we got on really well. And then every night after that, whenever he'd finish rehearsal, he'd kind of show up. We had a few more dinners, he sent me flowers, and the relationship took off from there. He was in London for six months, and we actually ended up spending pretty much every night together.

I don't know why Amanda thought it would be a match. Another reformed bad boy, I suppose. He'd done his time with sex, drugs, and rock and roll, and now he was clean and sober.

Divorced, he had two kids about the same age as Minty, a boy and a girl. He lived in a house in Brentwood owned by the mother of a guy he met in rehab, so it was all very arrested development, which was a little worrying. They lived in the bedrooms meant for children, which for me had echoes of the basement in Belgravia. The guy whose mother owned the house served as Christian's assistant/manager/best friend. Also in the house was the guy's girlfriend from South Carolina, who was even less sophisticated than he, and I think the two of them spent a great deal of time worrying that I was going to take Christian away from them. When I visited L.A., Christian would stay with me at the Peninsula, and we'd watch episodes of *Entourage*. We were in on the joke.

Christian was great for that moment in time, but fundamentally we had very different worldviews, and we wanted different things. He'd grown up in New York, where his father was an actor and his mother was a casting director and producer, and he'd been in the business his whole life. But he had very simple tastes. I went to baseball games with him, trying to be a good sport, but I have to say I was bored out of my mind the whole time. Hot dogs? Cracker Jack? Not for me.

In the middle of our relationship, I was forced to hire Bert Fields and file a civil suit against my mother in California. We still had not resolved the question of the 32,000 shares allocated to the wrong trust, the millions misallocated supposedly to protect my assets during the divorce, and the completely gratuitous £4 million in cash frozen because of the dispute—all of which led to some very nasty letters between my mother's lawyers and mine.

Occasionally, either side would make a proposal. Mine was to put the money at issue in a trust for Minty. Essentially, I told my mother, "You don't touch it, I don't touch it. It goes straight to the trust, and then your granddaughter gets the benefit instead of these lawyers."

But my mother wouldn't do that. Her response was always, "No, no. If anything ever happens to Tamara, we'll look after that little girl," words that filled me with horror.

Their counterproposal was to set up Marqueta II, a separate trust designation for charity. They even proposed the Elton John AIDS Foundation as beneficiary, which showed that they'd done their homework. But the way it was to be set up, they could shift the money back over into my mother's trust anytime they pleased. So the conversation went nowhere.

The whole affair felt like a chronic illness, with pathogens from my mother trapped in my body. I was so tense that my back was always going out on me. Sometimes it felt as if a giant snake were wrapped around me to keep me from taking a full breath.

. . . .

OUR FIRST HALSTON SHOW WAS in February 2008, but not even this legendary brand could sustain the burden of all our dreams and anxieties. In setting up the company, the investors had spent $3 million just on legal documents, so they were feeling strained and nervous going in. And then the first reviews were less than stellar.

After the catwalk, and before the buyers came by for closer inspection, Bonnie took it upon herself to redesign the collection. She mixed and matched and moved everything around and it was awful.

Selfridges had been negotiated previously based on the hype, but orders from the show itself were weak.

Pure panic soon set in. I was in the airport on the way back to London when the screaming phone calls began, and no one can scream like Harvey.

The trouble with Mr. Weinstein is that he never trusts the people he hires. He'll go out and ask everyone what he or she thinks, so he gets a dozen different opinions, often conflicting, and then he blows hot and cold every which way from one notion to the next. So, as if things weren't bad enough already, his next impulse was to set up an advisory board that, fortunately, never came into being.

On the creative side, all was not sweetness and light. Rachel's primary job was to shop for vintage Halston in L.A., but an article in *Harper's Bazaar* London quoted her to the effect that she was the creative director, which clearly upset Marco.

Bonnie was, in fact, driving our designer nuts with contradictory directives, second-guessing, and interventions, her relationship with Rachel was deteriorating, and I must confess I did not have my eye on the ball, too busy with Jimmy Choo, among other matters. I was so exhausted and overloaded that the best I could do was to ask Rachel to back away, which I've always felt really bad about because it made her seem the scapegoat.

And that was just the first season. There would be more to come.

11

I n the spring of 2008 Christian and I were in New York and, on an impulse, I said, "Let's just go out and have a look at the market and see what's out there. See what apartments are selling for."

I'd been thinking about relocating to New York for some time, but I hadn't really been ready to buy, and then I fell in love. Edgar Bronfman Jr. was selling the top two floors of a small structure on the Upper East Side. Built in 1913, it had once been a private academy. It reminded me so much of my apartment in London that I bought it on a whim.

With Christian living in L.A., certainly New York had advantages over London as a base for me. But there was more to the idea than that. At the time it just seemed that everything was pushing me toward the city, particularly with regard to Minty. I had no family left in London, and when Matthew and I got divorced, he ended up moving to New York, and I think it is very important for girls to grow up with their dads. I also found it difficult not to have an extended family because when I had to travel for business, there was no one around for Minty but the nanny. If we were living in New York, she'd not only have her dad, she'd have uncles and aunts and cousins. We'd already been going to Rolling Rock each year, the Mellon estate in Pennsylvania where she gets to meet dozens and dozens of other little Mellons. It was important to me that she would grow up with a sense of belonging to something more than just the two of us.

Given the nature of my business, it didn't make any difference whether I worked from London or from Manhattan. Then again, relocating to a different city, in a different country, would be incredibly complicated, and it wouldn't happen overnight.

Back in London, I went to dinner with Josh at Cipriani and I said to him, "How do you feel about moving the operations to Manhattan?"

Josh was from the city originally, and he was intrigued by the idea of coming back himself. He said, "I think it's a great idea."

But then he had a conversation with TowerBrook, after which he did a 180-degree turn.

I think TowerBrook objected for the usual reasons: They were afraid of losing control. The most they could abide was my own personal relocation, but they insisted that it not affect EBITDA, that Holy Grail of private-equity exit opportunities.

What they failed to take into account, of course, was that I was already flying across the Atlantic every few weeks and I was burned out. When you go back and forth through so many time zones so often, you're in a permanent condition of jet lag because you're never in one place long enough to fully recover. You're lost in this dopey netherworld, a state in which I realize I've probably spent the greater portion of my adult life.

So I stayed in London for the time being, and that summer I rented Tom Cruise's old house in Beverly Hills. It was a lovely place, English Tudor style on three or four acres off Sunset, with a long winding drive. Christian moved in for the month of August, and things were looking up. He had a new series about to launch, a secret agent thing with a

Bourne Identity twist called *My Own Worst Enemy.* I was even contacted out of the blue by the luxury goods holding company Labelux, offering £350 million pounds for Jimmy Choo.

At Halston, however, things continued along their dismal path. Just in time for the kickoff of our second season in August, Marco resigned. We still had to present the collection, so I called Charlotte and asked her to come help style the show. She and I flew to New York, and we didn't do a full fashion show but rather a presentation at the Museum of Modern Art that managed to salvage things, at least for a while. Even Emmanuelle Alt from French *Vogue* picked up on the look we'd created.

Back in London again, I was at a charity event, having dinner with Lord Jonathan Marland, a major shareholder in Hunter, the company that makes the famous Wellington boot. I said, "You know we should do a collaboration. We'll infuse your Wellies with the DNA of Jimmy Choo."

I'd seen a stylist at the Oscars the year before wearing Wellies with a denim miniskirt, and I thought it was a great look. Not long after, Kate Moss showed up in Wellies at the Glastonbury Festival, so the boots were definitely coming off the farm and out of the garden and onto the streets.

Eventually we worked out the details and were able to take the traditional Wellie, the green rubber boot, put a faux crocodile print on it, and schedule it for sale in January 2009.

At the end of the summer Josh and I went to Paris to open a new location on rue Saint-Honoré, then we moved Milan to a better location. We were still opening stores in North America, but now with forty locations, we were pretty maxed out. Still, we anticipated sales of over $200 million and EBITDA of $44 million.

Then came September 14, 2008. Lehman Brothers collapsed, the world economy crashed, and the luxury goods business dropped off a cliff. People just stopped buying. It got so bad that even the customers who were spending money asked for plain brown shopping bags so they wouldn't be seen walking down the street festooned with a luxury logo. Business fell by 30 percent.

TowerBrook saw the same kind of drop-off in all their businesses, so it wasn't as if they could flog us in particular. But they had saddled Jimmy Choo with £80 million in debt. The covenant we'd signed obligated us to pay a million a month, so the most important thing was to maintain a highly reliable, steady cash flow.

Not too surprisingly, Labelux stopped calling, though I think they were simply hoping to wait out the economic storm and pick us up at a much lower price than the £350 million they'd initially proposed.

Remarkably, I think the crisis drove a need for quality in the luxury marketplace. Customers were looking all the more for great brands they could rely on and trust. The market was now for investment pieces rather than whimsical purchases.

Eight years earlier it had been the presidential daughters who wore Jimmy Choo to their father's inauguration. In January 2009, it was First Lady Michelle Obama who attended the swearing-in ceremony in patent leather Jimmy Choo pumps.

Shortly thereafter, the Jimmy Choo Wellie hit the stores, and even though they sold for £250 per pair, the line did fantastically well for us. The boost to the bottom line was a huge factor in seeing us through the economic downturn, and it was a turning point for Hunter, too.

Not long after, H&M approached us with an even bolder idea.

H&M is the Swedish retailer with two thousand stores selling clothing at a very, very low price point. They wanted to do a collaboration, and with the new mood of austerity—if not global depression—the timing could not have been better. We could broaden our audience while also doing something that was feel-good and fun. But they wanted us to do not just shoes but an entire line of clothing, which I also thought was brilliant. Jan Nord and Jorgen Anderson, their collaborations people, said, "We'd like you to do a full look—all the way to menswear."

Josh was reluctant, but I loved the challenge of designing for the whole woman, as well as her husband or boyfriend. So I pushed. Ultimately, it would show that collaborations could not only garner attention but also, through the miracle of licensing, drive profits that aren't accompanied by any increase in cost to us.

I'd just gone on an inspiration trip to Miami with Alvaro, our bag designer, and I'd been absorbing all the bright colors and the art deco design, buying from thrift shops like a madwoman. So it was a very serendipitous thing that I'd just put this rail of clothes together with sequined dresses from the fifties, fringed suede from the seventies, and cardigans from God knows when. I had Charlotte come over and we picked the favorite shoes and bags and we styled the collection with the clothes, and then we presented that to H&M.

We were reimagining these shoes, bags, and dresses from an earlier era, updated to suit the Jimmy Choo woman. Again, H&M would do all the manufacturing and invest the money on the advertising, and we'd simply take a percentage while benefiting from an avalanche of favorable press.

Not long after we set this in motion, Nordstrom gave us the award for Brand Partner of the Year, and Josh went to Seattle to collect it. As he was going through the store, he came upon some industry people trying on UGGs, and he called me up and said, "What do you think about a collaboration with UGG? Would it hurt our image?"

This one was a little risky, because UGG had become very mass. Then again, they have the virtue of crossing all the barriers. Every woman from every income bracket, provided she has a closet and a charge card, has a pair of UGGs, so I put them in the category of guilty pleasures. I decided this could be really fun.

We began thinking about how we would carry through, and then for whatever reason Sandra arbitrarily decided to do her own designs and send in the sketches without really going over them with me.

Next thing you know, Josh called me in a panic and said, "You have to come in and fix this." The UGG executives hated what they'd seen.

So I did a set of designs that more effectively captured the Jimmy Choo DNA and sent in the new sketches. Everybody was happy.

To launch the collection, we hired photographer Inez van Lamsweerde to capture Amber Valletta on a motorbike wearing her Jimmy Choo UGGs with cutoff jeans and a vintage leather jacket. Our sales went through the roof that quarter, and £4 million dropped to our bottom line.

The Oscars were by now a regular part of our routine, and we were so well established in Hollywood that we didn't have to push. Managers and stylists would simply come to our hotel suite and pick their shoes. But we'd always done other celebrity gifting throughout the year. I would sit down and say, "Send this to that person," but as the business got bigger, we needed someone to track what the women we wanted associated with our look were up to, and that's when I brought on Amanda Kyme to help us.

We had a list of targeted actresses, and we would try to match the style of the product to the style of the actresses. Our thought was that if they really liked what they received, they were far more likely to talk about it: who's having a baby, who's doing which movie, who's going off to India, what works best with whose personal style. The same concept applied to gifting fashion editors before they went to the shows, trying to ensure that they'd be photographed carrying our latest bag.

But it was not just the marketing of fashion, but fashion itself that was changing. Shoes were no longer just what you bought to compliment the dress; they became a sexy centerpiece of the look. Then again, it was no longer just Manolo Blahnik competing with us in luxury shoes. Dior, Dolce & Gabbana, Prada, and Gucci had caught on. Chanel was repositioning its shoes for the younger woman. Pierre had left Hermès to start his own line, and Diego Della Valle of Tod's had revived the Roger Vivier brand, to be designed by Bruno Frisoni.

Christian Louboutin was the most powerful of these competitors. He had a dozen or so boutiques, all over the world, including space in Harvey Nichols, which had once been all ours.

Department stores like Saks and Bloomingdale's were now devoting entire floors to shoes, and Brown's in London opened an entirely separate store for footwear. More affordable brands like Nine West and Piperlime were also trying to make their presence felt with shoes that were sexy and fun.

Our US business now consisted of twenty-two stores plus the wholesale operation. Brian Henke from Prada was brought in as president of the North American subsidiary. Josh also hired Lisa Bonfante from Chanel to oversee merchandise planning. Buying would now be organized by region. Each of the regional heads would come to Milan every year to see the new collection.

At Halston, we shot a music video of the spring/summer collection to send out to all of the editors, which was actually rather pioneering. We filmed on an outside lot at Pinewood Studios in London, and with winter coming on, the models were all turning blue. I raced home and collected every fur coat I had and brought them in for the girls. I let them use my apartment, I paid for extra models—I did all I could.

· · · ·

THEN RIGHT AROUND VALENTINE'S DAY, my friend and financial adviser Adrian Harris called to give me the grim news that I had just about enough cash to live on for another six weeks.

Before the financial crisis I'd put almost all my available cash into hedge funds, which were now frozen because the funds had put up firewalls to keep investors from withdrawing their money. The £4 million I'd cashed out during the TowerBrook deal was still frozen because of legal disputes with my mother. I was already paying hefty lawyers' bills, and I was expecting those to skyrocket as the showdown approached. I'd just bought the apartment in New York, I was still paying rent in London, and in addition I had moving expenses, plus maintenance expenses on the new place.

I wasn't insolvent, just illiquid, but still, I felt very exposed and uncomfortable with the state of my finances.

What made it all the more galling was that the agent of so much of my misery was the person who had always seemed to relish making me miserable: my mother. Without her narcissistic scheming, I would have had plenty of cash to weather any storm.

I stepped out of my home office feeling dazed, only to find Christian and Minty having a shouting match through her bedroom door.

I think my daughter had been internalizing all the stress around her because she couldn't sleep, and she wanted to come out and be with me, but Christian was camped outside her room, insisting that she get back in bed.

Christian had very traditional views and had set himself up as something of an authority on child rearing, having been instructed on the virtues of "tough love" by the South Carolina girlfriend from his entourage back in L.A. She considered herself an expert because she'd done some babysitting in high school. I don't think his mood was improved by the fact that *My Own Worst Enemy*, his secret agent show, had been canceled in December after nine episodes.

I thought Minty needed cuddling, not isolation, but Christian told me I was being too lenient. I told him to back off and that I had much bigger issues at the moment. That's when I told him what I'd just heard about my finances, which led to a huge fight that I truly didn't need. What I needed was someone to hold me and tell me that it was going to be okay.

The upshot of all this was Christian's announcement that he had to be on his own. His declaration of independence did not, however, stop him from using my car and driver to get to the airport to fly back to L.A.

This was one of the worst moments in my life, and this was the moment Christian chose to walk out on me. I know he resented the long hours I put in at Jimmy Choo, but given the guilt already surrounding the enterprise, you just don't criticize a single mom's mothering. Ultimately, he simply never understood my life, and I suppose I never understood his. But I think the only way it ever works with an actor is to be his nanny.

To make matters worse, the ugly letters from my mother's lawyers did not abate just because the other crises in my life were piling up. In fact, the letters were becoming increasingly vile, with more and more intense bullying and threats. "You'll be on the stand for five days," her lawyer wrote. "Don't think this will be easy."

Given the circus my life had become, it was all I could do to put one foot in front of the other and keep plodding on. For months I would wake up in the middle of the night and have to change my pajamas because they were soaked with sweat. I was in a very dark and danger-ous place, and I'm sure the only thing that saved me was Minty. I was actually kneeling by my bed to pray each night . . . and I'm an atheist.

But at least I had enough sense to reach out for help. For the past couple of years I'd been seeing a therapist named Martin Freeman, who specializes in addictive behaviors. Matthew and I had gone to him back when we were first married. Now I began talking to Martin every day. When we met face-to-face I could see him really taking on all that I was going through, so much so that I worried that I would cause him to have an empathic panic attack. But my sessions with Martin helped me enormously to process and to sort and to gain perspective.

I kept going to work, and I attended all the meetings, and I kept coming up with creative ideas in the design process, and this is where the mask I'd developed so early in life served me well. No one knew just how vulnerable I was—or how much I was dying inside.

Before the six weeks were up I took an advance on the rest of that year's salary, borrowing £100,000 from the company to stay afloat.

I also went to see Richard Pegum, very successful in hedge funds, for a bit of financial advice. He reminded me that I was accruing interest on the millions I'd reinvested in Jimmy Choo and that all that interest was simply rolling over. I should be able to access that, he said.

So I swallowed my pride and I went in and asked Ramez for a loan based on some of my accrued interest. He said no. He said he didn't want Robert to know.

I went back to Richard, who told me to go back to Ramez. "He has to do it. You're his partner. He needs your head in the game. It's the logical thing to do."

So I tried again. With the lawsuit coming up, as well as the move, and not knowing how long the hedge funds would be frozen or how long until TowerBrook made their exit, I asked for £3 million.

Ramez said, "Okay. We'll loan it to you at 20 percent."

My face must have drained of all color, and he must have noticed, because he then tried to laugh off the absurdity of the interest rate.

"My money is expensive," he said.

But he knew full well how much my shares were worth, which was a huge multiple of what I was asking for.

"I've got to justify it to my investors," he told me.

Eventually, we negotiated the rate down to 13.2 percent. We set up a credit line so there would be no interest on any money until I took it out, but still I would be paying $50,000 a month in finance charges. Bottom line: I was loaning the company money at 11 percent and borrowing it back for 13.2.

In the midst of all this, my "glamorous" life representing Jimmy Choo had to go on, which included attending the Oscars. I was in L.A., hosting a lunch at Cecconi's with Valentino and Elton and a bunch of actresses when a FedEx package arrived containing affidavits from Daniel and Gregory. Just when I thought the whole thing couldn't go any lower, my two brothers were basically selling me down the river to please my mother.

My brothers were being led, but there was also a kind of willful naïveté, or wishful—even magical—thinking. As in, "Dad always said everything should be split evenly, so we should get half of whatever Tamara has." But the 64,000 shares at issue had not just "turned up" in my trust. I had put millions at risk to earn those shares, and I'd also signed on to work like a dog. Of course they shouldn't get half of that. They'd already got their half.

Everything they were saying was such gibberish. I kept thinking, all they have to do is explain to my mother how it really works. But no one ever did.

We even sent a memorandum of the Lion deal to Joshua Rubenstein, my mother's lawyer in New York, and he acknowledged that I was right, that my cash, plus the shares attached and stapled to the bond, equaled what my mother cashed out, so the split was fifty-fifty, just as it should have been. But then he was acting for my mother, and under her instructions he was going to ride this dead horse for as long as it would last.

That's when I knew I had to go ahead and get out of London. I simply needed a change.

Before the move to New York could happen, we needed to transfer my employment contract to Jimmy Choo USA. So I had a meeting with

Josh in my office in London and we were discussing how this was all going to work. Are we going to have one assistant in London? One in New York? How would we go back and forth?

I had already planned to stay at a friend's house in St. Bart's over Easter, so even though I was broke, Minty and I went to the islands. She was changing schools, which meant that we were able to spend the whole month together, which was so needed after all the stress and travel and long hours. I still well up with tears when I think about her being at home with no one but a nanny during all this time.

And yet that month in St. Bart's was not pleasant. I had Ramez dangling the loan and meanwhile extorting concessions, I'd run out of money with a court case looming, and I was stressed out of my mind. The only thing that saved me was Minty.

No island is really an island in the age of global communication, and Bonnie called and asked if she could fly out to see me. Nothing had improved with the creative team at Halston, our next "look book" for the fashion editors was terrible, and her relationship with the rest of the staff had started to fray. But ultimately, I just didn't have the bandwidth to deal with it. Every day I was on the phone to my lawyers in the case against my mother, telling them to just get rid of it. Settle. Whatever. I just didn't care anymore.

Then another FedEx package arrived, this time with a document from TowerBrook. Instead of just transferring the language of my previous employment contract to the American company, they'd revised the agreement to include details from my conversation with Josh, now codified before me in fine legalese.

My lawyer, Andrew Roberts, looked it over and said, "Did you know there were going to be all these changes?"

None of the alterations was earthshaking; it was the process that upset me. It was that everything I said was instantly reported back—almost as if my phones were bugged—and then the changes made official without any actual discussion with me. There seemed to be a complete absence of goodwill, and certainly no trust.

I called Ramez and said, "When I was talking with Josh about logistics, I didn't realize I was negotiating a new contract. I'm not signing this."

He responded in typical Ramez fashion: "I'm not sending you the money you want to borrow unless you sign that contract." Ramez was now in a position to make me painfully aware of who was in charge, and he seemed to enjoy doing it in the crudest and most bullying way.

So I was forced to sign an agreement I didn't want to sign in order to take out a loan at an exorbitant rate of interest. Remind you of anyone? I felt like I was in an episode of *The Sopranos*, lucky not to be left in the trunk of a car parked at Newark airport.

. . . .

IT WAS MAY 2 WHEN Minty and I arrived in New York, the day before the Costume Institute's benefit gala at the Metropolitan Museum. People call this "the fashion Oscars," because you have the entire fashion world as well as the younger and more glamorous reaches of Hollywood.

My furniture had arrived, but the apartment was so much bigger, and all the empty space around me seemed to reflect the sense of isolation, of devastation, really, that I felt. I had no network, no support from the office, and I felt a bit like a castaway, clinging to the flotsam and jetsam.

But the show must go on, so the next night I was looking my best and smiling into the cameras as I walked up the red carpet to enter the museum. Thank God my London nanny was there to take care of Minty, and my new assistant came over to help set up the place, guided by my great friend Elika Gibbs, who'd founded a company called Practical Princess to address just this kind of organizational challenge.

Eventually, I was able to extract a bit of money from the hedge funds, and Société Générale used some of it to pay off my loan, but they did it at a terrible exchange rate. This wound up costing me dearly and did nothing to counter my suspicion that, in many areas of banking, finance, and fiduciary stewardship, basic competence is inversely proportional to the rate of pay.

By this time, Nick Morgan was no longer in the picture. My mother had moved the Marqueta Trust from CI Law to RBC Wealth Management, also in Jersey, where she began to work with a new trustee named Mike de Figueiredo. I'd moved Araminta to a different firm, Ogier, where Simon Willing was my trustee.

Martin and I met with de Figueiredo at Claridge's in an attempt to settle, and for a moment I thought we'd have a deal, but he was just as bullying in person as he had been in his lawyer's letters. I had to assume that this was all bluster and that they would capitulate because they were so clearly wrong. But facts had never done much to overcome my mother's profound narcissism and sense of entitlement. I offered to give them half a million simply to get them to go away. They countered with a demand for three of the four million that had been frozen. That I could not abide.

Much of the case would turn on what was said at the shareholders' meeting in November 2004, when we had met in the Jimmy Choo conference room and decided to accept the offer from Lion Capital.

We assembled affidavits from various players, including David Burns, who'd been there, who could be explicit about what had been said, how the deal structure had been explained, and how the proceeds to Marqueta and to Araminta would be equal, the only difference being that Marqueta was taking £22 million in cash, while Araminta was taking an equivalent amount divided between cash and equity. There were no further debts to be settled, no "extra" shares. I also got a statement from Lyndon and from Ramez (though I had to twist his arm), who could speak to what the norms are in such dealings.

As CEO, Robert had, of course, led that November meeting, and my lawyer said to me, "It would be really helpful, you know, if you could get an affidavit from him."

"Oh God." I cringed. "That's going to be *really* difficult."

But I swallowed my pride and I called Robert and we, too, met at Claridge's, and I said, "Listen, I need you to give an affidavit to the court."

He gave me the strangest look, and I said, "All I'm asking you to do is tell the truth."

He took a sip of his champagne. "I'll do that for you," he said, "if you buy my shares for £4 million."

I did not leap to accept his generous offer.

"You know," he said, "this could go the other way. I could give an affidavit for your mother."

I said, "Are you blackmailing me?"

He said, "Call it what you want. That's the deal."

In truth, I would have loved to have bought his shares because I knew they were going to go up in value, but I didn't have the money.

On June 13, 2009, I sent him an e-mail:

> Having reflected on our meeting I have to say I'm really disappointed that you were unwilling to help me in telling the truth, without wanting something in return—maybe it was naive of me to have thought otherwise. However, in principle, I have no problem increasing my stake in the business at a commercially acceptable price, but I cannot respond to your request immediately for a variety of practical reasons, especially the shortage in the amount of meeting time. My deadline for your statement, which we didn't really want to ask you for but my lawyers said would be useful, is this week, Thursday the 2nd of July. If this deadline passes without your cooperation it's hard to see why I should have any motivation in helping to meet your request. So, Robert, I feel that it's really your call as to whether any goodwill can exist between us, to move things forward.

He responded with an e-mail complaining that I'd "trashed" his name and reputation in various interviews. He summed up our relationship this way: "Although there is nothing you can say that can hurt me in the industry, you can understand that all of this hasn't disposed me very favorably toward you."

That summer we did another collaboration with Elton called the PEP Project, an effort to increase awareness of "post exposure prophylactic drugs," that reduce your chance of infection, even after being exposed to the HIV virus. We designed a funky print that had Elton and me on it, the British flag and the American flag, and we put it on shoes, flip-flops, and bags. We raised about £150,000 with that print, but we sold out so quickly, I think we actually underestimated the demand. I wish we could have sold more.

In August Minty and I went to L.A. for a vacation. Tamara Beckwith, who is Minty's godmother, was going to be there and I thought it would be fun to go to Disneyland and be tourists with our kids. One day we were sitting by the pool at the Beverly Hills Hotel, and I was playing in the water with Minty. When I looked up, there was my mother sitting in the café not thirty feet away. She was with a friend, their chairs turned toward me, looking like Bette Davis and Joan Crawford on a stakeout. This was no accident. She'd heard that I was in town. But rather than call up and say, "Please bring Minty by," she chose to spy on me. I ignored her, and she sat there for an hour, and then she went away.

I found it all so terribly sad. She had not seen her granddaughter in six years. Was she secretly hoping that I'd bring Minty over and let her say hello? But then she'd never engaged with Minty any more than she'd engaged with me.

The traffic in e-mails, the discussion of witnesses and affidavits had been consistent for a couple of years, but now it had ramped up, relentlessly.

We ultimately booked court time, and soon the case would proceed to trial.

···· 12 ····

My mother comes from St. Albans, which is a very middle-class suburb of London, comfortable but not rich, where her father had run a construction business. When my mother was still quite young, her mother developed breast cancer and went through a radical mastectomy. I don't know exactly how that affected my mother's early life, but I think it's safe to say that Ann Davis did not have a carefree childhood. I try to take that into consideration, and I know that I'll never be free until I'm able to forgive her for how she treated me, but, as I said at the outset, I'm still working on it. I think my mother was simply born a narcissist whose extraordinary beauty only made her solipsism that much worse. But how solipsism turned to sadism toward me remains a mystery.

It would have been so much simpler to have taken the bad deal that we'd discussed with de Figueiredo, but the feud had cost me too much, not just in terms of lawyers' fees but in terms of lost sleep and ruined health. And now, with the booking of court time and all the attendant costs of preparation, the stakes were escalating into serious money. I felt like a character on the lam in a Western or a gangster film. I had to stop running. It was time for the final showdown.

The proceedings on the island of Jersey were to begin on Monday, the eighth of November, and I flew over from Gatwick the day before. Technically, the case was between RBC, the company that managed my mother's trust, and Ogier, which managed mine.

There was no certainty I'd be allowed into the court—ordinarily those likely to testify are not permitted to listen in until they've made their statement—but I felt compelled to witness every moment of this spectacle. Even though it was very difficult to be away from Minty, I wanted Nick Morgan, the trustee, to see me in court. I wanted to see my mother's face as she tried to justify her claims. And mostly, I wanted to get to the bottom of this. What the hell had been going on with these trusts and my money? Somehow, I think I knew that finding the answer might offer some insight into what had been going on my whole life.

Jersey is like a dreary old people's home, and the weather was grim and blustery as I arrived and checked into the island's only five-star hotel, Longueville Manor, which, despite its pedigree, reminded me far too much of Fawlty Towers.

The weather did not improve during the nearly four weeks I was there, so after breakfast each day a car would pick me up and take me to the rather medieval town square where the high court was located. Happily, the opposing lawyer, Beverley Lacey, an advocate from St. Helier, agreed to let me observe, but otherwise she gave me a very chilly reception.

To offset that lack of warmth, on the first day the usher leaned toward me, extending a small piece of paper. "Ms. Mellon, I wonder if you'd mind signing this for my niece. . . ." It was the receipt for her first pair of Jimmy Choos.

The legal system in Jersey is medieval French. You don't have a jury but rather two upstanding citizens known as jurats, who serve the function of jury, though they decide only on matters of fact, not matters of law.

As I sat and listened to the opening remarks of my lawyer, Anthony Robinson, also from St. Helier, I was impressed by the clarity with which he laid out the issues. This case would revolve around what was discussed at two meetings—the first held to approve the sale of the Phoenix shares to Lion, and the second at the Pelham Hotel to review how the proceeds of that sale were to be distributed between the two family trusts. Also central would be the validity of a certain document, a "declaration of trust" my mother's side claimed gave her clear title to the 32,000 shares misappropriated to her. Once a declaration of trust is signed and stamped by the trustee, it is considered irrevocable.

On our side, we were counting on the elucidation of the financial technicalities and terms of art that were at the heart of the case: the shares, the "deep discount bond" or loan, and the "institutional strip" that represents the shares and was stapled to the loan note. The eight-hundred-pound evidentiary gorilla in the room was the fact that the shares and the loan notes in these transactions were always stapled together *because one was a marker for the other.* This single bit of evidence showed without question that the shares had everything to do with me and my reinvestment in Jimmy Choo, and nothing at all to do with my mother.

In contrast to Tony's mastery of detail, it sounded to me as if my mother's lawyer had no understanding of any of this. She seemed hardly prepared, which made we wonder: Was this some kind of sham to exploit my mother's delusions? A Potemkin village of a case, taken on just for the fees? Which might have helped to explain all the blustering and bullying—they knew all along that they had nothing.

I had asked my therapist, Martin Freeman, to come along with me for the trial, and I think we were both surprised by just how similar the whole experience was to rehab. When you're trying to free yourself from narcotics or alcohol, they regiment the day to help you overcome the chaos of your life. Rehab helps you regain a routine that respects day and night. It forces you to take time for meals and other rituals that provide structure.

On Jersey, the court proceedings were virtually identical from one day to the next. Then each afternoon, after adjournment, Martin and I would go back to the hotel, have a pot of tea, nibble at the shortbread biscuits and smoked salmon that seemed to be the only decent thing on the menu, and spend an hour or two processing both the facts and the feelings. Then I'd have a workout and go to bed.

My mother was the one suing me, so after two days of opening statements and submissions, her witnesses would go first. This is what I wanted to hear: how this elaborate fantasy had been construed, and how my mother had drawn so many other people, including professionals who should have known better, into it.

Raj Patel, the accountant for the trusts, was the first to take the stand. Asking questions from a dozen different angles, Tony Robinson began to scrape away like an archaeologist with a dental pick, gradually revealing each of the artifacts of truth he was looking for. Through that tedious process, he was able to isolate and demonstrate where the lies and the false assumptions were hidden, and to make the solid facts emerge, incontrovertibly, on our side.

Eason Rajah, senior counsel from London, sat behind Tony, slipping him notes from time to time. At the end of proceedings each afternoon, they'd get together to read the transcripts of the testimony so far and to work out the questions for the next day.

It shouldn't be surprising to hear someone speak the truth under oath in a court of law, but right from the start, Raj's admissions were so damaging that I was blown back in my chair. When Tony asked him directly, "Did you make false accounts?" his answer was, "Yes." When Tony asked, "Are these sham accounts?" again, the answer was, "Yes."

My immediate thought was that we should push for criminal prosecution, but Eason advised me not to. "Raj will hide behind Nick," he said.

I could only speculate about how my mother must have worked over Raj, who was not exactly the pick of the litter when it came to accountants, but I can well imagine it all starting with his saying, "Do you realize how much these shares are worth?"

Their greed, or ignorance, willful or otherwise, was then compounded by my mother's delusions, as well as her ability to either charm or intimidate others into accepting her highly idiosyncratic, and egocentric, view of the world. Madness, combined with stunning beauty, gave her an air of certainty and rectitude that certain men had always found difficult to withstand.

"I'm Tom's wife!" I can hear her saying. "You know how much Tom wanted to provide for me."

On Monday, the sixteenth, the next witness to appear was Timothy Gere, who managed investments for us. He had been at both meetings after the Lion deal, but he hid behind confidentiality agreements and revealed very little.

But then on the seventeenth, Nick Morgan took the stand and was grilled for three and a half days.

He managed to maintain a modicum of credibilty, at least for a while. The heart of his testimony dealt with the declaration of trust that assigned the shares to Marqueta. Supposedly this document had been executed on September 5, 2005, but then Tony was able to demonstrate that it had been written much later and backdated. "Oh," Nick said. "The original got lost."

This obvious gap in credibility would all be sorted out later, Beverley Lacey said, by a lawyer who had actually witnessed the signing. I waited eagerly for this bit of testimony.

Adding to the incongruities of Nick's posture was the fact that, at the very beginning, he had been very open about the mistake. Sitting in my lawyer Andrew Roberts's office years before, he'd freely admitted how he'd called my mother to say there's been a mistake and that he was going to have to put the 32,000 shares at issue back in Araminta. We can only imagine her response. "Do that and I'll sue you," is my best guess.

It was on the third day of Nick's testimony that my mother and brothers flew in to give theirs. Though the weather had been grim all along, I couldn't help but notice that just as my mother's plane passed overhead, the skies turned absolutely black and the clouds assembled to disgorge wind and rain. It was like the Wicked Witch appearing in *The Wizard of Oz*.

We had been warned that my mother had made reservations at the Longueville Manor, so we thought, "Well, that's going to be awkward." Beverley Lacey, my mother's advocate, suggested that we move. My response was, "No fucking way. Let my mother get her own hotel."

As a precaution, we did arrange to seal off a lounge as a private sitting room.

The manager said, "That's going to be expensive."

I said, "We can handle it."

Ultimately, my mother chose to stay at another hotel, the Atlantic, so we'd won the first round.

On that first blustery morning after they'd arrived, I was walking across the cobblestone square from Tony's office, he in his long black robes a bit like Harry Potter, when we came upon my mother and brothers in her black Mercedes. I saw the three of them ducking down behind the tinted windows, trying to avoid being seen.

Arriving on the same plane with my mother was Joshua Rubenstein, the trust lawyer from Katten Munchin Rosenman in New York, who had set up Marqueta II to reduce my mother's tax liability during her move to the United States. He was the first witness that next day, and he was presented as the kind of expert on trusts who speaks at all sorts of international conferences.

But he was dancing to my mother's tune. Even the maddest delusions have a right to expert representation.

There's an old lawyer's adage that says, "When the law is on your side, argue the law. When the facts are on your side, argue the facts. When neither the facts nor the law are on your side, attack the other person." Unfortunately, that's the tack that my mother, by way of Mr. Rubenstein, chose to take with me.

He had written an affidavit that was so demeaning to me personally— busloads of men I'd slept with, wild parties I'd attended—that the judge refused to allow it to be read in court. Of course, it was all rubbish provided by my mother. She was utterly shameless about trying to shame me, presenting me to the world as evil, conniving, and utterly immoral. And how lovely it is to have your own mother portraying you as a slut in a public dispute.

With character assassination disallowed on the stand, the main line of argument in Rubenstein's testimony shifted to my supposed insta-bility. Fortunately, Tony was brilliant in cross-examination: Exactly how many times have you met with Ms. Mellon? For how long? And how do you come to this assessment of instability? Is that a judgment based on some professional qualification?

Rubenstein kept dodging the "how do you know this?" questions by saying, "It's my opinion." Tony responded brilliantly: "Given that you are not privy to the sort of factual background," he admonished, "do you not feel uncomfortable in having sworn an affidavit in this court advancing these theories? You are a professional man. You are a lawyer, Mr. Rubenstein. All the court requires of you is for you to express in a neutral fashion your understanding of the facts. Not venture your opin-ion based on hearsay information from Mr. Morgan or Mrs. Yeardye, which may have got twisted in the telling. Do you still feel comfortable with this?"

Rubenstein replied, "I feel comfortable that that is my opinion as to what happened."

My mother had brought Daniel and Gregory to testify against me, but when they took the stand she repaired to a café across the street. It was a bit like throwing her sons to the wolves.

As I listened to Daniel answer the advocate's questions, I couldn't help thinking about all the times I'd paid for him to go to rehab and how I'd bought him a car when he first moved to L.A. And then I thought about the time when he'd relapsed and kicked my mother out of her own house, refusing to let her back in, so that she had to go stay with a friend for three or four days.

And then there was the image of Gregory, having to share a room with her for six months at the Peninsula because she was too cheap to pay for an extra, and he was too much of a weakling to move out. He'd had a date one night, and when he got back she threw a fit, screaming and flinging all the wooden coat hangers at him, *Mommie Dearest* style.

Why they'd never found the wherewithal to escape from her clutches and live their own lives, I don't know. They were both big guys, well over six feet, and here they were in the thirties, still clinging to their mother's skirts.

I remember Daniel saying much earlier, "It's so unfair. It was my turn next when he died," by which he meant that it was his turn next for Dad to "make him successful." What they've never understood is that someone can invest money in your idea and give you some guidance, but you still have to come up with the idea, and then you have to get off your ass and execute it. This means years of hard work that no one, neither your mother nor your father, can ever do for you.

My brothers' testimony harped on the fact that my father wished for the investment income from Jimmy Choo to be split fifty-fifty. Tony's counter was: Right. No one is disputing a fifty-fifty split. The issue is what constitutes fifty-fifty? You've already got your fifty! Remember that £22 million that showed up in the account?

But then they kept repeating the mantra of "extra" shares, as if someone had found a few pennies under the sofa cushions. Against all evidence, they could never quite comprehend that the shares they were calling "extra" had indeed appeared after the sale but not because they had been overlooked. They appeared after the sale because they emerged as the result of a new transaction that had absolutely nothing to do with Phoenix, or with my mother, or with them. I had reinvested my money in the new company being set up by Lion. The 64,000 shares at issue represented that new and entirely separate investment.

It was just not that difficult to understand, unless there was a demonic intelligence at work trying to make if difficult.

I was too exhausted to fly home for the weekend, but my pal Elika Gibbs came over to lend moral support and also to see the fireworks and the freak show.

The big event was to come on Monday when my mother would be the first witness on the stand. But having heard how her sons had fared none too well, she seemed to falter in her commitment to her delusions.

Elika and I were sitting in the courtroom, waiting for the trial to resume, when Rob Gardner, a vital part of our Jersey legal team, came out and said, "Can we have a word?"

I nodded, waiting to hear what he had to say.

"They'd like a conference. They want to give it one more try to settle."

Tony and I agreed, so then the lawyers began trying to find a room with a big enough table for all of us to crowd around.

A few minutes later both teams were assembled in full. On one side were my lawyers and trustees, Martin, and myself. On the other were Beverley Lacey, Mike de Figueiredo, Gregory (Daniel was disallowed for some reason), and, at long last, looking exquisite in a Chanel suit of black-and-white boucle wool—my mother.

I hadn't seen her up close in four years, and she looked amazing. Everyone ages, so God knows what she'd been doing to retard the process. Then again, that's how she spends all her time.

Everyone held their breath through a long silence, waiting for her to speak, but somehow she couldn't even look at me. She sat with arms and legs crossed defensively, lips pursed, almost pouting as she looked away. She appeared profoundly uncomfortable because this was a situation in which she had no control. I studied her face, but once again I don't know what I was looking for. From my earliest moments I'd always looked for some sign of love, or even acceptance, but I had never received anything from this woman but pain.

Ms. Lacey started off the meeting with a rather saccharine introduction, talking about herself and her children. Obviously my mother had worked her over with the usual "my ungrateful child," and "my daughter's so terrible." Martin said, "Don't go there. This is not family therapy."

But actually the confrontation was far better than therapy. I'm sure, to everyone else, my mother seemed perfectly composed, but I had a visceral sense of her rage, and yet I wasn't turning back. I was facing down my most profound demon, and it was not through anodyne transference or by reconstructing childhood memories on the artificial stage of a therapist's consulting room. I was actually confronting the real person, here and now.

Right off the bat Gregory said, "Can we stop? I want to talk to Tamara."

Certainly I was open to that, so he and I stepped outside the building and we each lit a cigarette.

There was an awkward moment, the two of us standing on the courthouse steps in a bleak November drizzle. I broke the ice by saying, "I understand the monster you're dealing with."

I could see his eyes well up. He'd written his affidavit in February, and now it was November, and seeing me seemed to soften his stance. "This is crazy," he said. "I don't want this. I don't care about the money."

He looked down and then shook his head. "What a cunt," he said.

I had to laugh. Neither of us ever used this word, but it was the only one that would do. "Yeh," I said. "What a fucking cunt."

It was a moment of sharing, a verbal bond like our use of "the House of Pain" to refer to wherever she was living.

We went back in and Gregory said, "I don't want to talk anymore. Let Tamara have everything."

But that was a bit further than Ms. Lacey was willing to go.

We hemmed and hawed a bit, and then de Figueiredo made his offer: Drop the suit and use the £4 million that had been frozen to cover everyone's legal fees.

Our side went into another room to discuss this new proposal. But it took all of about thirty seconds for us to come to "This is nonsense. Let's get on with it." Our case was going well, and this offer was a step backward. Why should we stop now?

As we left that meeting, Martin turned to me and said, "This is the first time I've really understood what you've been dealing with. My God, Tamara. I think your mother is a sociopath."

My eyes widened as I took a deep breath.

Laypeople throw around psychological labels all too freely, but in this moment Martin was speaking quite literally, and as a professional.

I returned to my seat in the courtroom beside Elika, and once again we waited for the proceedings to resume. Then my mother walked in and was immediately called to the stand.

"She does look good," Elika said. "I hope these old dogs aren't going to be fooled by this."

The fundamental issue of my mother's testimony dealt with whether or not all the details of the sale from Phoenix to Lion had been properly explained to her when we met in November 2004 to approve the transaction. She was claiming that she'd been left in the dark and that if she'd understood matters more fully, she might have made a different choice between cashing out and reinvesting. In reality, of course, she was never offered that choice—not because I had concealed anything, but because Lion wanted to clean house.

Tony presented into evidence a copy of Nick's agenda for that November meeting, and on it were the trustee's copious notes, showing in excruciating detail just how carefully all the points had been explained.

Tony also introduced the fax I'd sent to my mother in California setting out all the options, such as they were, including the fact that rolling over her equity was probably not going to be possible.

As she was walked through this evidence page by page, she seemed dismayed by the law's insistence that what mattered were the facts, and that neither her wishes nor her grudges nor her beauty held any sway. She kept saying, "I'm the chairman's wife," as if that explained every-thing, and that this prestige position entitled her to allocate the spoils as she saw fit.

When it came time for her comments about me, she pivoted to what she thought the judge would want to hear, what would be expected of a "good mother." In so doing she went off script, saying, "I'm proud of my daughter. She's worked hard for what she has." She didn't seem to understand how praising me undermined her case, and certainly con-tradicted all the slander she'd tried to introduce by way of Joshua Rubenstein.

In truth she seemed utterly bewildered. She was looking to others to confirm the voices in her head, meanwhile playing the part of el-derly, vulnerable, victimized, but always loving mother. In a context she can control, my mother can come off rather well, even when she doesn't have a clue what's going on. But here she had run the fantasy of injustice into the ground.

Normal people are confined by the independent reality of the other individuals around them, which is very useful. A normal concern for others narrows the boundaries of your imagination and reins in any lurking pathology.

My mother thought of me as a hypochondriac. She had always said that I was the one who was crazy, that I was imagining things, and that all the awful things I attributed to her were simply a reflection of my own immaturity. But here an actual judge in a court of law was seeing my mother looking so perfectly put together while at the same time being completely out of it. It was like Gloria Swanson at the end of *Sunset Boulevard*, perfectly groomed and staring into the police lights, saying, "I'm ready for my close-up, Mr. DeMille." It was the madwoman revealed, and the perfect cliché climax for a courtroom battle.

After my mother left the stand there was little more to say, but then, as if merely to complete the farce, Ms. Lacey produced the solicitor, previously announced, who was said to have witnessed the signing of the declaration of trust. Only he looked like he'd been dragged out of a hedge. This man, too, was no longer a lawyer and as he sat before the court, a large portion of his suit jacket was actually ripped off at the shoulder and hanging down. This lawyer from the hedge maintained that he'd witnessed the signing, but then on cross examination he admitted that, technically, he'd "witnessed" it without actually being present.

If it hadn't been costing me millions of dollars, the farce would have been quite entertaining. But I didn't know whether to laugh or cry.

I was physically and emotionally exhausted, but so far, we'd heard only my mother's witnesses. Tony would begin to present our case in the morning.

My mother and brothers took a flight back to London, and Martin and I repaired to the Longueville Manor for our usual session of "facts and feelings" in our private sitting room.

At around five p.m. Mike de Figueiredo called and asked if he could come over. We got Tony's approval, and it was around seven when Mike showed up. I will admit we kept him waiting a bit. Martin added another note of censure by refusing to shake his hand.

We sat down and the trustee tried to put a brave face on it, never admitting how he'd made a real dog's dinner out of it. He approached our discussion with a combination of bluster and evident fear that I was going to press on to the bitter end.

He said, "It's not over yet, you know. You'll still be in the witness stand for days."

I said, "I'm fine with that."

He was grasping for face-saving straws, all the while hinting at what he'd really come to say.

"Can't you give me anything? What if you leave some money in trust for Minty?"

"That's where I started years ago," I said.

Finally, he came to the point: They were folding. "We're going to withdraw," he said. "You take the money that's owed you, and each side will cover our own legal fees."

I didn't leap to accept. I could still fight on in the hope of getting a judgment against them that would require them to pay my fees. But I was just sick of the whole thing. Accepting this offer would spare me another ten days in Jersey, and my £4 million would be released without claim. And given all the absurdities so far, there was no guarantee that, if we pressed on, we'd prevail.

Tony advised us to accept, and we agreed to sign an agreement the next morning.

That evening, Martin and I looked up the definition of "sociopath," and as I read all the characteristics of the diagnosis, my mother ticked every box. For added clarity, Martin rang up his friend Dr. Marco Procopio, a consultant psychiatrist, and asked him to comment. What he had to say rang all too true: "A sociopathic personality disorder is the only personality disorder in which the individual with it experiences no suffering. Instead, all the suffering is experienced by those around them."

Amid all this family drama, packages of sketches had continued to arrive from London, and I found it hard to believe I was sitting in a hotel room in Jersey trying to make decisions about shoes and bags. I'm normally pretty good at categorizing and compartmentalizing, but everywhere I looked there was confusion, chaos, and betrayal.

The whole trial had been like the distortion of addictive behavior transposed onto the real world. Addiction consumes space. If you have space, you can begin to see details more accurately and sort through them. But addiction wants to keep you preoccupied with acting out or other compulsions that make reality a blur.

When I walked into the conference room the next morning Beverley was there, and she and I looked at each other and burst out laughing. It was the release of anxiety from pure embarrassment. That's how absurd their case had been. And that's when I noticed she'd come with a Jimmy Choo handbag.

Half the £4 million I recovered went for lawyers' fees, but for me it was the principle. I didn't want my mother to steal from me or my daughter. And I simply had to do something to expunge her toxic influence from my life.

We filed legal proceedings against Nick and his company for recovery of the fees. Eventually we reached a settlement and recovered a substantial sum for part of the costs, although there were no admissions of liability. A professional complaint against Raj Patel for producing the false accounts is still under way.

As happened in rehab, when the evidence is overwhelming, sometimes people at last face the truth. There was no question that I had won, but there was no joy in demolishing my mother in a courtroom. That's simply not the kind of relationship I wanted to have with the person who was supposed to be my nearest and dearest relative. She did exit my body, though. Before the trial in Jersey I used to feel her in my chest all the time, but now that constriction was gone. After forty years we were at last severed. With my money finally under my own control, and with her money no longer invested in my enterprise, there was no more basis for extortion or manipulation.

I was the last one standing, but as I emerged onto those courthouse steps on that gray November day, it was nothing like Rocky Balboa dancing exultantly with arms raised after running up the steps of that museum in Philadelphia. There was no cheering crowd, no sense of exuberance or celebration. I could see nothing but wreckage all around, and I felt empty and alone.

The one silver lining behind all the clouds was that the collaboration with H&M had just appeared in the stores. Coming back to the dismal Longueville Manor on the dismal island of Jersey, I turned on the television and saw lines of people outside the shops. In fact, they'd started lining up at three or four in the morning with sleeping bags. The entire collection sold out within twenty-four hours. H&M said it was the most successful collaboration they'd ever done.

···· 13 ····

For years before the case in Jersey, I'd been having massive anxiety attacks and night sweats. With the trial behind me and even with a positive resolution, none of that went away. In fact, my symptoms ratcheted up to suggest true posttraumatic stress. I couldn't sleep. I was so distracted that it could take me hours to dress. I couldn't make decisions or stand to be with people.

After all the storm and stress, I felt it was time for a lark, and it was during this dark period that Karl Templar, the art director of *Interview* magazine, rang me up and said, "We'd love to do a feature with you." He added, "You look like you're in such great shape. How about doing the photo nude?"

I thought the suggestion rather cheeky, but I'd already nearly bared my all for "4 Inches."

"We could get Terry Richardson to shoot," he went on. "A Jimmy Choo bag or whatever placed strategically. What do you think?"

I thought that having a nude taken while I was young and fit, by one of the best photographers in the world, with one of the best stylists in the world, was an offer that was not going to come around again.

I said yes.

I did the interview, posed for the photo lying on my back with my

Jimmy Choos, a cigarette, and a cat, and then I went to St. Bart's for the holidays. Unfortunately, the residual anxiety from the past few months came with me. I'd feel it when I woke up, and then it would build throughout the day. I was like the survivor of a near-miss car crash. You drive on, and then afterward, when the excitement and danger have passed, you start to shake.

Through the winter into spring, each month was worse than the one before.

At Easter, at Diane von Furstenberg's home on Harbour Island in the Bahamas, Matthew married Nicole Hanley, formerly a stylist at Ralph Lauren. They'd been together for quite a while, and I was very happy for them. In fact, they'd launched a fashion line together, Hanley Mellon, in 2008. Now Minty would get to be a bridesmaid, and soon she would have some half siblings to be a part of her life.

I was very keen on surrounding my daughter with as rich a fabric of friends and family as I could, and the reason why was impressed on me very dramatically just a few days after the wedding. I was in London, and I couldn't get home for Minty's birthday party because a volcano erupted in Iceland, stranding me and millions of others in clouds of volcanic ash. It was a good lesson in humility. When there's an act of God of that magnitude, it really doesn't matter whether you're in first class or coach, or you have your own plane. You're not going anywhere.

. . . .

JIMMY CHOO NOW HAD 115 stores and was represented in thirty-nine countries, but the economy was still struggling to come back. In 2009, Josh came up with the idea of relaunching our House Collection, renaming it 24:7, adding new styles and putting some serious ad money behind it. This meant putting more emphasis on the bottom of the pyramid as far as our collection was concerned, so he wasn't sure that I'd go along. But I said, "Let's do it."

The effort was a huge success, and it triggered an enormous growth spurt, pushing our EBITDA up from £13.5 million in 2006 to £50 million in 2011.

The downside of this explosion in growth was that our owners became greedy, and they began pushing us to improve our margins. They told us we could no longer use leather that cost more that 30 euro a square meter. But luxury brands should only use top-grade leather, which costs at least 50 euro a square meter. They pushed our factories to lower their prices, but they have to make money, too, so they were forced to use cheaper materials and otherwise cut corners in the manufacturing process.

This meant that our 24:7 shoes simply didn't have the perfect fit we were known for, and the brand overall was losing its fashion-forward edge. Now, 80 percent of Jimmy Choo's business comes from 24:7.

Alvaro was still designing marvelous bags, but then we'd have a side meeting with merchandising, after which I'd see that the quality was less than we'd initially specified. None of this stopped the product from selling—to the uninitiated it still "looked" like Jimmy Choo—but to me, what we were beginning to produce wasn't my idea of who we were. I feared we were becoming just another big commercial enterprise.

From Italy, Anna saw the decline in the manufacturing specs being approved. Through her brother Massimo she sent me the message "It's the beginning of the end."

The most important part of a luxury brand is innovation, creativity, and quality, but the bean counters that now controlled our destiny gave merchandising too large a voice. They always tend to look backward and then ask for new versions of old styles. But even when you're paying homage to vintage designs, you have to add that certain spark because fashion keeps moving on. To that point, a cleaner look had supplanted our distinctive hardware, but our merchandising people were afraid to go with the trend.

Their rearview focus became terribly frustrating for me, and then some of the newer people couldn't properly navigate the boundary between sexy and trashy. Jimmy Choo had always had an element of rock and roll, but it was never campy or tacky.

At Halston, Bonnie "borrowed" the House Collection concept to launch a vintage line she called Halston Heritage. This would be the Halston classics, but at a lower price point. The fact remains that there were just far too many conflicting visions for what Halston should be doing. I had too much on my plate at Jimmy Choo to contribute effectively, so I ended my relationship with Halston, though I did hold on to my shares.

At Jimmy Choo, the greatest surge of creativity often came toward the end of the design process for each collection. Eventually, we found a way to capture this surge, putting together a collection of special pieces called Catwalk, which consisted of these late-breaking inspirations, which we would sell slightly after the main collection. The buyers would have placed their bulk order already, but then they'd come back a few weeks later to buy Catwalk—the 10 percent of their buy that was really fashion forward.

Green shoots had been coming up in the marketplace for the past year or so, the mergers and acquisitions business had come back, and there seemed to be some movement in private equity. Soon enough TowerBrook was actively planning for yet another sale. But very quickly Ramez made it clear that he wanted me to stay out of it.

"Don't worry," he said. "We'll get you your money."

In the summer of 2010, we hit gold when Madonna was spotted coming out of a restaurant carrying the Jimmy Choo Blythe Leopard-Print Pony Hair Satchel. The publicity was worth millions.

About the same time I got a letter from the prime minister's office. "You're not allowed to tell anyone," it said, "but the Queen is awarding you an Order of the British Empire [OBE] for your contribution to the fashion industry." They suggested two dates in October for a ceremony at Buckingham Palace, and they asked me to pick one.

When my OBE was reported in the media, I got an e-mail from Ramez saying, "Bravo!"

A few weeks later, in August 2010, Ramez rang me up in the Hamptons to say, "We're selling without you."

I'd known this was coming. It was the same old story. In every transaction, my partners tried to sell the company without me, and then every time the buyer demanded that I be part of the deal.

Ramez actually told me that his plan was to tell potential buyers, "We've bottled the essence of Tamara, and now we can operate without her."

This, of course, played into the finance guy's theory, or fantasy, of how businesses work, which is that no one person is all that important and that all it takes is shrewd management, not a certain level of taste or a vision for the product, to make a company great. To which I would respond: Tell that to Steve Jobs.

Private equity simply doesn't want any one personality to have power, especially not someone on the creative side, because creativity threatens them by being unpredictable, and thus uncontrollable. As a result they fear it, and they try to diminish its status.

For all their attempts to throw me under the bus, the irony remained that I was the only individual who had her own money in the game. TowerBrook talked about "owning" the business, but they were just a vague collective that risked other people's investments and leveraged debt. Ramez had screamed out more than once, "I own this company, not Tamara!" But he had no visceral connection, either in terms of real, personal risk or in terms of concern for the product.

Shortly after the rather abrupt announcement from Ramez, Josh called me up to go over some plans for the year ahead, and somehow in that conversation I let slip, "Look, I might not even be here in a year."

Almost immediately I got another call from Ramez. Apparently Josh had called him up in a panic, and now Ramez was trying to smooth the waters all round. He was conciliatory, but he made it clear that as we approached the next sale, I was to remain decorative and silent.

. . . .

NOVEMBER WAS MY TIME FOR affirmations. I flew to New York to receive an Enduring Vision Award from the Elton John AIDS Foundation. Then I flew to London for my moment with the Queen.

I stayed at the Ritz, and I was very moved that David and Frederick Barclay, the owners, and old friends of my dad's, were on hand to wish me well. They were very sweet to Minty, telling her how proud her grandfather would have been.

I've never felt intimidated by the pressure to look a certain way, but if there ever was a quintessential moment for "looking one's best," it would be while appearing before the Queen as a representative of the British fashion industry. I faced the challenge in a vintage-looking Dolce & Gabbana polka-dot dress with a fur collar, and a large, black fedora.

I also invited my old friend Mark Bolland to accompany me. Now a major figure in public relations, Mark had once been deputy private secretary to Prince Charles, so he knew a thing or two about conducting oneself properly. He was the one who improved the prince's public image after Diana was killed, recasting him as a strong father for William and Harry, working out ground rules with the press to protect the boys' privacy, then getting a reluctant British public to accept Camilla Parker Bowles.

With a bit of moral support from Mark, I simply followed the rules, and where the Queen is concerned they make it very clear exactly what the rules are. The palace staff provides quite a bit of coaching, but, after all, I'd learned to curtsy at finishing school.

There's a line of people offstage who are being given the award, and one person is led out at a time. You have to go up and bow or curtsy, and the Queen puts a medal on you. She, of course, has someone behind her whispering in her ear, telling her who you are. As she handed me the award she leaned forward and said, "I hear you make shoes."

I said, "Yes, mum. And bags, too."

Then I shuffled away backward because you can't turn your back on the Queen.

After the ceremony I took the Jimmy Choo team to lunch at Scott's, and then that night I had a bit of a bash at the Savoy. It was short notice, but Nick Rhodes from Duran Duran was there, as was Philip Green from Topshop and Valentino, as well as Elizabeth Hurley and Elle Macpherson. I had to invite Ramez as a courtesy.

I gave a little speech in which I thanked everyone for coming. I said, "As you're all aware, my father died not long ago, our family has fallen apart, and I just want you to know that everyone who's here to celebrate this with me tonight will be etched in my memory forever."

There was a board meeting the next day, and Ramez was gracious enough to compliment the "human quality" of my speech. During the applause, Robert walked out of the room.

One of the agenda items at that meeting was the opening of a new store at Fifty-First and Fifth, and the need to refurbish others. Tower-Brook's response was, "That's not going to pay off during our time horizon" so they declined to make the investment. They still cared nothing about the long-term health of the business or the actual quality of the product. The only thing they cared about was protecting their EBITDA.

By this time we all understood their narrow focus perfectly well, but to actually admit to this tunnel vision in front of the management team—that's what was shocking to me. For the actual managers, Jimmy Choo was their career and their daily bread, and they not only loved the company, they couldn't possibly do their jobs without thinking about growth and innovation. And then on top of it all, to be told by their board, "We're simply running in place, waiting to cash out. Oh, but the rest of you . . . steady on! Really push yourselves!"

Our board, of course, was ten guys in suits and me. I'd tried to bring in Kris Thykier, the partner in Matthew Freud's hugely powerful public relations group, but they wouldn't have it. They had to be in control. Kris critiqued us once, saying that we needed to coordinate more. I passed along this assessment to Josh, who said that he agreed completely. The change had a huge impact on the business. Which suggests the kind of massive impact Kris could have had if TowerBrook had allowed him on the board.

Then, as if to add insult to my partners' perceived injury, the prime minister's office contacted me yet again, this time asking if I would accept a position of trade envoy for Great Britain. Of course I said yes, and the *Daily Mail* used the announcement as an excuse to reprint the nude picture from *Interview*. I think the combination of official honors and tabloid notoriety must have driven the TowerBrook boys absolutely nuts.

The responsibilities of a trade envoy are to go overseas to encourage investment in Britain and to educate British businesses about overseas opportunities and how to go about mastering them.

My first trip was to China to help introduce British brands to the Chinese market and British products to Chinese buyers. Our team was a diverse bunch, ranging from me in fashion to someone who designed airplane engines for Rolls-Royce. We would invite local businesses and do a presentation for Asprey, Aston Martin, Liberty, and so on, each of which had a representative along on the trip. We met with the mayor of Beijing and went to the opening of the design center. Later, I would speak at conferences in Brazil and in London to help entrepreneurs prepare for success. In New York I did a "British fashion" shoot with Anna Wintour and Victoria Beckham.

. . . .

BY NOW WE WERE BACK in our "repetition compulsion" of meeting with Goldman Sachs and Morgan Stanley to discuss the next sale. Like any other form of addiction, once you're hooked on private equity, you can't change the destructive behavior. You just plug in new people, one cycle imposing itself on the other.

For me, facilitating due diligence had become a tiresome second job. Meanwhile, our competition wasn't necessarily going through the same kinds of distraction and could focus on the real work of creating and maintaining quality and innovation.

Akeel at Rothschild wanted to handle the sale but Ramez didn't want to work with him because of past history. Funny enough, even though Akeel had taken up arms in Robert's conspiracy in the sale to TowerBrook, I thought he would have been the best person to represent us. He understood what we were all about, and I think he would have been able to extract the most value.

TowerBrook thought Morgan Stanley would do a better job, but they also wanted to keep favor with Goldman Sachs. In the end they found a way to work with both, having the two banks work together and split the fees. The transaction wasn't going to move the needle much for either firm, but it was a nice, glamorous, high-profile sale, and even the finance sector was still climbing out from the collapse of 2008.

We had no problem stirring up interest among buyers. We asked for first bids in March, and the players making bids ranged from Labelux (partnered with Investcorp), Texas Pacific Group (TPG), to KKR (Kohlberg Kravis Roberts), to Carlyle, to Li & Fung. Final offers would be evaluated in May.

I flew to London and stayed at the Ritz for ten days of dog and pony shows, which we held at Brown's on Dover Street. We presented to Labelux on April 13, to Jones Group on the fourteenth, and to TPG on the twentieth. Tom Barrack, a friend of mine who owns Colony Capital and bought Miramax from Disney, called a friend of his, David Bonderman, TPG's founding partner. Bonderman's personal wealth was estimated at $3 billion, and it was said that he never left the United States. But at Tom's suggestion, David came to our London presentation, and it was the talk of the town when he showed up.

From that first round three suitors emerged—Labelux (sans Investcorp), Jones Group, and TPG. Stupidly, though, Ramez and our bankers didn't check the Jones Group's balance sheet to see if they actually had the resources to play at this level, which they didn't. So when we actually got to the auction in May, we had only two bidders, which is an exponentially weaker position than having three.

I was secretly rooting for Labelux, who had first contacted me in the summer of 2008. They're not private equity but a luxury holdings group, owned by the Reimann family, whose über fund, Joh. A. Benckiser, had been in business since 1823. They owned Coty, and they'd recently acquired Bally, and I saw them as owners who might take an interest in the brand beyond how its EBITDA would look in two and a half years. But again, Ramez didn't want me to speak to anyone. He needed to be in control, and he feared that I might make demands that would put off a buyer or affect the selling price.

Whenever I was so reckless as to voice an opinion, Ramez would call me at home and scream at me. "I'm pulling this deal," he'd say. "You need the money and I don't."

But the fact is I was liquid again. I'd won the court case with my mother, I'd lost only about 10 percent on the hedge funds, and their firewalls were now coming down, which allowed me access to my money. More to the point, I had petitioned Ogier, the trustee for Araminta, to dissolve that trust so that I would have free access to that money as well. This was not something they were obligated to do, but because I'd built the wealth, rather than having inherited it, they agreed.

I was able to remain very calm and tell Ramez, "Okay, don't sell if you don't want to."

But I called Ron Perelman and asked him what to make of Ramez's threats. He said, "Forget it. He's way too pregnant with this deal. He's not pulling out. He's just grandstanding. Trying to bully you."

"Keep your eye on the prize" was Ramez's mantra, as if a big payoff was the only goal. But I actually cared about the business we were in. The product. The people. I wasn't merely passing through. I'd rather pay people properly than see them burned out, crying in the office, and saying "I can't take it anymore," even if it meant I would make less on my investment.

We were getting closer to the endgame, with the pressure increasing, when I called Ramez and said, "I want you to know I've hired some people to come in and negotiate on my behalf."

He went nuts. "I don't want anyone you hire coming in and screwing up my deal!"

When we were able to speak in more civil tones, I said, "It's highly unlikely that my guy will 'screw up' your deal. He just negotiated the three-billion-dollar acquisition of Tommy Hilfiger."

"You don't trust me," Ramez whimpered. "You don't think I'll get you a good deal."

The fact of the matter was I firmly believed that "a good deal" for me wasn't even at the bottom of his list of considerations. Every time I'd brought up any issues about how the management team was to be compensated, I was silenced, if not literally shouted down.

Toward the end of the conversation Ramez admitted, "Well, I suppose you do have the right to protect yourself."

The adviser I brought in was Joe Lamastra, who for fifteen years had co-invested in various projects with Tommy Hilfiger and overseen all his business, real estate, and tax matters.

Labelux, through Akeel, had been trying to contact me, but for the longest time I honored my commitment to have no side conversations with any of the bidders. I wouldn't even call them back, but after a while I said, "Fuck it. Ramez is throwing me under the bus as usual. So all bets are off. I'm going to take up my issues with Peter Harf."

Harf was the chairman of Labelux, and when I called about a meeting, he offered to book the restaurant. I said, "No. I don't want to be seen in public together."

So he took a hotel room instead, at the Mark, between Fifth and Madison on the Upper East Side, and he had the bed removed and a table for two brought in with waiters coming and going, and it was one of the weirdest dinners I've had in my entire life.

I talked to him about why I'd launched the brand, tried to describe my passion for it, and tried to explain that, while I wanted to make money, I also cared deeply about the business. And then I made my proposition.

"No one will buy this brand without me," I said. "I'll tell TowerBrook that I'll only do a deal with Labelux, which will get you the business. But there are certain things I want."

"I'm all ears," he said.

"My life is in the States now," I told him. "I live in New York with my daughter, and her father lives here as well, and I think it's not unreasonable to move some of our operations to New York as well."

He said, "We're all worldly, sophisticated people. That's a nonissue."

Then he went offtrack a bit, probing for information that was more strategic. "There's only one other bidder, right?"

He wasn't supposed to know that, but obviously he had his spies. I said, "No, not really. There's another."

The fact was this third player was not in the same league as the other two. Investcorp had come in initially, then dropped out. But then they called Ramez and said, "If you do an IPO [rather than another sale], we'll come in and buy one hundred million pounds equity pre-IPO."

I let that information settle, and then I said, "I want to have more equity in the business. So I'd like you to loan me $25 million, which I'll pay back with interest on the exit."

Harf looked at me, then asked, "How much money have you made so far?"

I told him, and then he said, "You're rather rich for a woman. Why do you need more?" He saw my face blanch, and he tried to cover. "Well, rather rich for anyone, really," he said.

But I thought it was one of the dumbest, most sexist comments I've ever heard an intelligent person make.

Then he fumbled and mumbled.

I said, "Well, if you won't loan it to me, I'll find it elsewhere."

And he said, "Where will you get it?"

I said, "I have friends."

So he agreed, or at least he gave me the impression that he agreed, summing up our conversation with, "You'll be very happy with your compensation."

With that assurance, I walked out feeling really great. I called Martin and told him how good I felt. "You know that feeling in films where people punch the air?" I said. "I feel like I can work with these people."

During the second round of bidding, in May, I met with Josh at the Jimmy Choo offices, and a simple comment from me triggered the only fight we ever had.

By now we were both totally exhausted and overwhelmed by the stress of the exit process, which consumes every ounce of energy. But no one had consulted me, and I had to make my concerns known.

I said, "One of my conditions is going to be that part of the office will move to Manhattan," never expecting that it was going to tip Josh over the edge.

I knew the business plan had been written the way that Tower-Brook wanted to present it, which was nothing more than financial engineering to elicit maximum value. Any curveball from me, such as moving the office to New York, would be a capital expenditure large enough to affect EBITDA, and therefore the purchase price.

"Be honest," I said. "You want to move back to New York. You told me so. So why are you pushing back now?"

Of course I knew the reason. He was just doing his job. But even as an investor I was more than willing to go off plan and restructure for the long-term benefit of the company. I certainly didn't care about TowerBrook's fees and their "carried interest" tax advantages. I didn't care about TowerBrook because they didn't care about the business or the people in it. To me they were nothing more than another pack of private-equity vultures just passing through, trying to pick off for themselves everything they could.

The final bids were due May 13, and Labelux came in at £550 million. TPG bid £475 million. Narrowing the gap, Labelux added £25 million in deductions for costs they said they were going to have to absorb.

But Labelux was the clear winner, and now we had nine days for one-on-one meetings between our management and our new partners to be. Even so, TowerBrook insisted that I not speak to anyone from Labelux without one of their bankers present. So effectively, I was still being quarantined, prevented from voicing my concerns about a move to New York and about the financial package for management.

Our team had worked far too hard to be thrown to the wolves, and I was dismayed by the way the lawyer representing the management team rolled over on every issue. I e-mailed Josh and said that I didn't understand her position, because he was going to be financially damaged just like everyone else. And the deal on the table was absurd. Management could invest their own money, the shares would run for ten years, but nothing would become vested until five years down the road. You could pull out before then, but you'd realize no gain in value.

Even if you waited to cash out until your shares were fully vested, they'd organized the structure so that these management shares were taxed as income rather than as capital gains. This was cheaper for the business, but it would cost each individual from 20 to 30 percent.

I asked him to be a more forceful advocate, while I hired KPMG on the side to do a study to show how they could structure the management equity plan as capital gains.

Given all the screaming I'd had to endure, Joe Lamastra, my adviser, decided that keeping me away from Ramez was not a bad idea. Anyone who wanted to talk to me would have to do it through him.

So Ramez had his deputy, a decent fellow named Kareem, call Joe and ask for a meeting.

Joe said, "She's not coming if you're going to bully her."

They promised to be on their best behavior, and so, with very low expectations, I took a car to the TowerBrook offices at the bottom of Haymarket.

The moment I walked in Ramez launched a vicious, verbal attack about my wanting to move the office. He was pounding the table with his fist as people began to arrive for a second meeting, and Joe looked on, appalled.

I could barely focus, thinking, "I can't believe we're having to go through all this again."

Joe and I started to leave, but there was a scrum of people, and unbeknownst to Joe, Ramez pulled me aside. "We need to have a word."

I was still so upset with him that I walked away, heading down the hallway to the lift to go downstairs. Just as the door was closing, this foot jammed in to make the door reopen.

"Oh, God," I thought. "More torture and I'm trapped in a little metal cube."

"I'm sorry," Ramez started in. "I was angry. We're okay, aren't we?" He was like a man who hits his wife, then shows up with flowers.

I said, "You know, Ramez . . . Robert must have really done a good job on you."

I went downstairs, and when I finally caught up with Joe, he looked grim. "I've never seen anything like this," he said. "I don't care what kind of deal it is—we've got to get you away from this lunatic."

I flew back to New York only to have to immediately turn around and come back to London to talk to Reinhard Mieck, the Labelux CEO. All I wanted for myself was fair market value, and to be sure of my footing, I called several other women who'd founded similarly sized companies and worked at my level, and I asked about their compensation. Their packages ranged from $2 million to $3 million; my first salary offer from Labelux was £320,000!

The papers were to be signed on Sunday, and Labelux kept me waiting for my meeting with Mieck until Saturday. I was so stressed out that I kept my father's black cashmere sweater with me. In the evenings I'd rub it against my face and take in the scent of him. I missed him so desperately.

As the week came to an end, just before we were to talk, Mieck suddenly had to race off to Germany, and Joe was forced to jump through hoops to track him down to get him to discuss my package over the phone. I could now see that TowerBrook and Labelux had kept me out of the process once their bid was accepted, and that in our meeting at the Mark, Harf had been little more than a stalking horse.

After some artful persuasion by Joe, Mieck agreed to improve the offer, but even so, I now had less than twenty-four hours to review the details. I responded by saying that I would sign, but that I'd like a good faith commitment that post-deal they would review the report on executive stock options that I'd commissioned from KPMG. They said they would.

When Sunday came, after the stress of a week spent fighting to be treated with more respect, I could hardly muster the strength to leave my hotel room.

I asked Martin to call Joe. "Can't they just send the papers over?"

Joe's response was, "You know, they're spending five hundred million pounds. I think you have to show up."

I put on a pair of jeans and a shirt and I went to the Morgan Stanley office in Mayfair. It was four in the afternoon on May 22, 2011.

The only other woman present was Josh's lawyer. Otherwise, it was a sea of blue suits, and all these soulless men strutting about to see who was going to be the silverback gorilla.

They had a table set up for three—there was Reinhard Mieck from Labelux, there was myself, and there was Josh. The signing was largely ceremonial so that Josh could close the chapter.

Earlier in our discussions, Ramez had said to me, "I'm a fair guy, I always leave something on the table for my partners." So before I signed I said, "Ramez, what are you leaving on the table?"

He sort of laughed it off but clearly he was embarrassed.

After we signed, Ramez came over to shake my hand, and he said to me, "You've been a really good partner."

I looked him in the eye and I said, "I'm afraid I can't say the same to you."

His jaw dropped, so I knew I had his attention.

"You've been threatening all the way through, and you've handled this whole thing like a complete amateur."

I walked out with people chasing after me, and I got in the car and went back to the hotel. I couldn't fully release my anger until we were in the car, and then I started shaking. Normally I would have swallowed it, said nothing, and moved on. This was a major breakthrough. For the first time I'd faced down a bully and found my voice.

An hour later Andrew Roberts, my lawyer, called. "*What* did you say to Ramez? He's absolutely devastated."

I was the only one who paid my own legal fees. TowerBrook took £1.5 million out of the company to pay for their lawyers but didn't have the decency to try to negotiate a good deal on management's behalf.

These were midlevel private-equity people who hadn't yet learned that you can't just screw everyone. All they cared about was their own monthly fees, their 20 percent on exit, and their favorable tax rates. They were like feedlot farmers who don't care about cruel and squalid conditions or the hormones and chemicals flooding into their animals. Their only concern is that their livestock put on sufficient weight to bring top dollar when slaughtered.

Jimmy Choo meant everything to me, but now it was like a love affair in which your partner has cheated on you, physically abused you, and then run off with another woman. My partners had beaten the soul out of it with their lack of care for any of the individuals involved and their fundamental lack of respect for the brand. But it was the way Labelux behaved after the sale that was the final nail in the coffin.

We had a Cruise Collection presentation in New York, and I knew that Reinhard, the CEO, would be in town, so I suggested we have dinner. "We need to talk," I said.

He said, "I'll just see you at the presentation," but we never connected.

. . . .

IT WAS A NOSTALGIC SEASON for me, the fifteenth anniversary of Jimmy Choo. To mark the occasion we'd launched a feature on our Web site called "Choo Stories" where our fans would write in. My favorite was from a young female soldier in the British army who'd bought herself a pair of red patent Jimmy Choos to be sent to her while on tour in Afghanistan. She sent us a picture of herself wearing them with her uniform.

We also published a book with Rizzoli. The foreword was penned by fashion writer Colin McDowell, and I wrote the preface. It covered the entire history of the brand, with behind-the-scenes design sketches. Revenue was donated to the Jimmy Choo Foundation, which I'd recently initiated to help fight gender discrimination and the sex slave trade, and for gaining equal pay for women.

Josh also suggested that we go back into the archives, revive some of our greatest hits, and call the collection Icons. Of the thousands of shoes in the Jimmy Choo archive, some were seminal, either because they marked a moment in our history or they became famous because of the women who wore them. One of these was the "feather" shoe made famous when it slipped off Carrie Bradshaw's foot in *Sex and the City*. We got the artist Nan Goldin to shoot the campaign, and in our promotions we showed the vintage piece, then showed how it would have been designed if we started from scratch today. Our customers loved it.

In midsummer I went to L.A. for an inspiration trip with the design team, and I called Reinhard again. I said, "Time's going by. You haven't looked at my KPMG report. I'm not getting fair market value. And you're stalling on moving the office."

He said, "We're not moving the office."

So nothing I'd discussed with Peter Harf that night at the Mark was being carried through. They had completely dismissed my concerns.

With that I'd had enough. "I'm tired guys. . . . I'm tired of fighting you bastards for everything."

On August 1, 2011, fifteen years almost to the day since I'd gone to that first trade show in New York with samples too awful to show, I gave them my notice. And this is what I said:

Dear Peter and Reinhard,
After reflecting on my deal and looking at where I have actually landed up, I am very sad to say I am going to have to resign.
My father taught me two things in business:
1. Don't let accountants run your business.
2. Lawyers always ruin deals.
His words ring true now. I'm sure your lawyers and accountants feel they've done a great job, but they have forgotten that happy people are productive people.
Looking at the numbers, I do not feel motivated at all. The compensation is fixed in pound sterling, but I live in New York, so I feel I should be paid in dollars.
My compensation is still below market value, even though it has increased significantly from TowerBrook years. Over the last

decade I have basically worked for free, using my capital to live off. I can no longer do this.

It is a great pity that TowerBrook blocked access to negotiations.

The management equity plan is subject to income tax, which now approaches 50 percent. I have not worked this hard to pay income tax on my shares. I'm afraid the carrot has turned into a peanut.

Also for all the management team to put their own money in and then, at the end, pay income tax, I consider grossly unfair.

Peter and I discussed moving the office to New York, which I don't see for a long time to come. The travel is a totally false economy and I can't work to my full potential being burnt out.

At this stage in my life half measures avail me nothing.

Yours sincerely,
Tamara

The saddest part of my departure was that I was leaving before I was able to get the Jimmy Choo Foundation going in a larger way. They haven't done anything with it since. It appears there's no one left at the company with the motivation to work for women's empowerment.

···· 14 ····

The last collection I put together for Jimmy Choo was fall/winter 2012, and it was a very stressful four months during the time I was still working with the design team but couldn't say I was leaving.

The moment I'd told them that I'd reached the end, Labelux, in the typical fashion of abusive partners everywhere, expressed dismay and suddenly became very attentive. But their entreaties were too little too late. My notice period ran through January, but by November the strain was obvious, my resignation was made public, and I was gone.

Like TowerBrook before them, Labelux offered me large sums of money to sign a confidentiality agreement, but obviously I said no. However, my employment contract with them already included a one-year non-compete, which would begin in February 2012.

Despite the miseries I'd been feeling for years, it was when I stopped working altogether that the cumulative stress, exhaustion, and emotional turmoil hit me like an oncoming train.

In the world of rehab they speak of a "respite admission," when you really need just to check in (or check out), like some nineteenth-century aristocrat taking the cure at Baden-Baden. That's what my "non-compete" year was like.

It began at Thanksgiving, which is a holiday Minty always spends with her dad. Happily, Valentino was kind enough to invite me over, so I enjoyed a very traditional American feast at his apartment on Fifth Avenue. The group was mostly family, and we ate turkey and dressing and cranberries, and I had a lovely time.

In keeping with my own family tradition, though, I did my best to hide what I was feeling, which was a combination of anger, relief, mourning, and a profound sense of loss. The ancient Greeks reserved a time of quarantine for their returning warriors before they were expected to resume their place in society. I needed that same kind of buffer. And not just to recover, but to rediscover who I was, to come back to being me without all the pressure. I'd been on a fifteen-year voyage with Jimmy Choo, and when I finally jumped ship I was a different person.

Shortly after the holiday, Josh dropped by and we had a nice chat. Referring to Jimmy Choo, he said, "This was you . . . you created all this," kind words that I appreciated. Despite a bit of friction over the package for management, we'd always gotten along because he could always be human. Which is not to say that he never repeated favored phrases like "Everyone's replaceable," "It's TowerBrook who owns this company," and so on. But I knew once again that he was merely doing his job, passing along TowerBrook's message to me.

What I learned from Josh's visit was that he, too, had resigned. In their inimitable fashion, Labelux had not told me that he was leaving, and they hadn't told him that I was. Even at this point, Reinhard had tried to prevent him from talking to me, but Josh had insisted.

I WENT AWAY TO ST. BART'S for Christmas, and when I got back in January I really started spiraling down. My energy drained away until I could barely speak. When you're in the middle of so much stress, you rationalize how terrible you feel and you attribute it all to the job. But the body takes a while to let go and really feel the trauma it's undergone. Often the damage persists well after the pressure has subsided and you're no longer locked in battle mode, rising to the bell each morning and counterpunching all day.

With a full year off, not only was I able to reflect deeply, but I was able to take a long look at my health. The fact is, my sleep problems and issues with depleted energy had been with me since Heathfield. Back then I was always in the fog, and certainly never able to make it to breakfast. This was when my mother started saying I was a hypochondriac. This was when nothing could reach me—except, of course, drugs that acted directly to excite the nervous system.

Even as an adult, whenever I tried to get help from doctors about my lack of energy, their response was usually, "With all you're doing, how bad can it be?"

But the fact is, I'd launched a global brand while struggling to get out of bed each morning, then struggling all day to stay awake—which says something about the nature of existential fear, the power of feeling that if you fail, you're going to die.

I've suffered from insomnia, but more often my problem is that I sleep too much, and the sleep I get isn't refreshing. Left to my own devices, I can be out for fifteen hours at a time, but I wake up with that terribly foggy, jet-lagged feeling, as if it were three in the morning in a very alien time zone.

I'd delved into all the psychological factors that might have been causing this condition. I'd dealt with my most self-defeating patterns through therapy, and then, after the trial in Jersey, I felt as if a huge obstruction in my chest—my mother—had been surgically removed. But while everyone knows that psychological trauma can leave emotional scars, the fact is, relentless stress, especially in childhood, also leaves its imprint in the cells, disturbing how the endocrine and nervous systems operate. The "vacant" quality I'd always had when I was young was actually what psychologists call a "dissociative disorder," which is also a response to stress.

One of my doctors, a psychopharmacologist, suggested that I go to the New York Sleep Institute for a diagnosis. I spent the night there, wired up with sensors like an astronaut, and they determined that I have true hypersomnia, meaning that my "wake up" system doesn't activate, and, because I have attention deficit disorder, I exhaust myself trying to focus.

They also determined that, in addition to serotonin dysregulation, I have low dopamine—and suddenly the penny dropped. Dopamine helps control the brain's reward and pleasure centers. Serotonin affects mood. Both are affected by the adrenal system, and relentless stress can lead to something called adrenal fatigue. So all those years drifting through school like a zombie? And my particularly avid response to stimulants like cocaine and even tobacco?

During my sabbatical year I started taking dopamine supplements, along with my usual medication, and the change has been astounding. For the first time in my life, the morning is my favorite part of the day.

I also found that there's something in me that doesn't tolerate leisure all that well. So in an odd way, my time off was a bit like the experience of that bomb squad soldier from *The Hurt Locker* who comes home only to find that he really needs to get back into the thick of it. After spending half my life flying back and forth across the Atlantic and being constantly "on," suddenly having unlimited time to myself was unnerving. But then my diary quickly filled up with charity events, and with raising a child, and I began to think, "My God, how did I ever have time to work?"

One of the gratifications that came with announcing my departure from Jimmy Choo was that my in-box suddenly filled with messages from very serious people saying, "What's your plan? Let me know. Whatever you do next, I'd love to be in on it."

. . . .

JUST AS I'D BEEN INCUBATING the idea of Jimmy Choo while still at *Vogue*, even while nestled in rehab, I'd long ago started thinking about a new brand that would carry my own name. With the noncompete I couldn't really do anything with shoes or bags, or bring another product to market for twelve months, but I could start writing a business plan, and I could start talking to investors. What was nice about my legal restrictions is that I was forced to take it slowly. I also had the chance to think through what needed to be fundamentally different and how to avoid the mistakes of the past.

At Jimmy Choo we did shoes, bags, and other small leather goods,

fragrances, and eyewear. If I'd stayed on, I would have started
ready-to-wear: dresses, skirts, and blouses. I actually had a vision for
a full lifestyle brand that extended all the way to housewares. Ralph
Lauren, Armani, Versace, Vendi—they all do it. And now that's what
I'm going to do with my new brand, Tamara Mellon.

I feel that the fashion business has become a dinosaur. A fashion
house will have a runway show, and the images appear online that
same day, but the actual product doesn't get into the store until six
months later. By that point the merchandise is overexposed, and it
seems old and tired. The PR departments have sent it out to celebrities,
and it's been seen everywhere, so a customer thinks, "I don't want to
wear that dress. Why should I be the last person to this party?"

As a result, speed to market is now much, much more important.
So is changing the way the fashion business has always operated on a
set seasonal schedule. Women have been forced to buy their spring/
summer clothes in February and their winter coats in June. But atti-
tudes have changed. Customers don't want to think about a coat in
June, and if they don't want to think about it, they're not going to buy it.

For my new brand, I've created a business model that allows us to
actually sell in real time so that our customer can buy her coats in
September and her bikinis in June. Breaking from the established cycles
means going much more directly to the consumer.

At Tamara Mellon we're going to do a biweekly drop of clothes, and
because it's biweekly, the clothes will be slightly limited and more exclusive. It also means that every couple of weeks we'll be creating an
event to generate some excitement, which we hope will bring customers into the stores.

We're also going to have an aggressive presence online, with ten-second ads with a click-and-buy component. I love the fact that I'll be able to communicate directly with the customer through social media.

This time there will be no phantom namesake to complicate matters (while owning half the company): I'll be using my own name, everyone will know that I'm creating the collection, and I'll be free to speak to the customer in my own voice.

Trust me, I've learned my lesson: Private equity will not be part of the deal. If we're successful, then ten years down the line we might do an IPO, but what I've learned is to always retain majority ownership and, with it, control. I've set up Tamara Mellon as a privately owned LLC, with a few well-chosen minority partners putting in their own money, but leaving the creative vision to me. These partners include Sandbridge Capital, where Tommy Hilfiger is a senior adviser, and Tory Burch from the fashion world; Ronald O. Perelman from MacAndrews and Forbes; Michael Spencer, the founder of ICAP, probably the biggest brokerage in the world; David Ross of Carphone Warehouse; Lord Jonathan Marland, the prime minister's trade envoy; and Danny Rimer, Canadian tech entrepreneur.

I'd long ago come to the conclusion that private equity should stick with cement factories and soybeans and stay out of fashion. Certainly the only time to sell to private equity is when you want to divest entirely and walk away.

I think their brand of short-term thinking and exclusive focus on financials is a huge part of what's wrong with so much of the economy. You can't have sustainable growth and real innovation when no one cares about what they're actually producing or about the people who produce it.

The private-equity mind-set is just as delusional as my mother's because, like hers, it insists on redefining the world to suit its pathology. With it there's never an open dialogue between creative and financial. The exchange is always acrimonious, because it's always about dominance, ego, and control.

Even if its outcomes were always glorious for all concerned, the endless cycles of buying and selling are simply too exhausting. Private equity is like American politics: The endless campaigning, fund-raising, and positioning for the next contest is to the detriment of the job you're actually being paid to do.

If I'd had an MBA when I started Jimmy Choo, I think it might have given me more confidence to shut down the unimaginative and short-sighted bean counters when they wanted to interfere with the creative process. But having been through the ringer with three private-equity companies and four corporate sales, I now have all the confidence I need. I'm sure I'll make new mistakes, but I have too many battle scars to repeat those from the past. And as they say in the recovery movement: Sometimes you have to break down in order to break through.

After 2009, which was as close to a "breakdown" as I ever hope to come, I was able to move beyond the trap I'd lived in all my life. It was like I'd been stuck in a box, except that it was actually a triangle, one that has been known in therapeutic circles for a long time.

My psyche was shaped by a childhood in which there was a Persecutor (my mother), a Rescuer (my father), and a Victim (that's me). Because this dysfunctional pattern was never adequately addressed and dislodged, it carried over from my family of origin to any and all other relationships I might have, including those at Jimmy Choo.

When your designated role is to be the victim, and when that's all you know, you sometimes find a perverse comfort in it later on. When you're endlessly reliving an old pattern, you know what to expect, and you may still see it as the survival mechanism that helped you get through your childhood.

Moreover, the familiarity of the same old pattern, even when it's destructive, provides a degree of self-soothing because it gives you the illusion of control, though this kind of control is about as effective as a child trying to escape from a house fire by hiding in her bedroom closet. Deep down, your body is saying, "I know how this system works," and that sense of mastery lessens the anxiety of otherwise unpredictable, interpersonal encounters. And what are addictions and compulsions—drugs, alcohol, gambling, hand washing, promiscuity, avoidance—if not attempts to reduce anxiety and create the illusion of control?

For me, then, while being the victim may have been the road map of hell, at least I knew my way around. When your only experience of maternal attention is victimization, in your most perverse moments you might even see it as a substitute for love. And ultimately, when your psyche is conditioned for being persecuted, you will find plenty of applicants for the job.

Robert's approach to me was just like my mother's, but at the time I was unable to recognize it and fend it off. The same was true with Ramez.

To egg them on, and because of my fear of conflict, the only way I knew how to communicate was indirectly. So I never pushed back when they crossed the line. Instead I would withdraw, which was often viewed as compliance. Then, when I would reenter the discussion—sometimes with an outside adviser, or even a lawyer—they viewed my actions as narcissism, even betrayal. The lesson is that unless you make your boundaries clear, as well as your needs and desires, the other guys can't possibly know. And bullies will be bullies.

In my personal life, having idealized my father, I was always drawn to charismatic men who were emotionally unavailable. But, for me, the "triangle" trifecta was finding a charismatic, unavailable man who was also in need of rescue. Thus I could continue the familiar pattern while working my way up through the ranks to the more admirable role.

For whatever I may have learned, I know that I can't change my past. By the same token, I can change how I relate to my past, which allows me to do things differently in the future.

. . . .

IN SEPTEMBER 2011, I WAS at Ted Forstmann's "visionaries" conference in Aspen. This is one of the few places you can run into Queen Noor, Colin Powell, Michael Dell, Martha Stewart, Brian Williams, Tony Blair, and George Lucas before you're six paces into the room. The entire crowd of about three hundred people is at that level of recognition and accomplishment.

I was chatting with Tory Burch about the fashion industry when Michael Ovitz, best known for founding Creative Artists Agency and changing the way Hollywood operates, came over and began to chat. He was very close to Ted and had been on his board at Gulfstream.

We got together again the next evening, but then I had to leave early to go to China. He said, "When you come back, let's go to dinner," and so we did, and eventually one thing led to another.

For much of my career there's been no man in my life. Between Cedric and Matthew there were no relationships—there was hardly time for a date—and the same was true after Christian. But now it's such a relief to be with a real grown-up.

After years of being at the very top of the Hollywood power structure, Michael is completely done with the entertainment business, and now he's finding the same kind of excitement as an investor in the high-tech sector. He's based in Palo Alto, has a place in L.A. and another in New York, a magnificent art collection, and a boat that he keeps in St. Bart's, so our orbits overlap in many ways. And we simply have a lot of fun laughing and learning from each other. He's as knowledgeable about architecture and design as he is about art, and now he's learned a bit about fashion from me as well.

I truly enjoy being around someone who is so accomplished and whose interests are complementary to mine. I also get on famously with his three kids—Chris, thirty-two; Kimberly, twenty-nine; and Eric, twenty-six—and they treat Minty like a little sister. Michael, too, is great with her. Not long ago she was scheduled to have a sleepover at a friend's house while I was away, but then she changed her mind and called Michael and asked him to come pick her up. When he got there he asked, "You want me to drop you back home?"

She said, "No. I want to stay at your apartment downtown."

He said okay. But then he said, "How about we get some dessert?"

She smiled. "Okay, but first I have to change."

So he took her down to his apartment where she could put on her finery, and then there they were, the two of them at Max Brenner's chocolate bar in Union Square at nearly midnight, out on the town.

Is he a rescuer?

Thanks, but there's no need.

Am I out to rescue him?

Hardly. He's far from drowning.

In Hollywood, Michael was known as a tough cookie, but that's never been my experience—though some of my friends have joked that having a relationship with Michael Ovitz is like the final exam in the master class in self-actualization, the road test before they give you your license. It's true—you have to know what you want, who you are, and what you will accept. Michael knows where my boundaries are and where I draw the line.

Of course, with his strong business mind and his long experience in deal making, Michael has been a great sounding board as I put together the financing for my new venture. When one would-be investor was being difficult, I wondered out loud, "What am I going to do with this guy? Should we do what he wants?" Michael's response was always, "Do what's best for you and your business, and don't be afraid to be strong." So I kicked out the investor and I felt great about it.

Almost every mistake I've made in business has come from not trusting myself. But now I know that if something doesn't work for me, it's not going to work for the customer. It was often a struggle, but by ultimately making it "work for me," Jimmy Choo became the most successful private-equity fashion story in the industry—not just in the UK but globally.

. . . .

ANYONE WHO DOES ANYTHING WELL is probably compulsive to some degree, displaying the obsessive behavior otherwise known as "taking pains" and "getting the details right."

Obviously, this memoir is a by-product of the year I had the time to recover and reflect, and in writing it I've done my best to take pains and to get the details right. Then again, there does come a time when the publisher simply says, "Enough! We need the manuscript by Friday."

I've tried hard to make what I've written truthful, and I hope that it qualifies as "a good read." But I'd also love it if businesspeople, especially entrepreneurs, and even more specifically women entrepreneurs, find it useful. Women especially are flooded with clichés and conflicting advice, and it must be terribly confusing for a young person trying to determine early on just how much she should "lean in," and just how much she's supposed to "have it all."

As I'm sure you would anticipate by now, my most fundamental piece of advice to those young women is to follow your instincts. If you have the wrong instincts for what you're trying to do, that will become evident soon enough, and it may require you to change course, but being blown back and forth by the winds of conflicting opinions will get you nowhere. You have to know where you stand, and that your value as a human being does not depend on anyone else's assessment, and yet you must always remain open to learning and to growth.

Given all the cultural residues, it's incredibly difficult for women to understand and to accept their value, and even successful women can and do suffer from "imposter syndrome." Hoping to compensate for their assumed deficiencies (and perhaps still seeking to "earn Daddy's love"), they will silently work themselves to death, hoping that someday they will be noticed and rewarded for all their efforts.

But you can't just work and wait. You also have to speak up.

And there's absolutely no reason to tolerate bullying and belittling behavior. For years I tolerated abuse because in my early life that kind of behavior had been the norm. Today, I'd bounce the bullies in two seconds, because the first lesson of the school yard is that you have to confront them right away, in the moment. Being honest in the moment allows you to express displeasure at the first sign of transgression, which is when it can be addressed calmly and rationally, without fear of an explosion. When you speak up in the moment, you don't have to worry about overdoing it, because you're not expressing pent-up rage. You're simply stating a fact: "I'm not happy with this. This is not acceptable."

They say that when we reach our forties our life goals shift, with autonomy becoming the central issue. But at any age, being able to chart your own course rather than just responding to others' demands is a beautiful thing.

After Jimmy Choo had grown to a certain size, I used to have to sneak out of the office because there was always a line of people saying, "I only need five minutes . . ."

Those demands on my time have resumed as my new brand moves into high gear, but at least now there's no one in my diary that I don't like. Moreover, I have the clarity to recognize an intrusion before it happens and the wherewithal to deflect it.

At one time, my alarm systems were constantly overloaded, but now I give myself more space, and I refuse to make back-to-back appointments. Instead, I allow myself a moment or two to breathe, to reflect, to absorb my perceptions and intuitions. The body always knows more about any given situation than what registers in conscious awareness, and with a little practice, we can become more intuitive, then become brave enough to let our intuitions inform our decisions.

As I complete this project now, and as I anticipate the launch of my new brand, I realize just how fortunate I am to be where I am, with new worlds to conquer, a new home to enjoy, and in the meantime, the pleasure of watching my daughter's transformation into a smart, beautiful, and resourceful young woman. In the mornings when she comes in to kiss me before she's off to school, it's the greatest gift. Sometimes she'll even climb under the covers with me and give me a hug and we'll have a little chat before we start out the day.

We both adore the vitality and the variety of New York, the fact that we have such great friends, and that there are always great art galleries and fabulous parties to go to when the mood takes our fancy. But parties and especially business entertaining can get to be a bit much, and truth be told, I'd just as soon be home in sweatpants and a T-shirt watching *Downton Abbey*. That show is my guilty pleasure, and not just because of the costumes and the furnishings or the story lines. It's the sense of obstinate integrity that is a recurring plot element. Characters are always refusing to benefit from some windfall simply because it wouldn't be the right thing to do.

In 2012, I bought a place for summer and weekend getaways in Bridgehampton. It's a simple gambrel house with graying shingles and very English hedges on one acre in the village, just a short bike ride to the beach. It's Minty's and it's mine and it's our sanctuary. And I paid cash for it. There's no mortgage, so it feels solid and secure.

Minty loves the Hamptons, and she's obsessed with horses, so we stable a pony that she rides every day when we're there. We don't really go to the beach much since we usually stay at home by the pool. We go out to early dinners—but just very casual blue-jean dinners—we relax, and we watch movies. All her friends from school in Manhattan have family places nearby, so for her it's the same gang.

I feel truly sorry for my mother that she denied herself the pleasures of this kind of relationship. But just because I missed out on this kind of closeness as a daughter doesn't mean I can't treasure it now that I'm the mother.

I really don't hear much from my mother or my brothers these days, though I have heard that Gregory is in real estate, once again, in Los Angeles. But happily, I've remained close to the Mellons. Uncle Jay lives around the corner from us and every now and then we have lunch at the Four Seasons. Minty's Mellon grandmother lives in Palm Beach, and occasionally we all have Thanksgiving dinner together. Matthew lives at the Pierre, just a few blocks south of me, so Minty has ready access to both her parents, and I really admire his effort to stay clean and sober, which is so much harder to do when you're bipolar. He keeps fighting and coming back, which makes him much braver than his father.

. . . .

AS FOR THE REST OF our cast of characters:

Two colleagues from the very beginning have become like family to me, and their friendship is one of my greatest benefits from all those years at Jimmy Choo. Hannah Colman, who started selling for us at seventeen and went on to become one of our senior executives, holds a place in my heart as if she truly were my little sister. She always seemed to love the customers, and I know they still love her.

My other "sister" is Anna Conti, and I feel just as close to her brother Massimo. When Labelux bought the company, Anna set up a new agency called Matti, and then they had to renegotiate terms. Labelux handed her a list of other people in the business she would not be allowed to work with. My name was at the top of the list.

Harvey Weinstein and I are still friends, though perhaps not as close as we once were. In 2011, he sold his shares in Halston for fifty cents on the dollar, this after bringing in Sarah Jessica Parker for a stint as creative director. But there were already too many different people on board with too many different agendas and opinions. I left my shares in, and I noticed recently that they were opening a new store on Madison Avenue and still pushing Halston Heritage. There may be hope still, but profit or loss, the lesson for me is to never go through with a deal based on ego.

Martin Freeman is still on hand to help me process the "facts and feelings" I encounter in my life. As comrade veterans of the Battle of Jersey, we will sometimes go back over the transcripts of the trial, Martin doing the various voices as he reads aloud, the two of us trying to make sense of that intensely bizarre episode.

Josh Schulman is now president of Bergdorf Goodman, and clearly retail is the work he was born to do. At the age of eleven, or so I've been told, he used to walk through department stores and reorganize their displays. Bergdorf is owned by Neiman Marcus, which is owned by TPG, one of the original bidders for Jimmy Choo.

Robert serves on various boards and, along with Jim Sharp, invested in Bremont, a luxury watch brand. He also went back to Phoenix to acquire a lower-end British shoe brand called L.K.Bennett. I saw him not long ago at one of the BAFTA dinners we'd once sponsored, an event that continues to be one of the most sought-after invitations in London. Robert seemed so proud of himself for being there, as if he'd forgotten that we had once owned that dinner and he'd foolishly canceled it. The evening has been sponsored by Chanel for years.

Lyndon Lea had huge successes flipping companies like Weetabix and Kettle Chips, but his interest in frozen foods led to a certain degree of egg on the face. He was a huge shareholder in Findus, the Swedish company pilloried for selling horse meat as beef.

At last report, Jimmy Choo was still on Connaught Street and still making shoes.

Sandra Choi is still creative director of the company that bears her uncle's name, and she's still my biggest disappoinment. Every time she sees me she breaks down and cries. At Hannah Colman's wedding in Milan she came up to me in tears and I just looked at her and said, "Well, it didn't end well, but you know why." That must have hurt, because she's big enough to at least acknowledge her role in betraying me. But that doesn't mean that I have to provide forgiveness.

As for the company itself, it seems they've followed a rather Orwellian path in trying to rewrite history. I ran into some old colleagues not long ago who told me to check out the Jimmy Choo Web site. They were horrified to report that the company history provided there does not mention my name even once. I'd been written out of the script, re-placed by Sandra Choi in the creation myth they choose to offer.

As for me, enjoying my new life as much as I am, we have to remem-ber that even Eden had its serpent. Directly in front of my house in the Hamptons there are thirteen acres of land, which were supposed to be conserved and set aside for strictly "agricultural purposes."

When I was first interested in buying the place, I asked the Realtor, "Can you just make sure what's going to happen to that land?" It had just been sold to a new owner, so I was curious. "I don't want to buy the house if someone's going to put up a big fence or block my view or something."

So she called the new owner's lawyer and he assured her, "No, no. I've spoken to the landscape architect and they're going to respect the land and put in an apple orchard."

This sounded great, so I bought the house. But a while later I got a call from the broker, who said, "Oh my God, Tamara, the guy who bought the reserve—he's going to build an eight-thousand-square-foot stable. It's going to be huge, and he's going to be putting it right in front of your house. There'll be a monster fence, and horse trailers coming in and out . . . and I'm so sorry."

She gasped for air, and then to top it all off she said, "You must know this guy. He's going around saying he owned Jimmy Choo."

As it turned out, it was Robert Darwent, the bean-counting partner from Lion Capital that Lyndon sent in every month to check the numbers.

Our property lines are adjacent—he looks at my house, and I look at his.

It's the perfect irony, of course. But after everything I'd been through, and all the lessons I'd learned, you can rest assured there will be no "going along just to get along." The plot continues, but any issues along our shared boundary will be dealt with openly and with resolve.

If I have a bit of equanimity now, and if I'm better at standing my ground, it's only because I fought my way through the rites of passage until the monsters that tormented me were slain. It may have seemed that now and then I needed a rescuer, but over time, I learned to rescue myself.

ACKNOWLEDGMENTS

After so many years spent "biting my tongue," I must admit the idea of writing a memoir had been growing on me.

Then in the early summer of 2012, I met Portfolio's affable and intuitive Adrian Zackheim, who was so keen to publish my story that he offered me an agreement without a proper book proposal, outline, . . . anything. We simply had a chat, then continued in "cart before the horse" fashion, even to the point of his introducing me to an agent, the wily Rafe Sagalyn, and to a publishing lawyer, the skillful Richard Heller.

With Adrian having pulled together all the pieces, I had no excuse. And given that I was in the midst of a sabbatical, enforced by a one-year "non-compete" signed with Jimmy Choo, the timing could not have been better.

All I needed now was a professional writer to whom I could bare my soul, and from whom I could receive a well-crafted manuscript that gave my rambling thoughts a beginning, a middle, and an end.

Of course, it should be a woman, and a woman with enough life experience to identify with my struggles and my inner landscape, someone who understands deep down the business hurdles and gender discrimination a woman still faces.

Rafe supplied me with three names—but his shortlist consisted of two women and a man. I interviewed the two women first and knew which one I preferred. In fact, the choice was so obvious that I couldn't quite see the point of interviewing the guy. After all, how could some guy get inside my head and help me find my voice?

But then the day was upon us—my assistant had already scheduled the appointment—and the male candidate was coming in from out of town, so even though I knew this third interview was a waste of time, it would be rude to cancel, so I agreed to muddle through.

In walks this six-foot-three Texan who lives in some fishing village in the wilds of New England, and within five minutes I knew this was the one. Bill had a disarming ability to get me to open up immediately, and to tell the truth, so much so that it felt like talking to a great shrink. Bill "got" me and my story at such a deep level. More to the point, he was able to bring my voice to the page.

So the minute he left our first interview, I phoned Martin Freeman and said, "I've just found my writer." And what a fantastic lesson in life it was: Make no assumptions, stay open to the possibilities.

Let me thank William Patrick, then, for his incredible ability to grasp the complexities of my story so quickly, his attention to detail, his wonderful skill in "unpacking" each and every event, his always wanting to know more of what it was like "in my shoes," and his refusal to ever settle for the inauthentic. I also appreciate his willingness to dance around my hectic life, and to make himself available in the gaps that opened up. Indirectly, I also want to thank him for proving yet again that I should trust my intuition. If it feels right, it probably is right.

Thanks also to Rafe for sending Bill my way, and to Richard for sealing the deal, and of course to Adrian, who set the entire process in motion.

ACKNOWLEDGMENTS

As the months went by, though, I began to learn just how much help it takes to recollect the essence of one's life experience, while continuing to push one's present life forward. So I also want to extend a very special thanks to those who helped behind the scenes, and whose friendship, wisdom, and unconditional support I value so much: Hannah Colman, Elika Gibbs, Anna Suppi Conti, Massimo Conti, Charlotte Pilcher, Michael Ovitz, Mark Bolland, Andrew Roberts, Matthew Mellon, Tommy Hilfiger, Sir Philip Green, Ronald O. Perelman, Tory Burch, and Natalie Massenett.

Of course, more direct stage managers are also essential, and I could not ask for a better team to keep me organized and on time. Profound thanks, then, to my spectacular assistant, Irina Ponomarenko—ever present, never intrusive—as well as to my major majordomo, former NYPD detective John Vitale, who keeps me going with his reliability, consistency, and belief that "there are no gray areas" (except perhaps my own).

Closer to the action, I must praise the care and professionalism of the rest of the team at Penguin—Emily Angell, Katie Coe, Kristen Gastler, Will Weisser, and Allison McLean—thanks and well done!

And then hovering above the fray, but always available to swoop down like Zeus with a lightning bolt of perception, there is the priceless Martin Freeman, a master at keeping all the parts of my life moving, including certain jangly parts of my well-worn psyche. Thank you, Martin.

Above all, I must with all my heart thank my delightful daughter, Minty, for her love and understanding of a working mom who's been even more distracted than usual these many, many months!

MRS MONEYPENNY WITH
HEATHER MCGREGOR

MRS MONEYPENNY'S CAREERS ADVICE FOR AMBITIOUS WOMEN

Welcome to the world of Mrs Moneypenny, where it's all about who you know and what you know. Where you can't have it all, but you have to do it all. And where women wanting to reach the top need to learn to say 'no'.

The high-flying, uber-connected Financial Times columnist and star of Channel 4's 'Superscrimpers' is on a mission to help you get ahead at work.

In this incisive, hilariously frank book, Mrs Moneypenny tells you everything you need to know about taking control of your career. From nurturing your personal network and getting noticed, to the art of outsourcing and understanding numbers, she distils a lifetime's experience of running businesses and shaping careers into original, practical advice.

Whether you're just starting out or a rung from the top, whether you're a store manager or a CEO, let Mrs Moneypenny be your ultimate mentor - and guide you to success.

'Mrs Moneypenny. Working mother, businesswoman... just like me, really'
Elle Macpherson

'I wish I had ended up as worldly wise, energetic and well-connected as she plainly is' Bill Emmott, *The Times*

'Who needs Bond when Mrs Moneypenny comes to our rescue every Saturday?' Stephen Hester, CEO, Royal Bank of Scotland

'Mrs M is the FT's sexy little secret...she writes with great wit and deftness' David Yelland, Former Editor, *The Sun*

PHILIP DELVES BROUGHTON

WHAT THEY TEACH YOU AT HARVARD BUSINESS SCHOOL

What *do* they teach you at Harvard Business School?

Graduates of Harvard Business School run many of the world's biggest and most influential banks, companies and countries. But what kind of person does it take to succeed at HBS? And would you want to be one of them?

For anyone who has ever wondered what goes on behind Harvard Business School's hallowed walls, Philip Delves Broughton's hilarious and enlightening account of his experiences on its prestigious MBA programme provides an extraordinary glimpse into a world of case-study conundrums, guest lectures, *Apprentice*-style tasks, booze luging, burn-outs and high flyers.

And with HBS alumni heading the very global governments, financial institutions and FTSE 500 companies whose reckless love of deregulation and debt got us into so much trouble, Delves Broughton discovers where HBS really adds value – and where it falls disturbingly short.

'Delves Broughton captures an essence of HBS that is part cult, part psychological morass, part hothouse . . . His book is invaluable. Quite brilliant'
Simon Heffer, *Literary Review*

'A funny and revealing insider's view . . . his fascination is infectious' *Sunday Times*

'A particularly absorbing and entertaining read' *Financial Times*

'Horrifying and very funny . . . An excellent book' *Wall Street Journal*

JOSH KAUFMAN

THE PERSONAL MBA: A World-Class Business Education in a Single Volume

Are you searching for your next challenge? Are you tempted to go to business school? Before you do, save your money and read *The Personal MBA*.

Getting an MBA takes two years of your life. And most of it is spent on PowerPoint presentations and outdated financial models, rather than learning what it takes to run a real business.

The Personal MBA distils the most valuable lessons of the finest business schools and the best business books of all time into simple, memorable ideas and tools. It covers concepts such as The Iron Law of the Market, The 12 Forms of Value, The Pricing Uncertainty Principle, and The 4 Methods to Increase Revenue.

This book is all you need to learn the fundamentals of business quickly, and discover exactly how to apply them to transform your career.

'File this book under: NO EXCUSES.' Seth Godin, author of *Purple Cow and Linchpin*

'No matter what they tell you, an MBA is not essential. If you combine reading this book with actually trying stuff, you'll be far ahead in the business game.' Kevin Kelly, Founding Executive Editor of *Wired*

'Few people know how to get things done better than Josh Kaufman.' David Allen, author of *Getting Things Done*

SCOTT BELSKY

MAKING IDEAS HAPPEN: Overcoming the Obstacles Between Vision and Reality

Thomas Edison famously said that genius is 1% inspiration, 99% perspiration. Every day new solutions, revolutionary cures, and artistic breakthroughs are conceived and squandered by smart people. Along with the gift of creativity come the obstacles to making ideas happen: lack of organisation, lack of accountability and a lack of community support.

Scott Belsky has interviewsed hundreds of the most productive creative people and teams in the world, revealing one common trait: a carefully trained capacity for executing ideas. Implementing your ideas is a skill that can be taught, and Belshy distills the core principles in this book.

While many of us obsess about discovering great new ideas, Belsky shows why it is better to develop the capacity to make ideas happen - using old-fashioned passion and perspiration. *Making Ideas Happen* reveals the practical yet counterintuitive techniques of 'serial creatives' - those few who make their visions a reality.

'If you care about your art, your job or your market, you really have no choice but to read this book' Seth Godin, author of *Purple Cow and Linchpin*

'Ideas are easy. Implementation is hard. This book helps you with the hard part' Guy Kawasaki, former Apple guru and author of *The Art of the Start*

'This book is like a Swiss Army knife for ideas' Ji Lee, Creative Director at Google Creative Lab

'This is a book about execution, and when it comes to going from an idea to a real business, execution is everything' John Battelle, co-founder of *WIRED* and *BoingBoing*

RICHARD L. BRANDT

ONE CLICK: Jeff Bezos and the Rise of Amazon.com

Amazon's business model is deceptively simple: make online shopping so easy that customers won't think twice. It can be summed up by that button on every page: 'Buy now with one click'.

Why has Amazon been so successful? Much of it hinges on Jeff Bezos, the CEO and founder, whose unique character and ruthless business sense have driven Amazon relentlessly forward.

Through interviews with Amazon employees and competitors, *One Click* charts Bezos's rise from computer nerd to world-changing entrepreneur. It reveals how he makes decisions and where he will take Amazon next.

Amazon is a case study in how to reinvent an entire industry. It is one that anyone in business ignores at their peril.

'Richard Brandt compellingly profiles one of the great internet executives of the era' Stephen Leeb, author of *The Oil Factor* and *Red Alert*

'Meticulously researched and with breathless, pithy commentary. If you want to understand the Bezos phenomenon, this is an easy and efficient way to do it - just like shopping on Amazon.' *Management Today*

ERIC RIES

THE LEAN STARTUP: How Constant Innovation Creates Radically Successful Businesses

Most new businesses fail. But most of those failures are preventable.

The Lean Startup is a new approach to business that's being adopted around the world. It is changing the way companies are built and new products are launched.

The Lean Startup is about learning what your customers really want. It's about testing your vision continuously, adapting and adjusting before it's too late.

Now is the time to think Lean.

'Every so often a business book comes along that changes how we think about innovation and entrepreneurship. Eric Ries's *The Lean Startup* has the chops to join this exalted company.' Philip Delves Broughton, *Financial Times*

'Mandatory reading for entrepreneurs... loaded with fascinating stories and practical principles' Dan Heath, co-author of *Switch* and *Made to Stick*

'If you are an entrepreneur, read this book. If you are thinking about becoming an entrepreneur, read this book. If you are just curious about entrepreneurship, read this book.' Randy Komisar, Founding Director of TiVo

'*The Lean Startup* will change the way we think about entrepreneurship' Tom Eisenmann, Professor of Entrepreneurship, Harvard Business School